D0789065

WHY LITERATURE MATTERS

Why Literature Matters

Permanence and the Politics of Reputation

Glenn C. Arbery

ISI BOOKS
WILMINGTON, DELAWARE
2001

Copyright © 2001 ISI Books

"The Errand" and "The Rain Stick" from *Opened Ground: Selected Poems 1966-1998*, by Seamus Heaney. Reprinted by permission of Farrar, Straus and Giroux, LLC.

Cataloging-in-Publication Data:

Arbery, Glenn C.
        Why literature matters : permanence and the politics of reputation /
    by Glenn C. Arbery. — 1st ed. —
    Wilmington, Del. : ISI Books, 2001.

        p.   ; cm.

    ISBN 1-882926-59-5
        I. Literature — History and criticism. 2. Authorship in literature.
    I. Title.

PN45 .A73 2001   01-110952
809—dc21   CIP

Published in the United States by:

    ISI Books
    Post Office Box 4431
    Wilmington, DE 19807-0431

Manufactured in the United States of America

Contents

To my students at Thomas More College,
Merrimack, New Hampshire, 1986-1997

Acknowledgments

BACK in the 1980s, at a conference on Dante, I met a man who changed my perspective on literature. Bright and ambitious, sleekly dressed, with some of the glow of physical self-satisfaction that Oblonsky radiates at the beginning of *Anna Karenina*, he spoke of his ideas about Dante as though he had brought them to the conference "packed deep in hay and snow," like the oysters that Seamus Heaney says the Romans brought home from the North across the Alps. His interpretations were delicate commodities, and his aim was to release them in the right circumstances, to gain prestige with them, to make money on them, to afford better suits because of them, and to use them to elicit a deeper servility from the waiter or the maitre d'. His academic plans stemmed from tastes that he shared with, say, Donald Trump. Dante, on whose imagination he fed daily, obviously had no more effect on his perspective than the flames of the Eighth Bolgia had on Ulysses.

Years later, a former student wrote me from a graduate school where everything worked according to the conventional pieties peculiar to the 1990s, "I'm forgetting why literature matters." The implicit question was a summons. If literature were important only to fashionable academics and the "literature industry," it would be easy to forget why it ever mattered in itself. This book is for those who think of Priam kissing the hands of Achilles, or Beatrice unveiling her smile, or Ishmael squeezing out the lumps in spermaceti, as ways the world becomes more polysemous, more subtly knowable, not as "standing reserve" for a grade or a career. This book would not exist without those for whom such things matter deeply, including teachers of my own who made the profession of letters noble in my imagination. Among many, I think especially of George Martin, Marion Montgomery, and Louise Cowan.

And for urging this book into being, I want to thank, in particular, Brooke Daley of ISI Books, as she was known at the beginning of this process, but who by the end had become not only Brooke *Haas*, but a mother as well. Through Brooke, student and intercessor, I thank all the students to whom this book is dedicated. Jeremy Beer, Suzanne Wolfe, and Amy Fahey helped edit out its infelicities. Without my wife Ginny and her encouragement, these chapters would be barren, and without my children—let me name them: Joan, Lucia, Ruth, Sarah, Therese, Julia, William, and Monica—they would be fruitless.

Introduction:
The Money or the Mine

"**M**ILTON!" cried Wordsworth, a little desperately, in 1802, "thou shouldst be living at this hour: England hath need of thee." The England that made him look back to Milton had forfeited, not poetry, not great-souled men who could resist the pressures of the most contrary events, but something harder to describe: the "ancient English dower / Of inward happiness" (Noyes 316). Many who teach literature in our own hour seem to feel the same forfeiture. In the past few years, a number of books and essays have been published lamenting the abandonment of traditional canons, the domination of English departments by the proponents of literary theories centered on sexuality and power, the rise of amorphous "cultural studies," and the subsequent loss of literature itself as an ennobling discipline. Given the sense of loss that motivates these defenders of tradition, it is hardly surprising that they tend to have in common the stance of men looking back at a city still burning after its capture in the culture wars, a Troy whose great walls had seemed impregnable for generations.

In *Who Killed Homer? The Demise of Classical Education and the Recovery of Greek Wisdom* (1998), Victor Davis Hanson and John Heath show statistically that in the past thirty years, publications in classics about specialized topics, often with a postmodern emphasis, have ballooned, while actual enrollments in classical language courses have fallen with alarming speed. John Ellis argues in *Literature Lost: Social Agendas and the Corruption of the Humanities* (1997) that the current situation is worse than previous ones because, for the first time, new appointees in faculty positions "are for the most part not literary-critical faddists who would normally jump to the next fad when it arrives but true believers in the race-gender-class issue who are not interested in literature" (212). R. V. Young, showing how postmodern literary theory has affected constitutional interpretation in *At War with the Word: Literary Theory and Liberal Education* (1999), writes that "a decline in higher education portends a general moral and spiritual malaise in the culture of a nation" (143).

Ellis's title, in its allusion to *Paradise Lost*, makes the literature departments of a generation or so ago, when men and women loved the literature that they taught, seem Edenic in contrast to the polarized and suspicious departments of today. His book and the others have amply shown what has happened to education: they have exposed the proud leadership of transgression, the rhetoric of oppression and power and revenge, the ardent constituencies. Perhaps what is needed now is not so much the first two books of *Paradise Lost*, which also deal with these things, as a reminder of the perspectives of Book III. When He spies Satan on his way to tempt Adam and Eve, "Coasting the wall of Heaven on this side Night / In the dun air sublime" (71-72), the Father not only foresees the fallen angel's complete success at deconstructing the prohibition on the Tree of Knowledge, but calls the still-unfallen Adam "ingrate" for succumbing, when he was "Sufficient to have stood, but free to fall." Already, however, before the fall that the Father cannot prevent without taking man's freedom, the Son prepares a countermeasure: He offers to take on the penalty that Adam incurs and to become "a sacrifice / Glad to be offered" (270-71). By offering to confine his immortality within mortality, to undergo death, the Son transforms the abyss of defeat. Milton's insight is Christian, without question, but it is also epic and profoundly poetic, because, from the largest perspective, the restitution is already deeper and more capacious than the fall itself; in fact, one *falls toward* the ground of a greater good, as Troy falls toward Rome. This idea of the *felix culpa* or "fortunate fall" might seem singularly inappropriate now, when Milton himself, like so many others in the Western canon, is being abandoned. But the greatest poetry in the Western tradition, long before Milton, has found that this power of restitution is neither subject to culture nor ultimately, humbling as it may be, a matter of education—though the best education ought to make us trust in it. Cultures come and go, whereas the freedom that the great poets intuit is hidden in being itself, a paradoxical capacity not simply for renewal after defeat, but for immortal glory.

The current crisis in education has already had one fortunate result: it has made us ask again why literature matters. Asking this question differs in significant ways from asking what to do about restoring English departments. When I read, in John Ellis's last paragraph, that "the road back to a functioning literature program on American college campuses will be long and hard," I doubt that the real problem has been addressed. If all the ministers think that God is dead, but enjoy the life of the pulpit, then the continued existence of churches is a confidence game. Unless literature itself, not the academic industry around it, not the competition for tenured positions or endowed chairs, is the central concern, then perhaps the academy deserves to fall. Harsh as it is to say so, there would be no crisis if departments were not structured in a way that rewarded the very theories and practices now destroying them.

Neither Shakespeare nor Homer has an importance *bestowed* by literature professors and their universities. The true bestowal flows entirely in the other direction. What professors of literature *can* rightly bestow is honor, because meaningful praise has to come from those who know the excellences of things. In the *Odyssey*, the king of the Phaiakians thinks that his men "surpass all others / in boxing, wrestling, leaping and speed of our feet for running" (8.102-3). Finally taunted into competing by Euryalos, one of the rudest young men, Odysseus sends the discus whistling far past all the other attempts, and the Phaiakians begin to revise their opinion of their own merit; when he challenges any one of them to compete with him in boxing, wrestling, or running, Alkinoos modifies his claim: "always the feast is dear to us, and the lyre and dances / and changes of clothing and our hot baths and beds" (248-49). Not only is Odysseus himself better than they are, but he has known men better than himself. Those who have seen only their contemporaries might think them excellent and give them great honors; those who have known an Achilles cannot help judging by the greater measure. The confusion that now prevails in the humanities lies in the failure to distinguish between honor as a fluctuating, sometimes irrationally exuberant (or morose) gauge of value, like the price of Internet stocks, and honor as the reward for an importance and worth established by competition with the best of every age.

Giving honor is a political act so old that it virtually defines the earliest (some would say, pre-political) orders. Hrothgar keeps harmony among his thanes, for example, by giving rings and the honors associated with them. Agamemnon infuriates Achilles at the beginning of the *Iliad* for being unfair in giving out prizes. Contemporary politics in the humanities is occupied with exactly the same thing. What is called "multiculturalism" is the insistence that all cultures be treated as equals, ostensibly without there being a supervening Hrothgar-culture by which they are granted or permitted this equality. In effect, multiculturalism caricatures the process that has always been at work in any city or culture: the assignment of honors as part of what Aristotle calls "distributive justice." This kind of justice consists in distributing "honor, wealth, and the other divisible assets of the community" (267) equally. But as Aristotle goes on to point out, "it is when equals possess or are allotted unequal shares, or persons not equal equal shares, that quarrels and complaints arise" (269; 1131a). If Odysseus had to pretend that Euryalos was as good a runner or fighter as Achilles, the truth would still be there. A culture naturally honors what it thinks serves it best, but in some situations, like the one that prevailed in Athens in 399 B.C. or the one in the humanities in recent years, it might not consider itself well-served by what is best, simply. In "identity politics," the representative character of the author influences what is being praised. Both literary works and the reputations of their authors can sometimes have a cultural utility that has little to do with literature per se or with artistic excellence.

Like the excellence of discus throwers and runners, the measure of literary excellence lies in the doing, but also in the larger context of literature. Robert Frost, in one of his famous digs at his contemporaries, said that writing free verse was like playing tennis without a net. Any good writing, he meant, but especially poetry, had to have technical obstacles to overcome, but he also meant that it was a game; it was play, and with play, there had to be rules and a context provided by players who establish the measure of excellence within those rules. Robert Pinsky writes at the beginning of his new book, *The Sounds of Poetry*, "There are no rules." He says that there are principles, but not rules. Frost would not find the distinction helpful. Without a net, what would tennis be? Not *tennis*. This sounds like a kind of curmudgeonly comment about free verse: whatever *that* is, it isn't *poetry*. But I think he means it more seriously. Without a net, without the lines of the court, there would be no way to reveal the difference between controlled and uncontrolled power, force and finesse. The player steps onto the court as a space of measure, and the more he controls his shots and uses the limits of that space, the more intensely the form of the game emerges. At its upper limits, at Wimbledon or the U.S. Open, excellence ultimately has to involve not just athletic prowess but an extraordinary amount of preparatory hard work, a beauty of performance and a certain greatness of soul that not only withstand the measure but actually shine because these qualities have a form that can reveal them.

Or consider the batter facing the pitcher in baseball. Over home plate, what is called the *strike zone*, a supple volume of air that differs with any given batter, makes it possible to see the artistry and courage of the duel. Think of what happens, say, between Greg Maddux and Mark McGwire or between Orlando "El Duque" Hernandez fresh from Cuba and Tony Gwynn, returning to the World Series with the same Padres team after fourteen years. Power and control and character and personal history and city pride and cultural expectation are revealed in their pathos or glory because of that agreed-upon, heavily focused space. It brings together two acute acts of attention, two men in the mastery of two different physical acts that converge in the one space of their opposition. I don't want to make extravagant claims for sports. Donald Hall writes in *Life Work* that, when he isn't working on his poems, he cannot read mysteries (as T. S. Eliot did) or watch movies with any pleasure, but that "for sports, intellectually equivalent to *The Price is Right* or Judith Krantz, I sit with my mouth open, witlessly enraptured." The point I want to stress is that games like tennis and baseball create intense spaces and become capable of revealing engaging things about human excellence or failure within the boundaries of established and agreed-upon rules. Hall's rapture isn't entirely witless, in other words, and it relates directly to poetry, and through poetry to literature in general. Part of the pleasure of reading a sonnet is knowing, not so much the rules, but what the rules make it possible to see. The pleasure of watching sports is very similar. For someone who doesn't understand the rules of baseball—what constitutes an "out" or what "bases" are—it's meaningless when, in the last inning of the World Series, Jeter smoothly fields a grounder and flips it underhanded to Knoblauch on second base, who turns in one motion and jumps over the sliding runner to make the throw to Martinez at first for the double play. The play is over in perhaps three seconds: beautiful, fluid and exact, from a scoring threat to two outs. But suppose one has to explain it to a Russian guest who doesn't know the game. One is plunged into abstraction: a runner coming from first base (wait, what is "first base"? "base"?), a runner coming from first base is "out"—that is, he must leave the field of play without having completed a circuit of the bases—if someone in possession of the ball touches second base before he does, but only if a batter has hit the ball and is therefore forcing the runner to leave first.

The rules are obviously not what anyone enjoys in watching good baseball. Nobody ever enjoyed the fact of there being ten syllables in a line of iambic pentameter, either, or fourteen lines consisting of three quatrains and a couplet in a Shakespearean sonnet. The rules are work. Even to understand them is work, because they usually suggest a difficult and initially artificial level of consciousness. For example, there is a first level of difficulty simply in getting someone to hear a pattern of sounds that apparently has nothing to do with the meaning of the words. A sentence, "I can't believe he hit the ball to Jeter," when you scan it, becomes a pattern of unstressed and stressed syllables, analyzable into feet. At first, with this awareness comes a kind of uneasiness, a sense of intrusion on natural language. The act of deliberately writing fourteen lines that make sense in this kind of self-conscious pattern—and then getting the end words to rhyme—seems absurdly artificial. I still remember how taken aback I was when a teacher in my freshman year of college casually mentioned that Shakespeare had varied the stresses and used words hard to enunciate together in order to underscore the sense of his lines in Sonnet 73. It was a revelation about dimensions of language new to me:

> That time of year thou mayst in me behold
> When yellow leaves, or none, or few, do hang
> Upon those boughs which shake against the cold,
> Bare ruin'd choirs where late the sweet birds sang.

Nothing particularly remarkable, it would seem. A note on the poem, as I recall, mentioned that Henry VIII had despoiled the English monasteries and that many were roofless and empty, a fact which explained the reference to "Bare ruin'd choirs." But what impressed me was the teacher's point that the poem leads its reader to expect an unstressed syllable at the beginning of the fourth line, but instead Shakespeare uses a stressed one.

I suddenly *felt* the word "bare," how it cuts across an established expectation, the way a good tennis player catches his opponent leaning the wrong way, or a pitcher throws only fastballs, then gets the batter to swing at a change-up. Thinking about this play with expectation, I understood what a "line" was, or again, better to say I *felt* it, the way a child playing baseball first feels the significance and exact location of second base when someone is on first; I felt the way one line influences and plays off the previous one and the next one. With games as with art, understanding precedes the capacity to feel accurately, and accurate feeling includes understanding. In its current usage, "feeling" usually means something vague and not susceptible to much scrutiny. I will have more to say about this in a later chapter, but I mean by feeling an extremely acute mode of intelligence, the "quick" of the whole intellect, Pascal's "spirit of finesse" from the *Pensées*—the source from which most of our insights are unfolded. When I understood that Shakespeare was not expected to make every line a succession of unstressed and stressed syllables, but that he was allowed and expected to make all kinds of variations—to substitute spondees, trochees, pyrrhics, even anapests, for iambs—or in other words, to vary his pitches—I felt it, and formal poetry immediately became interesting to me.

But perhaps that way of putting it is too abstract. What interested me was much more complicated. This was the first male English teacher I had ever had, a man who always held an unlit cigar, who wore cardigan sweaters and work boots, and who spoke with sardonic, impatient intelligence in a slow, dry, middle-Georgia accent. This man knew and cared deeply about the arts of language and wrote both poetry and novels himself, I discovered later. He was middle-aged, and strange to say, his physical presence made it plausible that Shakespeare could write three lines of more or less regular iambic pentameter about getting old, that he could be deliberately indecisive about those leaves and get the word "hang," after all those changing-his-mind commas, to hang there, that he could emphasize "cold" with the rhyme, and that he could suddenly, at the beginning of the fourth line, write on purpose, "Bare ruin'd choirs, where"—a glutinous sound clump, a gobbet of near-rhymes full of r's that have to be laboriously pulled apart. I still do not know how the visual metaphor—the stripped boughs of a tree as the roofless choir—can be so clear and airy while the sound is thickly dissonant yet perfectly appropriate for what a "ruined choir," having lost its art, might sound like. This sound, "Bare ruin'd choirs where," then this one overlapping it, "where late the sweet birds sang": how can the end of the line call up so effectively the way that choirs ought to sound, as though breaking free and ascending, a bird-flock of words?

To the extent that literature is a serious game, a form of high play, a *ritual*, it has rules that focus attention, set up expectations, allow surprising meanings to emerge in the revelatory space of its structure, and enable its readers to feel with the greatest range and accuracy. What is true of the meter and form of a sonnet is true also of works within the Aristotelian genres, as Louise Cowan has explored and expanded them in her theory of lyric, tragedy, comedy, and epic. But with genres, Cowan would argue, Pinsky's dictum about principles rather than rules is more accurate. Shakespeare was chided by neoclassicists for breaking the supposed rules of tragedy, when in fact he was expanding the range of the genre. Establishing the right kind of praise for him means not only understanding the particular play, but the genre that informs and is informed by it, not to mention the context of his fellow Elizabethan and Jacobean playwrights, and the prevailing opinions of his age, political, religious, and otherwise. Most of all, though, it means acknowledging, if it is true, how fully the work in its revelation of a spiritual landscape intuits what is hidden in one's own life, how well it provides a measure for one's own time, and how completely it gives form to the very way certain kinds of complex character and experience can be thought.

SOMETIME in 1862, perhaps around the time that she wrote a letter to Thomas Wentworth Higginson telling him that the idea of publication was as foreign to her thought "as Firmament to Fin," Emily Dickinson composed a poem demonstrating that immortality—the same kind of immortality in art that concerned Shakespeare in some of his sonnets—was very much on her mind:

> Some — Work for Immortality —
> The Chiefer part, for Time —
> He — Compensates — immediately —
> The former — Checks — on Fame —
>
> Slow Gold — but Everlasting —
> The Bullion of Today —

Contrasted with the Currency

Of Immortality —

A Beggar — Here and There —

Is gifted to discern

Beyond the Broker's insight —

One's — Money — One's — the Mine — (Johnson #406)

"Time" offers immediate compensation, the metaphorically literal "Money," to his employees. Those who labor for "Immortality" and its "Slow Gold — but Everlasting —" might have to do so, like Dickinson, in complete obscurity. Why? Not because they lack "the Broker's insight," but because they want freedom—even if it has to be a beggar's freedom or a monk's or, like Faulkner's Ike McCaslin, the freedom of the deliberately dispossessed. Those who want immediate fame eventually get the gold for their very coins from the few who work for Immortality. Higginson, once a famous activist and editor of *The Atlantic Monthly*, is now largely a footnote to the woman whose verses he found too "odd" and "delicate" to publish. By the time that she wrote him, Dickinson was already deep in her fabulous mines, not leading a "starved life," according to Allen Tate, but "one of the richest and deepest ever lived on this continent" (286). To change the metaphor and adopt the language of James Joyce that Seamus Heaney imagines speaking to him in "Station Island," she was already well past the boundaries, sending out "'signatures on [her] own frequency, / echo-soundings, searches, probes, allurements, // elver-gleams in the dark of the whole sea'" (*Ground* 246).

Her whole *habitus*, in a sense that I will discuss later, was the freedom of her art. The posthumous uses of Emily Dickinson can serve, for that reason, as a compelling illustration of the ironies at work in the distributive justice of literary praise. Dickinson's poems were discovered after her death neatly bound in "fascicles"—groups of poems written on letter paper into which Dickinson had punched holes and bound the pages with string. Along with her longtime correspondent Higginson, her first editor was "the wife of an Amherst professor," as Dickinson's editor Thomas Johnson describes her,

Mabel Loomis Todd, who unbound and shuffled the fascicles in selecting poems for the first edition of the poems, dividing them into four comfortable categories: "Life," "Love," "Nature," and "Time and Eternity." Todd and Higginson altered many of the poems, conventionalizing punctuation and substituting a more comfortable diction to make Dickinson seem a little less odd. Mabel Todd was also, as it turned out, the lover of Dickinson's married brother Austin, and therefore the mortal enemy of Dickinson's sister-in-law and closest friend, Susan, to whom many of the poems had been written. A rival edition to Todd's was published by Susan Dickinson's daughter in 1914, as well as a counter-edition by Todd's daughter in 1945. Family honor, in other words, dominated the early stages of the quarrel: to whom should Emily Dickinson's fame redound?

Thomas H. Johnson's 1955 variorum edition established texts of the poems that restored their original diction and punctuation, including the famous dashes, and introduced a much edgier, more potent poet than one could have suspected from Todd's version. This freshly emerging Dickinson coincided after the 1960s with the rise of deconstructive and feminist criticism, not to mention a new emphasis on sexuality. By 1990, Camille Paglia's notorious chapter on Dickinson in *Sexual Personae: Art and Decadence from Nefertiti to Emily Dickinson* had transmogrified the prim, Victorian image of Dickinson by comparing her—not altogether without reason—to the Marquis de Sade.[1] But the texts themselves became the burning question. In his 1960 one-volume edition, Johnson had imposed his editorial decisions about definitive texts on Dickinson's deliberate undecidability, according to later critics. If Dickinson refused to publish, did she not thereby express a suspicion of the male-dominated literary world of the time? If she left various versions of the poems, did she not therefore intend to deconstruct the idea of poetic closure and of definitive texts? If she left the poems privately bound in fascicles, might those orderings not provide important clues about her real intentions?[2]

In 1998, R. W. Franklin published a 1664-page variorum edition of Dickinson's poems that presents all the versions of the poems and attempts to honor contemporary concerns with Dickinson's "private" intent. In an appraisal of it for *Women's Review of Books,* Vivian Pollak, author of *Dickinson: The Anxiety of Gender,* wrote that some years before, she had first met Franklin at the Houghton Library at Harvard, where he "was using a small instrument—was it a micrometer?—to measure puncture marks [in the paper of Dickinson's manuscript pages] for the string [that bound the fascicles]. The size of the punctures entered into his calculations as he reconstructed these conceptually baffling units." For all the scholarly care that one might conceivably admire in Franklin's efforts, the scene strikes me as something out of Jonathan Swift. Pollak, I think, means to make the male scholar's positivist concern with little measurements look absurd. But for that matter, Pollak's overly intimate defense of Dickinson's privacy might also have a place in Book III of *Gulliver's Travels:*

> to those who identify with a woman poet unseen and unheard in her own time, *the disciplinary function of typographical reproduction* is suspect. Those who honor Dickinson's resistance to institutionalized norms of literary and social and gendered behavior want to experience her realities and not anyone else's. Yet despite a widely shared desire to draw closer to the reclusive poet's actual hand and body, few of us would wish to restrict ourselves to photocopies of her manuscripts, which are notoriously difficult to decipher. For most practical purposes, we need to take the journey Emily Dickinson took as a reader—into *the more disciplined world of print.* (My emphasis)[3]

"Discipline" in Pollak's usage goes back, not to Emily Dickinson, but to Michel Foucault's *Discipline and Punish: The Birth of the Prison;* typography becomes a "gendered" social mode of converting the personal presence of the "actual hand and body" into formal print—a standardization that eradicates or imprisons individual (female) identity.

Given her perspective, Pollak's concern is not absurd: lovers, for example, prefer the peculiarities of handwriting to a perfect typescript. "Typography," writes Pollak, "can never replicate the unprecedented appearance of Dickinson's poems on the page. Her handwriting, including the size and spacing of individual words and letters, is unique. Its genre is intimate and personal." But the question is exactly what we are talking about. It is true that Dickinson began a poem, "This is my letter to the World / That never wrote to Me —." But when she implicitly trusts that the poem will someday be known by the "Sweet countrymen" she addresses later in it, does she also expect them to read her "letter" in manuscript?

In honoring Emily Dickinson, then, should one "honor" (in the modern ideological sense) the intensely private, feminine reclusiveness out of which the poems were handwritten, or the poems themselves?[4] She obviously knew from experience that poems, even without the actual handwriting of the author, have an uncanny ability to engage a reader. She seems to have anticipated that her own poems would establish such intimate bonds, but their ability to do so would depend on a respect for *her* conventions, her own particular freedom inside the rules of the game. She must have hoped, when she imagined being published, not for an escape from typography per se, but for an editor who would leave her punctuation alone and try to approximate the halts and emphases and rhythms it suggests. Johnson, for example, restored the dashes and capitalizations that Todd and Higginson had removed from this poem:

What Soft — Cherubic Creatures —
These Gentlewomen are —

One would as soon assault a Plush —
Or violate a Star —

Such Dimity Convictions —
A Horror so refined
Of freckled Human Nature —
Of Deity — ashamed —

It's such a common — Glory —
A Fisherman's — Degree —
Redemption — Brittle Lady —
Be so — ashamed of Thee — (Johnson #401)

Dickinson's dash after "Soft"—implying a pause before the exact metaphor comes to mind—leaves the "Cherubic Creatures" hovering, but the capitalization makes them considerably more looming and ominous than the plump, sexless baby-angels of sentimental paintings. Like Mrs. Newsome from Henry James' *The Ambassadors*, they are formidable, entirely proper, full of exactly this refined horror at "freckled Human Nature." Dickinson imagines the Gentlewomen's haughty rebuff-in-advance of all unruly desire, a rebuff so effective that "One would as soon assault a Plush," but she also recognizes the Gentlewomen's *shame* that any self-respecting Deity would actually adopt that freckled nature—then employ that *Fisherman*, for heaven's sake, who had never attended Harvard! Common salvation without an earned Degree!

In this poem, Dickinson seems to me to draw an analogy between God and sex and poetry in the sense that poetry, too, affords what the "Brittle Lady" would scorn as "a common — Glory." Far from being exclusive and recondite, this glory comes, it seems, almost despite the Gentlewomen's efforts to suppress it. But for poetry to be effective, thoughts need to be seen in their freedom, outside their usual fabrics. Dickinson once wrote to Higginson about her poems, "While my thought is undressed, I can make the distinction; but when I put them in the gown, they look alike and numb." If even her own way of writing seemed a conventional "gown," one of Mabel Loomis Todd's dresses would have seemed to her a Plush indeed. Her poetry's oddities are surely meant to reveal a world everywhere accessible and everywhere cloaked by a little too much learning. Its common access might require the removal of one's Dimity Convictions. But to be ashamed of reality for offering "a common glory," as a woman might, or God, is to lose the possibility of essential rescue.

T HE cherubism of nineteenth-century respectability almost rivals the darker angelism of Dickinson's contemporary defenders, different as their fabrics might make them look. Today, sexuality in any unusual form—the body having been made a kind of self-theorizing construct— earns high academic praise in some circles, but Dickinson's acutely Christian understanding of the contradiction between intellectual pride and redemption, none at all. The unassailable Plush of contemporary correctness has its own Dimity Convictions, and I cannot go farther than Dickinson herself does in confuting them. It is strange to think that she would approve the champions of her privacy who build their careers by publicly exhibiting their every speculation about the details of her carefully hidden life. What exactly is being honored? Dickinson as poet, or Dickinson as sacrifice? The great problem with the loss of poetic form as the measure to which criticism looks is that the author's life, without the protections of that form, becomes an endlessly violable corpus for academics charged with appeasing the more ravenous idols of fashion.

This book attempts to show why literature matters in giving us "manners, virtue, freedom, power," as Wordsworth thought Milton might do—though, with John Crowe Ransom, I confess some reservations about the efficacy of the great Puritan in that regard. Beginning with the novelists and poets now attempting to bring literary form out of the tensions of our contemporary cultural situation, I shall move toward the permanent contemporaneity of the greatest poetry. My approach is like the one that Shakespeare describes in *The Rape of Lucrece* when Lucrece sees a painting of the Trojan War: "for Achilles' image stood his spear, / Griped in an armed hand; himself behind / Was left unseen, save to the eye of mind" (1424-26). What follows will be synecdochic, in other words, rather than comprehensive. For contemporary writing stand Tom Wolfe, Seamus Heaney, and Toni Morrison; for Shakespeare and the tradition of English literature, *Othello*; for the ancients, the *Iliad*. In each case I am concerned with the way that literary merit, both within the works and as a question about them, is affected by the kinds of cultural pressures that decide what will or will not be honored.

I will be looking first at those honored in different ways by contemporary culture—Wolfe with the money and immediate fame of the bestseller, Heaney and Morrison with the Nobel Prize. Then, in turning to Shakespeare and Homer, I will be asking about the kind of honor that should still be given to permanent excellence, especially given the demands of multiculturalism. I will circle back, when the time comes, to consider Emily Dickinson. She seems the fitting figure both to introduce and conclude a book that concerns itself with those put to the test of extraordinary prominence. How sardonic the one photograph of her seems, to the mind's eye, beside the white-suited figure of the first of these other writers, Tom Wolfe. Wolfe toughly faces the demands of his own notoriety and takes on the reality of globalization that has now entangled everyone, from the most retired scholar to his Charlie Croker, in bottom-line thinking. But the question is whether Wolfe—or Heaney, or Morrison—has faced the excruciating demands of Immortality as unsparingly as Dickinson did. The first half of this book will be an attempt to discern, like a gifted beggar, beyond the "Broker's insight" of contemporary valuation. The latter half is all the Mine.

I.

Why "Literature"?

IN December of 1998, William Jefferson Clinton was impeached at about noon on Saturday the nineteenth, but on the morning of that same day, the incoming Speaker of the House had already resigned, to the amazement of all the commentators, because of revelations about his own past adultery. Early the next week, as Clinton's popularity was ballooning to new heights in the polls, pundits were citing Nietzsche's description of the "last man" in *Thus Spoke Zarathustra* to assess the indifferent populace. Two ex-presidents were calling for censure as the Senate tried to calculate how to handle the situation, and on Christmas Eve, Larry Flynt, publisher of *Hustler*, released the names that he had garnered by offering to pay vast sums to women who could prove that they had had affairs with members of Congress; most of the mainstream press avoided the revelations. Military personnel were assessing the actual damage done to Iraq after the bombings, squeezed in before the start of Ramadan, that had diverted public attention and delayed impeachment proceedings for a day or so. In Israel, as Benjamin Netanyahu's government was collapsing, missile strikes from Lebanon killed thirteen and peace seemed as distant as ever. The stock market kept soaring upward, like the mad uncle in *Arsenic and Old Lace* who believes he's Teddy Roosevelt charging up San Juan Hill. Two businessmen trying to navigate the globe in a balloon headed over China and out over the Pacific before getting stuck in a low-pressure trough and going into the "shark-infested waters" near Honolulu. Furby, meanwhile, was the season's runaway success of childhood covetousness. *You've Got Mail*, an e-mail romance starring Tom Hanks and Meg Ryan, topped the box office the weekend before Christmas. *Shakespeare in Love* was released on Christmas day. And the number one best-seller in *The New York Times Book Review* was Tom Wolfe's big novel about "decadent end-of-the-century American masculinity," as one critic called it, *A Man in Full*.

The critical debate over Wolfe's novel, in that rancorous December, was largely a repetition of the debate a decade before over *The Bonfire of the Vanities*, and the question was whether it transcended journalism, for which Wolfe had first become famous, to achieve the status of "literature." The issue was in part the tension between contemporaneity and permanence, in part the nature of literary art. Would the book be almost immediately dated, like news that loses its edge of suspense and immediacy once further events unfold, or would it have the strength to last? Was it well-constructed enough to "show virtue her own feature, scorn her own image, and the very age and body of the time his form and pressure," as Hamlet says? "Now this overdone," Hamlet continues, "or come tardy off, though it make the unskillful laugh, cannot but make the judicious grieve." The judicious were grieving. Because of Wolfe's past theorizing about the novel, his book stirred respected periodicals to commission important contemporary novelists to respond to it. John Updike in *The New Yorker* and Norman Mailer in *The New York Review of Books* weighed in with their almost embarrassed opinions that the book had opted to be a bestseller rather than a work of literature. Both were accused of envying Wolfe's success. Even their negative opinions gave *A Man in Full* a nimbus of respectability, but the very idea that it would be considered literature so rankled James Wood, the reviewer for *The New Republic*, that he lashed other periodicals for their tasteless concessions:

> The *Washington Post* thinks his new novel is "tough, demanding, uncompromising stuff," that it "calls to mind the work of Dickens" and gets "to the innermost human soul." *Newsweek* says: "Right now, no writer—reporter

or novelist—is getting it [America] on paper better than Tom Wolfe," while *Time* quivers that "no summary of *A Man in Full* can do justice to the novel's ethical nuances." *The New York Times* judges Wolfe to have written "passages as powerful and beautiful as anything written not merely by contemporary American novelists but by any American novelist." So it seems worth explaining that the gap between *Anna Karenina* and *A Man in Full* is not merely one of talent but of genre: a fountain against an aerosol spray. (38)

Wood's assessment of the novel had the kind of killing accuracy reserved for high crimes and misdemeanors of pretension. He demolished the comparison to Dickens with a few quotations; he showed that Wolfe's "realism" was in fact "a set of unreal devices, in which people breathe 'stertorously,' and think in conveniently spaced ellipses, and have two-page daydreams...."; he scorned "this bumptious simplicity, this toy-set of literary codes essentially indistinguishable from the narrative techniques of boys' comics" (42).

Writing in the online journal *Salon*, Elaine Showalter argued that Wolfe's real intention was not simply a testosteronic display but a turn toward transcendence, one that she explained by pointing out that "In August 1996, Wolfe had a quintuple heart bypass operation, followed by a prolonged depression from which he was rescued by Dr. Paul McHugh, psychiatrist-in-chief of the Johns Hopkins Hospital in Baltimore, and the main dedicatee of *A Man in Full*." Reviews like Wood's might have sent Wolfe back to Dr. McHugh, but, as when the "workout team" of PlannersBanc humiliates and intimidates the novel's protagonist Charlie Croker for defaulting on his half billion dollars of loans, too much was at stake for Wood or the other severe critics of the book to let Wolfe off easily: in this case, the very nature of literature. If Wolfe had not claimed so much for his kind of "documentation" so obstreperously and for so long (this is the fourth decade in which he has managed to be controversial), he might have been spared the attack. Wood argued that "The acceptance of this kind of writing as literature is dangerous not because anybody will confuse it with life, will think 'this is what life is like,' but because readers may read it and think 'this is what literature is like'" (42).

But what *is* "literature"? Why does it matter enough to fight for? Why should it need to be protected from *A Man in Full*? One way to an answer lies through what Wolfe himself believes "literature" to be. Late in the novel, a former teacher of nineteenth-century English literature at Emory University, now a stroke victim, bitterly tells the young hero Conrad Hensley that students do not realize to what extent literature is "an incalculable luxury." Old Professor Gardner and his wife, herself a specialist in European literature, have been improvident about saving for retirement, and within a few years after leaving Emory, they have ended up in a four-room house in Cabbagetown, where Conrad finds them in his job as a home nurse. Before he knows their circumstances, he does not understand why the old man would say that "Entire civilizations are founded without any literature at all and without anybody missing it. It's only later on when there's a big enough class of indolent drones to write the stuff and read the stuff that you have literature." Or that "Literature's a sort of dessert," whereas "Life's about cruelty and intimidation."

Wolfe's metaphor for "literature"—and his use of the word unmistakably recalls earlier attacks on *The Bonfire of the Vanities*—is the Gardners' precious collection of dolls and porcelain figurines "arranged on wooden knickknack shelves" on every wall of the house. "Conrad had no idea what the dolls might be worth, but he had only to look at the exquisite workmanship of some of the porcelain figures to know they must be valuable. Despite its dreadful layout, the little house's interior seemed like something lavish beyond all normal reckoning" (643). Where one might reasonably expect to find the Gardners' *books*, their "literature," one finds instead dolls and figurines, a fragile collection of miniatures that represents "incalculable luxury." The thug who intimidates the old professors has already destroyed a whole shelf of these figurines before Conrad can stop him. Once he discovers that they are being bullied into paying protection money to this man (apparently the real reason for the old teacher's bitterness), Conrad overpowers and intimidates their oppressor, using the practical brutalities learned in jail. The sweet old academic Gardners, dreamers protected for most of their lives by institutions that let them maintain their delicacies, are Romantics who now face an embittered old age without provision for the actual business of the world.

Ironically their protector is Conrad, reader of Epictetus! One of Wolfe's running ironies in the novel is that in prison (a long story! as Wolfe might say), the virtuous Conrad has inadvertently received a copy of *The Stoics* instead of the novel he had asked his wife to send. In the sayings and anecdotes of the Stoic philosophers, he discovers affinities with his own situation:

> Epictetus *spoke* to him!—from half a world and two thousand years away! The answer was somewhere in these pages! What little bit Conrad had learned about philosophy at Mount Diablo had seemed to concern people who were free and whose main problem was to choose from among life's infinite possibilities. Only Epictetus began with the assumption that life is hard, brutal, punishing, narrow, and confining, a deadly business, and that fairness and unfairness are beside the point. Only Epictetus, so far as Conrad knew, was a philosopher who had been stripped of everything, imprisoned, tortured, enslaved, threatened with death. And only Epictetus had looked his tormenters in the eye and said, "You do what you have to do, and I will do what I have to do, which is live and die like a man." And he had prevailed. (411)

Philosophical (not to mention theological) rivals to Epictetus aside, the point seems to be that only tough-minded books that confront real life's cruelty and intimidation can offer liberation from the prison of circumstance. *A Man in Full*, one infers, is such a book.

Imprisonment is the novel's central symbolic situation, homosexual rape its metaphor for the ultimate injury to the ego. One could argue that, just as the breeding of Croker's prize stallion to a mare in heat in a breeding barn is the comic apotheosis of post-Freudian literary sex ("The quake rattled their innards. The planets collided. The earth wobbled. Sex! Lust! Desperate! Irresistible!"), so homosexual rape and its corporate counterpart (the "workout") are the atavistic expressions of a primitive will to power. This theme turns up everywhere, but especially in the novel's central set piece on art. Both Charlie Croker, the novel's protagonist, and his ex-wife Martha are pressured by others into buying $20,000 tables for ten at the opening of the High Museum's new exhibition of Wilson Lapeth's homosexual prison art. The Lapeth show features a number of long-suppressed pornographic works that are now shown largely because Atlanta is afraid to seem provincial. Lapeth, a fictional Atlanta artist of the 1920s and a take-off on Robert Mapplethorpe, has become fashionable because his work fits the principles of contemporary "queer theory" derived from Michel Foucault, whose name the museum's new director, Jonathan Myrer, invokes with reverence in his introductory lecture:

> "How fitting it is"—
>
> Charlie looked about to see if everybody else heard what he was hearing. But even Billy's and Doris's heads were turned in a polite blankness toward the podium.
>
> —"that Lapeth chose the prison as the subject matter of the art treasures we see around us tonight. As Michel Foucault has demonstrated so conclusively in our own time—the prison—the actual *carcerel*, in his terminology—the actual center of confinement and torture—is but the end point"—
>
> Who? thought Charlie. Michelle Fookoe? He looked at Serena, who was turned about in her chair drinking in every word as if it were ambrosia.
>
> —"the unmistakable terminus—of a process that presses in upon us all. The torture begins soon after the moment of birth, but we choose to call it 'education,' 'religion,' 'government,' 'custom,' 'convention,' 'tradition,' and 'Western civilization.' The result is…a relentless confinement within 'the norm,' 'the standard,' a process so…gradual that it requires a genius on the order of a Foucault—or a Lapeth—to awaken us…from the torpor of our long imprisonment." (435-36)

By having Michel Foucault's fashionable theories filtered through the perceptions of the troglodyte Charlie Croker (former football star, famous real estate developer, freshly bankrupt), he skewers Croker, whose every move is based on power, at the same time that he withers critical fashion by looking at it through the plain-dealer's common sense. Wolfe puts into Myrer's mouth an inverted version of his own prison theme. Myrer's speech about

Lapeth provides an ironic contrast to the brutal homosexual rape of a boy nicknamed "Pocahontas" (because of his Mohawk haircut) during Conrad Hensley's incarceration. Lapeth's "prison," in other words, is a fantasized paradise of sexually pent-up men without women, hardly "the unmistakable terminus of a process that presses in upon us all." Conrad's Santa Rita prison *is* that terminus, a metaphor for man in the Hobbesian state of nature. For conservative corporate Atlanta to sponsor Foucault and Lapeth because of *fashion*, Wolfe implies, ultimately means to eroticize tyranny and perversely *seek out* imprisonment. Conrad Hensley, on the other hand, finds in the tradition and civilization derided by Myrer the means of his own liberation from a haphazard upbringing by shiftless hippie parents, not to mention from his poverty and his very literal imprisonment. Through Conrad comes the novel's strain of affirmation and its movement toward transcendence.

T HE word "literature" as both James Wood and Wolfe's Professor Gardner use it is a measure of the works of the poetic or "making" imagination, and it implies a distinction between mere entertainment and a deeply pleasurable mode of wisdom. To "have literature," in the sense of possessing a cultured understanding of books and letters, goes back to the fourteenth century, though the use of "literature" to denote imaginative works of high quality is more recent. As commonly employed, "literature" does not mean what is unpopular or incomprehensible, but what has in it the capacity to illuminate and surprise, teach and delight, in a lasting way. Some bookstores even separate "literature" from "fiction," for example, and the criteria for the distinction is probably that some works of fiction have been found to be worth teaching—that is, that they have made their way into academic respectability, out of the general culture. What keeps the name "literature" from applying to what Wolfe has written? Of the reasons one might cite, I will choose two, the first more obvious than the second: the art of the fiction and the novel's engagement with our time.

The passage about Croker listening to Myrer's speech already demonstrates fairly well one of the problems: Wolfe's rendering of perception. The events that he describes have to be filtered through someone's consciousness, in this case Charlie Croker's, which means that the reader's awareness has to exist in the fictional space created by what Charlie perceives, his bodily sense of himself taking it in, and the flow of his thoughts meeting it. For example, Croker hears Myrer mention Foucault and the *carcerel*: "Who? thought Charlie. Michelle Fookoe? He looked at Serena, who was turned about in her chair drinking in every word as if it were ambrosia." Insecure, Charlie plausibly glances at his wife to see whether *she* (as his judge and his cultural representative at once) knows the name he does not recognize. But the phonetic rendering of "Foucault"—an obvious failure to recognize the name as French—unfortunately does not bode well for the urbane simile. This description of Serena (who is twenty-eight, and as Croker has commented to himself earlier, "Less than half his age! Even from fifty or sixty yards away she had Second Wife written all over her!") requires Charlie to make the ironic comparison of Myrer's critical jargon to ambrosia, which means that he has to know the classical qualities of ambrosia, including its capacity to immortalize those who are allowed to partake of it. Is there something either in Charlie's down-home background or in his acquired tastes to make classical allusions spontaneous? (When I was growing up in Georgia not too long after Charlie Croker, "ambrosia" was a holiday dessert made with orange and coconut.) Are his self-references Olympian? Not at all: his favorite work of art is an N. C. Wyeth illustration of the wounded Jim Bowie fighting off Mexicans with his big Bowie knife.

If this were "literature," Wolfe would care about the provenance of Croker's comparison, but he wants to satirize the Types, the big developer and his sophisticated trophy wife; he wants Charlie's "Fookoe" and Serena's rapt (therefore sexual and threatening) appetite for intellectual fashion. The problem is that for *A Man in Full* to work, the reader has to care about the characters, and only the texture of convincing inner association could make Charlie and Serena come to life as more than types. Even the satirist or the writer of black comedy should find something more here. To the richly grotesque Georgia imagination of Flannery O'Connor, for example, the local simile would have been worth getting right.

Much ado about ambrosia: but the question is what immortalizes writing, and there are similar examples of indifferent art on every page, even in Wolfe's best descriptions. In the chapter called "The Breeding Barn," Croker takes the guests at his plantation to see his prize stallion mate with a mare. Mailer and others have commented on the vividness of this, the only sex scene in the novel. Wolfe's horses dominate and submit on an archetypal and overwhelmingly physical scale—huge bodies whose desire has no mediating intellect, no language. Charlie Croker, full of doubts about his financial situation and therefore his masculinity, brings the stallion into the barn himself as a display of his potency in mastering the horse:

> As they entered the doorway, the stallion breathed in the full overpowering smell of the mare in heat and launched into a ferocious show of machismo. He snorted, he rolled his massive shoulders, he flexed his neck up and down and yawed it back and forth, he did a little dance with his hindquarters, and he whinnied. He whinnied in anger, in agony, in des- peration and anticipation. Had he possessed bigger vocal cords, he would have sounded like ten trumpets. He bared his teeth, rolled his eyes, whinnied some more. He looked like an immense equine lunatic. Charlie set his jaws and tried to look totally in command and held on for dear life. His eyes were slow in readjusting to the gloom. Over here—a dazzling cone of light—the mare in the stock—the stable hands. Over there— slowly taking shape in the shadows—Lettie, Wally, Serena, Herb and Marsha Richman, and the rest of them—they were huddled together. Their eyes were like saucers. As he fought to keep the beast's head down, Charlie could feel its huge body shuddering—with lust!—the rawest, purest lust imaginable! (303-4)

Is this literature? It certainly engages one's attention. I remember hearing a radio story about the way that cocaine arouses pleasure and well-being by activating L-dopa in the brain, but uses up the brain's natural chemicals to such an extent that, without the drug, the addict is left like the knight in Keats' poem, "all haggard and all woe-begone." In the same way, Wolfe's fictional world is pumped, exaggerated, like a comic book, but the style blanks out the natural pleasure of perception. It is almost impossible to quote from the book without feeling that Wolfe used plastic and neon for his sentences instead of more expensive materials. Undoubtedly, Wolfe would argue that his style reflects the world he describes, with its hyped emphasis on everything from big money to sharply defined muscles. The problem is that this kind of exaggeration, like pornography, uses up the imagination and obliterates subtlety.

Compare this scene—its awkward similes ("like an immense equine lunatic"), its clichés ("held on for dear life," "Their eyes were like saucers"), its stagy literalness about the inner space of the barn, and its exclamatory style!—with the scene in Tolstoy's *Anna Karenina*, when Levin is going out hunting with his dog Laska early in the morning. Levin is still smarting from his bad luck the afternoon before, when his friend Oblonsky killed fourteen birds to his five. In the intervening night, he stayed alone in the peasant hut (the obedient, newly married man), while the equally married Oblonsky and a friend went out to dance and flirt with the peasant girls. Like Croker, Levin has something about his manhood to prove to himself and to the others, but Tolstoy does not coarsen his perceptual acuity because of his preoccupation:

> The path led him straight to the marsh, which was recognizable by the mist rising from it, thicker at one spot and thinner at another, so that the sedge and willow bushes looked like islets swaying in the mist. At the edge of the marsh the peasant boys and men who had pastured their horses in the night lay, covered with their coats, having fallen asleep at daybreak. Not far from them, three hobbled horses were moving about. One of them clattered its shackles. Laska walked beside her master, seeking permission to run forward and look around. When he had passed the sleeping peasants and reached the first wet place, Levin examined his percussion caps and allowed Laska to go. One of the horses, a well-fed three-year-old chestnut, on seeing the dog, started, lifted his tail, and snorted. The other horses, also alarmed, splashed through the water with their hobbled feet, making a sound of slapping as they drew their hoofs out of the thick clayey mud, and began floundering their way out of the marsh. Laska paused with a mocking look at the horses and a questioning one at Levin. He stroked her, and whistled as a sign that she might now set off. (589-90)

Granted, few writers could rival Tolstoy at this kind of realism, but Laska in this scene has a more unstudied interiority and a more convincing subtlety of *presence* than Croker does, limping on his bad knee, through Wolfe's whole novel. In Wolfe, the world ends just beyond the spotlight of what *Time* calls his "keen and boisterous prose," but in Tolstoy, one could stay and have breakfast with the peasants and walk home in an entirely undescribed direction. The sound of the horses' hoofs being drawn "out of the thick clayey mud" is the kind of detail that establishes a rich fictional redundancy, with eddies and depths that people ordinarily take in as *feeling*, incommunicably, at a pre-verbal level—the sound (a feminine *slapping*) of the horses' mild alarm at Laska's animal intrusion, the sense of earth and water, the freedom of motion of the hunters in contrast to the sleeping bodies and the hobbled horses. One *recognizes* in a scene like this one how much is actually present and unsaid in real experience. Wolfe, to the contrary, appears to believe that the intake manifold of perception needs some kind of concentrated artificial enhancement—"the rawest, purest lust imaginable!" As a result, the plot of *A Man in Full*, running out of adrenaline and testosterone, inevitably becomes implausible: Conrad Hensley converts Charlie Croker to the Stoicism of Epictetus, and Charlie gives up everything to become a Stoic evangelist popular enough in south Georgia and the Florida panhandle to be offered a syndication deal (*The Stoic's Hour*) with Fox Broadcasting. No, sir, I really don't think so: Charlie should have worked himself into the corporate seminar circuit, like Tony Robbins or Stephen Covey.

If Wolfe comes across as a lively animator rather than an artist of the novel, if his book is not "literary" and in fact wants to break through "literature" like Conrad Hensley escaping from Santa Rita prison after an earthquake, then the claims of his seriousness have to lie in another direction. From Wolfe's perspective, *A Man in Full* is not "literature" because it is neither closeted and precious nor perversely theorized into significance. "Wolfe believes that novels can still show us the way we live now," says *Time* magazine's citation of *A Man in Full* as the best novel of 1998. It takes on the great social realities—corporate ambition, the power and money associated with collegiate athletics, the problems black leaders have with being "too white," edge cities, the real effects of downsizing, the invasion of popular fashion by prison culture, the false heaven of trophy wives, the traffic in illegal immigrants, and so on—and centers them on a few crucial characters whose trajectories mean something about the state of our culture generally. It addresses head-on the central anxieties that men have about their masculinity, their identity, their relations to their wives and their children. It shows the vulnerability of the ego, the fragility of "success," the necessity of integrity. Like Frost's poem, "Provide, Provide," whose last stanza ironically recommends, "Better to go down dignified / With boughten friendship at your side / Than none at all. Provide, provide!" it satirizes the desperate vanities of wealth and power. It has much to recommend it: unlike the Gardners' porcelain luxuries, it can distinguish itself in the marketplace by addressing real concerns; unlike Lapeth's work and its theorizing advocates, it can affirm solid decencies for a large audience and perhaps give its readers a mirror for self-knowledge and encouragement. Readable and engaging, it manages the complexities of a large plot with considerable skill. Why should this novel need to be "literature" in some sense that satisfies the aesthetic criteria of literary critics, if it captures the great thrust of the world as it is in our own time, in its real risk and excitement?

My question is whether a novel can really "show us the way we live now" without being a work of art and therefore, like it or not, *literature*. Since my answer might be too hasty, since it might very well be determined by all sorts of unexamined influences, and since it might too easily adopt the "symptom," as Marjorie Garber would call it, of a distinction between high culture and popular culture, I am going to make the best case that I can *for* Wolfe's engagement with our time, then step back and reassess the claims for "literature."

More than the plantation or the art world or the jails that Wolfe envisions, the corporate world dominates the novel, and at this level Wolfe addresses the governing reality of the late twentieth century: an economy that crosses all former boundaries and owes no allegiance to any particular place. The problem with Charlie's conglomerate, "Croker Global," might very well be that Charlie has not sufficiently recognized the nature of this reality, if he is still trying to put his own name on it. According to some contemporary thinkers, this global competition puts individuals—in fact, man as such—in an entirely subordinate position. In an essay entitled "The Opposition of 'Individual' and 'Collective'—Psychology's Basic Fault: Reflections On Today's Magnum Opus of the Soul" first published in 1996, the archetypal psychologist Wolfgang Giegerich criticizes his discipline— the one that attempts to situate the individual psyche with respect to the "archetypes," rather than the types—for what he regards as its two more or less nostalgic tendencies in the face of the modern world: to try to recover the soul of the natural after modern physics; and to attempt to rescue the soul from the collective world that has forgotten "soul" altogether by working on "individuation." These are both mistakes, according to Giegerich, because "the road to the anima mundi is closed. Nature is 'out', at least in any psychological, theological, or metaphysical sense," and because the real magnum opus of the soul, is "not individuation, but globalization":

> the supreme value of today [is] *maximizing profit* in the context of global competition. Much like the Pharaoh in ancient Egypt, profit maximization is the sun around which we humans today have been assigned to revolve, by no means because of the personal greed of those who profit from this profit, but because the Copernican Revolution has redefined the role of humans as mere satellites. And this sun is, just as for Plato, *to agathon*, the highest good, the *summum bonum*. It is the only, exclusive value prevailing today; it has no other values, no other suns, before or beside it. It is an end, nay, *the* end in itself. It is our real God, our real Self. This Copernican Revolution is not bloody, but what is happening because of it is terrifying. Its violence is logical or ' psychological, we could also say metaphysical. Compared to it, the French and the Russian Revolutions were cozy.

In this complex and challenging essay, Giegerich argues that "The powerful dynamic of profit maximization...has nothing to do with people." What happens to Conrad Hensley in *A Man in Full* is an instance of what Giegerich means. Pressured by PlannersBanc, Charlie Croker decides to downsize the warehouse force of Croker Global Foods by thirty percent. As a result, Conrad is laid off, despite having just saved the life of a co-worker. His plans, his character, and his excellence as a worker mean nothing. As Giegerich says, "In the entire economy a radical and extremely powerful process of restructuring, of downsizing, of rationalization is going on. It is a process that renders hundreds of thousands or millions of employees redundant and assigns to those remaining ones the logical status of a collective maneuverable mass." In this global competition, he writes, people "are considered as an amorphous and continuously replaceable substance as is water, and no longer as so many human beings, each with their individual identity and personal dignity." This new view of man "is of an entirely different order. It is the logic of our reality, the logic or truth *we are in* (regardless of whether we are no more than the bewildered victims of this process or, as managers in industry or the like, active participants in, and contributors to, it)." Painful as it may be, says Giegerich, maximization of profit in global competition "is the real movement of the soul" in the contemporary world. Croker participates in it, Conrad suffers from it, but neither controls the nature of the movement itself.

Confronted with such a reality, archetypal psychologists, poets, and novelists have recognized with chagrin that both the world and the soul have been demeaned in the name of gain. Wordsworth's sonnet, "The World Is Too Much With Us" already articulates the essential problem:

> The world is too much with us; late and soon,
> Getting and spending, we lay waste our powers:
> Little we see in Nature that is ours . . .

And the poem points to the kind of redress attempted repeatedly in our century, even more than in Wordsworth's own:

> Great God! I'd rather be
> A Pagan suckled in a creed outworn;
> So might I, standing on this pleasant lea,

Have glimpses that would make me less forlorn;
Have sight of Proteus rising from the sea;
Or hear old Triton blow his wreathèd horn. (Noyes 317)

Before modern physics, Christianity first stripped the natural world of its gods and animating presences, its nymphs, naiads, satyrs, and fairies—a point that Giegerich also makes. Now, in the post-Christian modern world, science and gain dominate. The *soul* in its rich imaginative depth is left "forlorn," a word that Keats echoes in "Ode to a Nightingale" (1819), where he also complains that "the fancy cannot cheat so well as she is famed to do." Giegerich's argument is that the "creed outworn" is exactly that. Fantasy can re-divinize the sea with "old Proteus," and this animated nature can be present to the nostalgic imagination as part of "historical psychology," but it is not something capable of being achieved in the real world. Fancy cannot cheat well enough to overcome the "logic of our reality," and that reality has been present since the rationalizing logic of industrial capitalism first took hold.

But Giegerich does not simply abandon archetypal psychology as futile. Rather, he takes the reality of the world that seems so inimical to "soul life" *as* the movement of soul, and he detaches "soul" from its personalized human context. In other words, "soul" as he means it contains us, as the collective unconscious contains the individual manifestation of it, as history contains the private act, or as language contains and makes possible the speaker. This individually demeaning reality, profit maximization in global competition, is the soul's "shadow" in the Jungian sense. In archetypal psychology, one does not deny the "shadow" but submits to what it has to teach and works through it: "the shadow first of all needs to be acknowledged and investigated ('analyzed') *without reserve*, prior to any value judgment, in order to become fully known," says Giegerich. The great work in the contemporary world is not to moralize against the maximization of profit but to submit to the "logic of our reality":

> this process needs us, needs our heart, our feeling, our imaginative attention and rigorous thinking effort so as to have a chance to become instilled with mind, with feeling, with soul. It must not be left as something that happens

totally outside of us and apart from our consciousness.... The task is to (keenly and intelligently, not emotionally = sentimentally!) suffer the fundamental loss this process inflicts upon us and to allow it to work on us, as a kind of chisel that objectively and factually, not merely subjectively, works off our inflated egocentricity and subjectivism, our personalistic mode-of- being-in-the-world and along with it the entire 'anthropological fallacy'.... It must be more than an "idea" or "representation" in our mind that we subscribe to. It must conversely have inscribed itself into us. We come to a real knowledge only by having 'learned the hard way'.

Giegerich goes so far as to affirm this literally dehumanizing process of profit maximization in mythical terms as "our psychopomp guiding us *out* of the anthropological or ontological fallacy dominating the present consciousness and *into* a new form of consciousness."

In these arguments, Giegerich sounds strangely close to Foucault, who predicts the end of "man" as a constructed category at the end of *The Order of Things*. One might also reasonably argue that the quality of the times that he invests with such animus is simply what Plato calls "money-making" and that the man who gives himself over to it "makes it the great king within himself, girding it with tiaras, collars, and Persian swords" (*Republic* 553c). But the question with respect to Tom Wolfe's novel and the nature of literature is this: Can it be that Wolfe has grasped, as others have not, the extent to which the very existence of "literature" is a symptom of moralizing resistance to the logic of our reality? Is great literature simply one of "the political uses of nostalgia," as the cultural critic Marjorie Garber says? "Are great books most in need of being called 'great' when their link with the culture is most tenuous?" she asks. Making the argument that "Greatness is an effect of decontextualization" (removing a work or a figure from its modifying con-text), she writes, "It seems clear that anxieties about greatness in literature are closely tied to anxieties about national, political, and cultural greatness, and that the more anxious the government, the more pressure is placed upon the humanities to textualize and naturalize the category of the 'great'" (42-43). Garber is not debunking excellence of achievement. Painful as it is, her point, like Giegerich's, is a serious and chastening one: "greatness" *does* have its political and psychological uses, often disingenuous ones; it can be a mode of intimidation, a means of instilling self-contempt in those who threaten the expensive edifice of self-exaltation. (I think of the role of the statue of Peter the Great in Pushkin's "The Bronze Horseman.") Wolfe recognizes the self-serving, fantasized character of the ways we exalt ourselves and use "great" figures to prop ourselves up, as Croker does with Jim Bowie. What happens to Charlie Croker in *A Man in Full* contextualizes "greatness" generally, and what happens to the Gardners, one might say, contextualizes "literature." No one escapes what a co-worker of Conrad's calls "the bald man with the necktie," the embodiment of the impersonal, dehumanizing character of global competition for profit.

In facing the "shadow," the global Pharoahism of profit and its disintegrating effects on individual personalities, has Wolfe done what none of his contemporaries would dare to do? Can it be that Wolfe has deliberately eschewed the "fineness" that Updike found lacking because the inner style of our culture is not fine but naïvely promotional and exclamatory? Has he perhaps refused a more subtle consciousness to Croker and the other characters because a Tolstoyan richness of texture is really a compensation—and already was in Tolstoy himself—for what is missing in actual experience? Is the refusal to call *A Man in Full* "literature," much less "great literature," really a way of saying that it contextualizes itself too much to disguise from its audience the logic of our reality and the real work of the contemporary soul?

OF course, there are different ways of being tough-minded. Confronting the exigencies of one's time is admirable when it occasions virtues, and the virtues that concern a novelist are those of his art, his making of a thing, the novel. Taking on the magnum opus of the soul under the limitless global reign of market competition may be noble in itself, but formal excellence—that pitiless demand of the judging mind—remains the test of whether that task has been effectual in making a work. Playing a stolen violin in a concentration camp as an act of defiance, however nobly intentioned, would be a pathetic gesture unless it were perfectly self-forgetful music, given over entirely to the chance of excellence. In this regard, the "fallacy of imitative form" (intentionally bad art that reflects the lack of sensibility of its subject or its audience) exerts the iron rule of the permanent market: intention does not matter. The imitative form, in Wolfe's case, has to do with the parallel between Charlie Croker's big "edge city" project without tenants and Wolfe's big novel, hyped for years in advance. Croker's depression and disintegration *in* the novel all too clearly echo Wolfe's depression (as Elaine Showalter mentions) and the disintegration *of* the novel. Wolfe tries hard to disguise his failure to end the novel well, but eventually, there are no excuses for not achieving form, a respect in which it resembles telling the truth. For the novelist, the swarming vanities of the present—the big Germanic Zeitgeists—world-historical forces—solemn, cliff-like logics of profit with their frisson of the sublime—are only part of the material that the art has to shape. Eventually everything comes to rest on the artistic virtue of the novelist in his fidelity to the nature of the made thing. This sounds so old-fashioned that even saying it is like a dream of being naked in a public place.

The idea of form has been attacked on every side for decades, from De Man's criticism in *Blindness and Insight* that the form of a work can never be fully apprehended, that it exists not "in" the work but as part of the hermeneutic circle, and so on, to the general view running through contemporary theories of various kinds that "form" is really a conservative ideological term symptomatic of a nostalgia for a past untroubled by questions of race, class, and gender. "Form," in contemporary theory, is the name of a disguised pharisaical moralism. As a dimension of the "ideology of the aesthetic," it describes the tweedy haven of those who have no engagement with the moment, but who hunger with an unrecognized and highly deconstructible desire for the kind of safe "true world" outside becoming, the weak desire for metaphysical "rest" already decried by Nietzsche. Those who concern themselves with form, the thinking goes, are the guilty aristocrats in the lifeboats of the Titanic.

But form, like spelling, is the condition of intelligibility. Consider Wolfe's rendering of the South Georgia dialect of a white man named Durwood:

"'Tale you what. If you'n Mr. Stroock ain't too hongry yet, ahmoan swing on ovair fo' we git to the Gun House. 'At's the biggest, kickin'est dayum foal—I ain' never seed one 'at big, not fer no dayum two days old, anyhows'" (83). Spelling is arbitrary, culturally determined to the highest degree, subject to all kinds of abuses in the way that it perpetuates barriers of class and so on, but on the other hand it is the natural and undetermined condition of alphabetic writing, necessary for meaning and endemic to the combining and discriminating structure of the mind. Unless letters form a word at least phonetically, they signify nothing at all, despite the intention of the writer, and if the combination of letters violates the "dayum" conventions of spelling (even when it succeeds in denoting the word), it merely surrounds the word with connotations of ignorance or otherness without adding anything to the meaning—unless we are talking about *Finnegan's Wake*. On its minimal level, achieved form *disappears* into the unfolding of meaning, like spelling into significance. On its higher levels, in the balances, elevations, and depths of its address to the whole imagination, achieved form *appears* as the culmination of meaning in a way that transforms its own conventions. Put another way, the meaning of a work of literature is its form, and the apprehension of it is a recognition, very much like Platonic *anamnesis*, that is a promise of analyzable complexity and knowledge. Form involves an apprehension of the whole articulation in time that cannot be shortened to another kind of statement, any more than a sentence with many balances and delays, in which the sense pauses and slowly drops through many qualifying clauses, like a ship through the locks of a canal, can be adequately conveyed otherwise than in its whole rhythm. The form of *A Man in Full* is "ovair," in the sense that the intention can be discerned over there, but the meaning of the whole, compromised by exaggeration and contrivance, is ultimately conventional. A novel that does not succeed at being literature cannot fruitfully address the actual condition of the world. Why? Because it has not addressed, with sufficient awareness and care, its own actual condition as a made thing. There is no reason to trust it as wisdom, and its inflated contemporaneity will eventually hit a low pressure trough and drop into the waters where not even the *Rachel* will be looking for orphans.

In the chapters that follow, I will be asking why *literature* matters, and my initial concerns will be with an exacting double measure: the logic of reality and the logic of form. The first two writers that I will treat, both winners of the Nobel Prize, have been caught up, to one degree or another, in circumstances external to their art. These circumstances have focused attention on them in ways that allow ill-disposed critics to dismiss their honors. Seamus Heaney might not have become so prominent had he not been a Catholic from Northern Ireland writing during the renewal of violence there in the late 1960s. Toni Morrison, as a highly literate African-American woman writing in the decades following Martin Luther King Jr. and Malcolm X, is susceptible to the suspicion that she has been the beneficiary of a literary affirmative action. Yet for each of these writers, "lucky" not quite in the sense that Jacques Maritain applied the word to Dante, what stands or falls once one removes the scaffolding will be the work itself and what it permanently brings to culture. To the degree that the work achieves form and excellence, it also has much to say about why literature matters, precisely in the most difficult times and circumstances.

2.

Seamus Heaney and the "Grand Elementary Principle of Pleasure"

SEVERAL years ago, I met an Irish priest—let us call him Fr. O'Connell—at the seventeenth-century convent in Rome where our college's sophomores spent a semester. The nuns always segregated the professors from the students at dinner, and Fr. O'Connell, who was teaching a theology course, had full freedom—in between the interventions of the nuns' gruff Calabrian helper urging upon us great scoopfuls of rigatoni— to quiz me on the book I was teaching at the time, Joyce's *A Portrait of the Artist as a Young Man*. I had thought that he might worry about my teaching a book that centered on Stephen Dedalus' rejection of the church, but instead he wondered if I remembered the name of a town near Castletownroche mentioned in the book, the site of an athletic contest. I couldn't remember the name, but I knew that Stephen Dedalus' friend Davin had walked back from there and had a strange nighttime encounter with a woman at the door of a cottage. Fr. O'Connell told me the name of it, then said that it was his own birthplace. I had not been to Ireland, as he soon discovered, and he pointed out the necessary corollary, that these place-names were all abstract to me. I admitted it. Names like "Derry" and "Lough Derg," for instance, meant little to me, and I asked what he thought of the poet I associated with them, Seamus Heaney. He waved his hand dismissively.

"He won't last. He's gotten himself in with all the political establishments."

Some of his critics, I said, had made similar accusations.

"Well, it's not on that basis I make my judgment," he was quick to reply, "but on what I see of him. Of course, he's drawn attention since he won— what was it?—the Nobel Peace Prize. Do *you* like him?"

When I admitted that I was teaching some of his poems later in the week, he looked at me with amused speculation.

"Do you think he'll *last?*" he asked me.

"I think he's a good lyric poet," I said. "Some of his poems will last."

I had the strong impression that Fr. O'Connell had never actually read Heaney, who won the Nobel Prize for Literature in 1995. Still, both the confusion about prizes and the suspicion of his reputation were revealing, since reputations are often made and prizes bestowed on a basis that has less to do with literary merit than with the restless Warholian-Hegelian spotlights of the historical and cultural moment. To ask if a poet will last is to ask whether the writer is being honored for the work itself or for its appropriateness to a "politics of recognition."

David Lloyd dismisses Seamus Heaney exactly on this basis. His essay "'Pap for the Dispossessed': Heaney and the Post-Colonial Moment" confidently encompasses the poet and his work in a wider view of cultural change. Lloyd understands Heaney's popularity as part of a vast, homogenizing cultural reductionism that makes poetry a deeply compromised part of the "literature industry," instead of a means of imaginative freedom. Trying to account for "the elevation of a minor Irish writer to a touchstone of contemporary taste" (137), Lloyd argues that Heaney's popularity stems from several qualities in his poetry and essays: his emphasis on a personal freedom that "finds its image in gratuitous creative work"; the fact that his poems "respond compliantly to analysis based on assumptions about the nature of the well-made lyric poem"; and his use of rural Ireland's "less deracinated, less cultivated regional sensibilities" (135, 136) to make readers feel that they are experiencing an authenticity lost to their own circumstances. All of these, according to Lloyd, in fact contribute to an "imperial ideology," because Heaney writes the kind of thing that can be analyzed in classrooms or read alone with a pleasurable sense of self-affirmation and emotional coherence in the presence of a poetic "voice." In this way the poems promote what Lloyd describes with obvious contempt as "the right of private judgment" that allows one "to develop one's best self. The illusion of a free-market economy, where taste pretends to be an expression of the consumer's uncoerced judgment, thrives in the pedagogical method that furnishes the core of those literary institutions which in fact arbitrate cultural values" (135). For Lloyd, the reader is encouraged by the pedagogical method of schools and colleges to think that he has the "freedom" to engage in an apparently "private arbitration of value" when he reads, whereas in fact he likes what he is taught to like—the kind of poetry that Heaney writes.

Lloyd's evidence? The "unprecedented homogeneity of 'taste'" (136) about Heaney's poetry. The poems draw on a regional vividness and fresh vocabulary, but for Lloyd this very fact "dulls perception of the institutional and homogenizing culture which has sustained its apparent efflorescence at the very moment when the concept of locality...has become effectively archaic" (136). In other words, Heaney's "regionalism" does not recover the primal sources of culture, but it does make Heaney more marketable. In Lloyd's view, Heaney's reputation ends up being explainable because he *seems* to be giving back the local texture of being, the particulars lost in the universalizing and flattening tendencies of the modern worldwide market economy, whereas in fact he is writing exactly the kind of consumable poetry that this culture wants.

Two things seem to me ironic here. One is the complaint about the popularity of poetry, because Heaney's "marketability" must reach into areas of readership not ordinarily associated with the poetic subculture of which Dana Gioia and others complain. Even more ironically, Lloyd's argument is precisely what would sell in the intellectual market for which it was written, and his fashionable cultural-historical point of view, with its affinities to Raymond Williams, Frederic Jameson, and Michel Foucault, is much more snug with the contemporary "theory industry" than Heaney's rather old-fashioned views. Lloyd bets everything on a kind of cultural analysis in fashion; he counts on an eventual vindication of his theoretical perspective and on his judgment (along with Fr. O'Connell's) that Heaney is merely a marketing phenomenon. By contrast, Seamus Heaney bets everything on the prospect that in the future, as in the past, people will live in houses, drink water, have marriages and children, long for freedom, and worry about their loyalties and responsibilities. He thinks that poets should voice the meanings of these things, live into them imaginatively, criticize them, disclose them, and "extend the alphabet" of experience in a space made by the pleasures of their art. By Lloyd's standards, this older, essentially conservative view of the poet's purpose cannot be valid, because it involves too much collusion between the academy and the market, the critic and the poet, about what poetry is supposed to be. What would he have said in his essay if he could have seen Heaney's dedication of *The Spirit Level* (1996) to Helen Vendler, his colleague at Harvard and the major American critic of contemporary poetry? What could be more obvious, he might ask, than the fact that Vendler's book on Heaney appeared in the same month (November 1998) as Heaney's *Opened Ground: Selected Poems 1966-1996*?

I N an odd and surely unintended way, Lloyd's criticism, like Fr. O'Connell's, echoes both Tom Wolfe's suspicion of the literary establishment and, more importantly, some of the ancient criticism leveled against poetry and poets. Philosophers and theologians envied poetry's power to charm the mind and shape opinions about the most important things, but they feared and mistrusted it because, at the same time that it was the best medium the city had for bringing about "homogeneity of taste," it was also protean and disloyal, capable of being turned from serving the good by self-interest and the glamor of power. Its charm, in particular, made it dangerous, like an Alcibiades. Socrates wanted to expunge from his imagined city's education such passages as Odysseus' praise of full tables and good wine, or Demodokos' delightful story of the entrapment of the naked Ares and Aphrodite (*Republic* 390 a-c). Both passages, not coincidentally, are closely associated with the "fulfillment of delight" that Odysseus praises: a whole people sitting in order, full of joy (*euphrosyne*), listening to the inspired singer (*Odyssey* 9.5-8). Poetry's appeal to the senses and the passions, the sheer *pleasure* that gave it the power to entrance the souls of a whole people, made it both necessary and suspect for the ancient world. One of St. Augustine's early rebukes of himself in the *Confessions* is that he was too moved by the *Aeneid*. "What is more pitiable," he cries, "than a wretch without pity for himself who weeps over the death of Dido dying for love of Aeneas, but not weeping over himself dying for his lack of love for you, my God, light of my heart, bread of the inner mouth of my soul?" (15).

Would it be a consolation to St. Augustine that enjoyment of the *Aeneid* is by now a snag in no one's examination of conscience? In the market-driven world of entertainment, to argue that poetry matters now as it did for Augustine is like warning people about the moral peril of painting minia-tures on ivory or doing scrimshaw. What can it hurt enough, or help enough, to earn it serious attention, unless someone like Heaney comes along with the threat of actually being read? What effect can it have on people who have no knowledge of it and no impulse whatsoever to read it? The question is to some extent misleading, because what the ancients meant by poetry would encompass everything now comprising the entertainment industry: not only fiction, but film, stage drama, opera, and popular music. Poetry in this sense is more powerful than ever, its effects on the young more hotly decried: it matters to everyone. But in its most common contemporary definition, "poetry" means verse, and the crowds in Borders or Barnes & Noble, the audiences at concerts or films, are in general respectfully uninterested. "To the general reader," writes Dana Gioia, "discussions about the state of poetry sound like the debating of foreign politics by emigrés in a seedy café."

When Gioia published "Can Poetry Matter?" in *Atlantic Monthly* almost a decade ago, he incensed many in the profession by arguing that poetry had

achieved its success as an academic subculture at the expense of its larger
cultural importance. American poetry had quarantined itself from the
larger body of readers without knowing it. "A reader familiar with the novels
of Joyce Carol Oates, John Updike, or John Barth," he wrote, "may not even
recognize the names of Gwendolyn Brooks, Gary Snyder, and W. D. Snodgrass."
He went on to pose the question directly: "How does one persuade justly
skeptical readers, in terms they can understand and appreciate, that poetry
still matters?" With its specialized audience, poetry is "literature" par excellence, so much associated with high culture that even very good readers believe
they do not *really* understand it. And there are good reasons for their unease,
especially since poets themselves, without a sense of responsibility toward a
larger audience, feel altogether liberated to be "entranced to the exact premonition," in Robert Frost's luminous phrase. Jorie Graham, for example, seems
to draw her language from a vital phloem just under the bark of ordinary
consciousness; her verse is prolific, (apparently) unedited, with something of
the unexpected, instantaneous inventiveness of the dreaming mind. Although
her forms constantly vary, she uses the typographical resources of spacing,
section division, parentheses, and omission of words ("Did you see that did
you hear that (wind in the / ____ ____ ____?)") as a means of accentuating
particular qualities of consciousness. The beginning of "Self-Portrait As
Demeter And Persephone" can stand as an example:

> So Look I said this is the burning bush we're in it it has three faces
> It's a day's work it's the hand that takes and the other one
> The other one the mother the one whose grief is the visible world
> a wound she must keep open by beginning and beginning (Graham 59)

Yet, much as there is to consider (the identification of the burning bush of
Exodus with the narcissus that Persephone plucks, the Trinitarian imagery,
the idea of the visible world as a wound, the question of the self as both mother
and daughter), a reader who might submit with humility to the stream-of-
consciousness in certain sections of Toni Morrison's *Beloved* would not read
this poetry for pleasure, even if what Fr. Mapple in *Moby-Dick* calls "top-
gallant delight" promises to be the inmost quality of it. Graham's is therefore

not a poetry that Dana Gioia could use in arguing for the importance of verse in the larger culture. Too taxing for most readers to find pleasing, Graham has no public responsibility, only a private one to a small audience and the demands of an exacting imagination.

But missing from her poems is a local quality that Heaney found in reading Patrick Kavanagh's poems about his own region: "the unregarded data of the usual life. Potato-pits with rime on them, guttery gaps, iced-over puddles being crunched, cows being milked. . . ." What he experienced reading Kavanagh, he writes, "was not some hygienic and self-aware pleasure of the text but a primitive delight in finding world become word" (*The Government of the Tongue* 8). When most readers take up Graham or Gluck, they suspect at a glance that, like ordinary people at a wine-tasting party, they lack the subtlety of appreciation necessary for the true "pleasure of the text." Primitive delight is an entirely different matter than "literature" of the usual sort. Contrasting Kavanagh's effect to what happened to him when he read Louis MacNeice, Heaney says that "MacNeice did not throw the switch that sends writing energy sizzling into a hitherto unwriting system. When I opened his book, I still came up against the windowpane of literature. His poems arose from a mind-stuff and existed in a cultural setting which were at one remove from me and what I came from" (*Government* 8). Like Kavanagh's or Robert Frost's, Heaney's poems seem primarily derived from a specific delimiting place rather than from "a mind-stuff." Graham, on the other hand, freed from wondering whether her language will be used in some incendiary way or get her imprisoned like a Mandelstam, can follow the precise "come-hither" of her own concern with the implications of states of consciousness. There is something in a poem like "Room Tone," for example, that the writer concerned with a politically charged public cannot afford to do—not that Heaney's tastes run in this direction in any case. Graham addresses her reader directly; she explicitly removes the windowpane of difference between her self-awareness as a writer and the reader's consciousness in order to draw an analogy between the imaginative space created by poetry and the "room tone" of divine presence:

will you
speak back to me,
will you look up now, please?
Dear reader, is it enough for you that I am thinking of you
in this generic sort of way,
moving across the page for you that your eyes move,
moving in and out of these rooms that there be a *there*
for you?
Is it less fearful that you are held in mind
even if only as an instance?
Can you pray to it?
Can you give yourself over? (Graham 73)

Next to Graham's, Seamus Heaney's imagination seems more standard and workaday, more distinctly conventional, and, if more solid, less brilliant, less likely to explore genuinely new spaces in the strangely transcendental "between" of writer and reader.

What interests Heaney, as his comment about "world becoming word" makes clear, is a more orthodox and readily comprehensible mimetic pleasure. Like Robert Frost forty or fifty years ago, Heaney has gained an audience. One can scorn his readership, as Lloyd does, for having a middling taste informed by large collusions of colleges with market forces, but it is almost certainly an audience that, reader by reader, finds a kind of primitive delight in what Heaney does with language. Because he has rejected, on the one hand, the pressures to become a political advocate, and has been spared, on the other, too private or introverted an imaginative temperament, Heaney is the only poet writing in English who has felt his work increasingly under the scrutiny of a global readership and who has consciously borne a large public responsibility for the past three decades. He has a political impor-tance, ironically, because he has done his best not to exacerbate the hatreds of his vexed homeland, Northern Ireland. As Jonathan Allison puts it, "To regard Heaney as a poet of self-division has become a critical commonplace. His poetry is said to mediate between, oscillate between, chart a course between, struggle between, and voice the conflict between certain opposing choices. (These phrases come from a random selection of critics.)" What is not generally acknowledged is that, in fending off political pressures to take sides, Heaney has instead taken what Robert Pinsky calls "the gift of pleasure" and its implications as seriously as any writer in the second half of the twentieth century. The focus that came to rest upon him because of his arising precisely in that troubled place has made it possible for him to articulate a very different and unexpected emphasis: "When it comes to poetic composition," Heaney writes, "one has to allow for the presence, even for the pre-eminence, of what Wordsworth called 'the grand elementary principle of pleasure,' and that pleasure comes from the doing-in-language of certain things" (*The Redress of Poetry* 24).

Wordsworth's argument about the poet's obligation to serve pleasure in "Preface to the Second Edition of *Lyrical Ballads*" could be taken, up to a point, as Heaney's own. According to Wordsworth,

> The Poet writes under one restriction only, namely, the necessity of giving immediate pleasure to a human Being possessed of that information which may be expected from him, not as a lawyer, a physician, a mariner, an astronomer, or a natural philosopher, but as a Man.... Nor let this necessity of producing immediate pleasure be considered a degradation of the Poet's art. It is far otherwise.... It is homage paid to the native and naked dignity of man, to the grand elementary principle of pleasure, by which he knows, and feels, and lives, and moves. We have no sympathy but what is propagated by pleasure: I would not be misunderstood; but wherever we sympathize with pain, it will be found that the sympathy is produced and carried on by subtle combinations with pleasure. (438)

Twenty years later in the *Biographia Literaria*, Coleridge wrote that "A poem is that species of composition, which is opposed to works of science, by proposing for its *immediate* object pleasure, not truth" (471),[1] and Wordsworth here insists on the same thing. He echoes and secularizes, or perhaps simply literalizes, St. Paul's description of the God "in whom we live and move and have our being." This indwelling divinity is everywhere near at hand and constantly moving us toward it with "the grand elementary principle of pleasure," a pleasure available to all without need of church or tithe or priesthood. It constitutes the very power, not just of feeling, but of knowing, of life, and of motion. Understood in the Wordsworthian sense, natural pleasure is therefore the evidence of a blessing, like the "gentle breeze" that begins the *Prelude*, an accord with the spirit that "rolls through all things," as he writes in "Tintern Abbey." Opening the deepest affinities of human nature with the "burden of the mystery," this pleasure has almost nothing to do with sensuality. The poet's obligation of "producing immediate pleasure" means that he should bring the reader of the poem a feeling somewhere between Rousseau's "sweet sentiment of existence" and the pang of the Beatitudes.

Heaney seems, like most contemporary admirers of the Romantics, to recognize and honor the mood of this thought but to find its actual claims untenable, as Wordsworth himself did a few years later. When Wordsworth attempted to make a natural theology of pleasure, he did not recognize suf-ficiently how much his experience owed to "the doing-in-language of certain things," as Heaney puts it. In his own insistence on the primacy of pleasure, however, Heaney is also asking his readers to think about the metaphysical implications of the "primitive delight" that accompanies the conversion of world into word. How does one pursue these implications? Heaney has re-frained from taking up the theoretical debate that has famously and fashion-ably raged through Saussure, Wittgenstein, Heidegger, Levi-Strauss, Chomsky, Lacan, and Derrida, to name a few, but his affinities, should he lean in this direction, might be with the early Walter Benjamin ("Of Language As Such and of the Languages of Men") or the late Heidegger in his essays on the revelatory powers of poetry.[2] When Heaney writes about the way that poems come, his concerns are more with "the divining, vatic, oracular func-tion" of poetic composition, than with "felicity in the choice of words" (*Preoccupations: Selected Prose 1968-1978* 48-49). "A poem," he writes, "can sur-vive stylistic blemishes but it cannot survive a still-birth. The crucial action is pre-verbal, to be able to allow the first alertness or come-hither, sensed in a blurred or incomplete way, to dilate and approach as a thought or theme or phrase" (49). This first alertness of poetry means, in large part, an attentive-ness to the characteristic music of the dilating thought or theme or phrase. Writing about a passage in the *Prelude*, he argues that "the paraphrasable content of Wordsworth's philosophy of nature would remain inert had he not discovered the sounds proper to his sense. Nature forms the heart that watches and receives but until the voice of the poet has been correspondingly attuned, we cannot believe what we hear" (*Preoccupations* 69). If the poetic pleasure "comes from the doing-in-language of certain things," those things are likely to involve "feeling into words" and "the makings of a music," to take the titles of his own essays.

What things, then, are they for Heaney? Over a thirty-year career, the changes of Heaney's own pleasure in language have been considerable; every poem obviously has its own inner impulse. "Had a reader gone into hibernation in 1966," writes Allison, "after having read *Death of a Naturalist*, and woke up in 1991 and read *Seeing Things*, he or she would not believe the same poet had written these two books, since the former evokes the speaker's relationship to the earth and the natural landscape and since the latter evokes the world of the spirit." Some poems in between, though, have taken on a revelatory importance, like tracers in a night fighter's machine-gun bursts. They indicate where his aim is and what its self-corrections have been. In the title poem of his first volume, "Death of a Naturalist," the pleasures come from the sheer density of sensation that gives the town flax-dam its appeal in memory:

> Daily it sweltered in the punishing sun.
> Bubbles gargled delicately, bluebottles
> Wove a strong gauze of sound around the smell.
> There were dragon-flies, spotted butterflies,
> But best of all was the warm thick slobber
> Of frogspawn that grew like clotted water
> In the shade of the banks. (*Ground* 5)[3]

Like Theodore Roethke's greenhouse root cellar, this childhood place constitutes the primordial ferment of his imagination—its image, its content. A rich fusion of decomposition and generation: fertile rot, strangely intimate and interior with its gargling surface and gauzy texture of sound, the fetid wound-smell, quick motion of dragonflies, the vivid lightness of the butterflies—then in the hand, "warm thick slobber / Of frogspawn." Memory surprises itself with its metaphors and amplifies the language into more and more complex pleasures of recognition. Heaney loves the noises of his flax-dam; take this line simply for its sound: "Bubbles gargled delicately, bluebottles…." The word "bluebottles" wobbles upward after the comma and the sense moves on toward the gauzy sound that the insects make in the next line, but the sound here (not "blue bottles," but, because of "bubbles" earlier in the line, a ballooning *blueb*…ottles) bulges and eructs beneath the delicate gargling.

One could argue that Heaney simply repeats on Irish soil a Romantic discovery of childhood already two centuries old. Although the poem revisits a Wordsworthian idea, I would argue that it does so in the same way that a Shakespearean sonnet revisits a Petrarchan idea: to take it up, accept it, mock it, change it. After the theft of frogspawn for display "on window-sills at home" or "shelves at school" where finally the "fattening dots burst into nimble-/ Swimming tadpoles," the boy visits the flax-dam one day to find it invaded by angry bullfrogs and a coarse croaking:

> The air was thick with a bass chorus.
> Right down the dam gross-bellied frogs were cocked
> On sods; their loose necks pulsed like sails. Some hopped:
> The slap and plop were obscene threats. Some sat
> Poised like mud grenades, their blunt heads farting.
> I sickened, turned, and ran. The great slime kings
> Were gathered there for vengeance and I knew
> That if I dipped my hand the spawn would clutch it. (*Ground* 5)

All those distanced "windowpane" pleasures of collecting and displaying frogspawn suddenly get nasty. In part, this turn echoes Wordsworth's "Nutting" or the rowboat episode of the *Prelude*, but here one does not feel a high realm of natural Forms correcting him for the violation done to them. The poem is called "Death of a Naturalist" because of the killing repulsion that the boy feels. The grossness of the sexual underworld of the body affects him as the ugly Furies affect Apollo when he finds them sprawled about the omphalos at Delphi. Not feminine but distinctly male—Catholic,

Darwinian, and Freudian at once—the scrotal Father-Furies of maleness come in reprisal. He has entered their underworld of spawn with his newly guilty adolescent pleasures, and the theft has charged the landscape with bodily metaphors that ruin his Apollonian communion with the remembered image: "if I dipped my hand the spawn would clutch it." He is hooted out of the violated garden, out of his innocence, by an Aristophanic chorus, "the great slime kings." But the higher pleasures of the poem derive from this complicated narrative recognition of the moment of expulsion and shame.[4] In the poem's drama, the boy suddenly alienated from nature has more affinities with the guilty, pear-stealing Augustine of the *Confessions* than it might seem. Being cast out is the occasion of peripety, perhaps of conversion.

Jung calls the work of art an "autonomous complex," that is, an independent construct that exists within the psyche and draws upon its contents as the child in the womb, moving toward separability, draws upon its mother's body for nourishment. As Heaney writes in his introductory essay to *The Government of the Tongue*, "The achievement of a poem, after all, is an experience of release. In that liberated moment, when the lyric discovers its buoyant completion and the timeless formal pleasure comes to fullness and exhaustion, something occurs which is equidistant from self-justification and self-obliteration" (*Government* xxii). To my mind, the early poems from *Death of a Naturalist* and *Door into the Dark* that most achieve this "timeless formal pleasure" are the ones engaged, not with himself, but with a deliberate attempt to salvage the world that he observed around him in his childhood. David Lloyd is right that the concept of locality has become "effectively archaic" by the time Heaney writes these poems; the critics who attribute Heaney's popularity to the same forces that have popularized health foods and ecological movements probably have something to them as well. But it is also important to recognize that it is not locality per se that Heaney means to redress. Particular arts of work attract him—churning, divining water, smithing, thatching—because each one has an inner pleasure that constitutes its genius. In each, he finds the unstated analogy between its doing and the doing of the poem. In "The Diviner," for example, the moment of the "pluck,"

like a sudden, sharp desire, is also the impulse that draws the poetic imagination toward a new poem. When the diviner with his "forked hazel stick"
circled the terrain,

> The pluck came sharp as a sting.
> The rod jerked with precise convulsions,
> Spring water suddenly broadcasting
> Through a green hazel its secret stations. (*Ground* 12)

What moves Heaney, though, is the recognition that the "pluck of water"
needs the diviner's particular gift. It is not independently verifiable. Not just
anyone could feel it on his own. But neither is it private in the sense that it is
confined to the diviner: when others asked to try it, the rod "lay dead in their
grasp till, nonchalantly, / He gripped expectant wrists. The hazel stirred."
The communicability of the experience is the most profound thing about it,
this marvel of *knowing* that moves along its arc equidistant from the diviner's
self-justification and his self-obliteration. In the foreground is not the "self,"
not the practical benefits to follow this discovery of water, but the gift and
the magic it throws over the world it helps to make possible. The pleasure here
is not something distanced and "aesthetic." For Heaney, I suspect, much of
it comes in feeling the strong downward pluck of his spondees, line by line.

Helen Vendler has said that Heaney's work is full of revisitings and new
versions of old poems that she calls "second thoughts." Among these second
thoughts are some surprising omissions. "The Forge," for example—another
poem about an art being lost—furnishes the title for Heaney's second books
of poems, *Door into the Dark*, but Heaney left it out of his *Selected Poems 1966-
1987*, perhaps because it embarrassed him. Perhaps it seemed to him, in the
wake of criticism like Lloyd's, that he was nostalgically claiming for himself
a level of manly, rustic craft and solidity inaccessible to, say, Jorie Graham. In
the last lines, the old smith who had been leaning out on the jamb, recalling
"a clatter / Of hoofs where traffic is flashing in rows," dismissively "grunts
and goes in, with a slam and flick / To beat real iron out, to work the
bellows." I suspect that Heaney, on second thought, found transparently
disingenuous the speaker's implied ignorance at the beginning:

All I know is a door into the dark.
Outside, old axles and iron hoops rusting;
Inside, the hammered anvil's short-pitched rings,
The unpredictable fantail of sparks
Or hiss when a new shoe toughens in water. (*Ground* 20)

The implication—perhaps embarrassing to the older Heaney—is that, schooled in the real forges of his childhood, he, by god, knows more about the right respect toward the process of making what lasts—real iron, real poems—than the flashy traffic of citified literati who pass as poets these days. But Heaney reinstated "The Forge" in *Opened Ground,* probably because its central lines are indispensable:

The anvil must be somewhere in the centre,
Horned as a unicorn, at one end square,
Set there immoveable: an altar
Where he expends himself in shape and music. (*Ground* 20)

This anvil-altar, virginal, an "immoveable" omphalos, combines private memory with a mythology of *poiesis* that goes back to Wayland and Hephaistos. It is the center that sacralizes the labor of any making in which the maker expends himself "in shape and music."

"Timeless formal pleasure" comes from the achievement of the "shape and music" for which the poet expends himself, the form that reaches its "buoyant completion" apart from him in the poem itself. Obviously, "The Diviner" or "The Forge" did not simply come into existence *ex nihilo*; it has its provenance in late-twentieth-century Northern Ireland. But when the poem has *form*— that deconstructed and historicized but still numinous phoenix—it transcends both the author's "self" and its specific "historical circumstance." When the poem stirs, it is because some otherwise inaccessible power increasingly passes through the poem by means of the poet's work. Something has been intuited, some "pluck of water," and the poet has intuited it by the poem's means, and the poem has become the locus in which the green hazel, the diviner, the hidden water, and the bystanders who suddenly feel its communicated temper meet. Its language brings the reader into the quick of its own tremor.

Without the preeminence of the poem's pleasure, shoddy, resentful, time-serving, accountable work—the kind of indifference to natures that Richard Wilbur describes in "Junk"—will supplant the real thing. In "Thatcher," Heaney recalls the elaborate care with which the man, "Bespoke for weeks," who thatched roofs, would one day appear unexpectedly and begin to prepare his materials—the "sheaves of lashed wheat-straw" and the bundles of hazel and willow rods. After his honing, snipping, and sharpening, he would begin the actual work:

> Couchant for days on sods above the rafters,
> He shaved and flushed the butts, stitched all together
> Into a sloped honeycomb, a stubble patch,
> And left them gaping at his Midas touch. (*Ground* 21)

At stake in the question of pleasure is the very nature of quality. Unless the "couchant" artist (rendered heraldic, like a lion) can pursue what *pleases him*, instead of merely being serviceable, this "Midas touch" will disappear. Unless the poet resists the urgencies that make others turn to him for his words, unless he comes when he pleases and takes his time, he will destroy the freedom of his art and thus have nothing communicable in his gift. Flannery O'Connor says much the same thing about fiction when she writes, "The great novels we get in the future are not going to be those that the public thinks it wants, or those that critics demand. They are going to be the kinds of novels that interest the novelist. And the novels that interest the novelist are those that have not already been written" (*Mystery and Manners* 49). Poetry as a mode of knowledge depends upon the primitive delight of world newly becoming word. Without it, the poem has nothing to convey. It is impossible to consume its "meaning" without being taken through its range of pleasures, as it is impossible to know what is being conveyed in a meal—what kind of love— without the sense of taste. The knowledge comes only through the pleasures.

Much has been written about Heaney's ambivalence toward the "bass chorus" of his tribe and the "responsible *tristia*" that he traces through his 1975 volume, *North*, but perhaps too little about what kept him a poet through it. Whenever Heaney responded to political pressures, he did so in a way that kept the preeminence of "doing-in-language" ambiguously in the foreground. For example, in the widely anthologized "Punishment," Heaney intimately identifies with a young girl executed for adultery in first-century Denmark and preserved intact until she was exhumed from a bog in 1951. Working from her description in P. V. Glob's *The Bog People*, he writes in short bursts of lines:

> I can feel the tug
> of the halter at the nape
> of her neck, the wind
> on her naked front. (*Ground* 112)

As he imagines what happened to her, he pictures "her drowned / body in the bog" under a stone that held it down, "her shaved head / like a stubble of black corn." By thinking of her both under the stone and also alive before her punishment, "flaxen-haired, / undernourished" and "beautiful," dead but also "alive and sinning" (as he will put it in a much later poem), "Punishment" almost pardons her and lifts the stone of her long captivity.

But Heaney withdraws this release: "My poor scapegoat, // I almost love you / but would have cast, I know, / the stones of silence." He recognizes in her, not only the woman of St. Luke's gospel taken in adultery, but the women of contemporary Northern Ireland punished for loving British soldiers and betraying the Catholic cause. He ends the poem by seeming to side with the condemning community against the girl. Her punishment reminds him of the way that he has

> stood dumb
> when your betraying sisters,
> cauled in tar,
> wept by the railings.... (*Ground* 113)

He knows that he would "connive / in civilized outrage" at the treatment afforded her. To be "civilized" is to identify with what is rational, cross-cultural, enlightened, universal. His actual feelings, however, are idiomatic, arising from his identity with the tribe. He can "understand the exact / and tribal, intimate revenge." His condemnation of the girl appears to be a refusal of the civilized response, as well as a proudly guilty (perhaps Romantic) recognition of how "primitive" he really is.

But the opposition between "civilized outrage" and "intimate revenge," civilization and tribalism, is misleading. In a review of *North* shortly after the book appeared, Ciaran Carson accused Heaney of ignoring the particular historical circumstances of Northern Ireland by turning the punishment of the "betraying sisters" into a ritual that could happen in any time or place, as it happened in ancient Jutland (Longley 78). If, for Heaney, the punishment of these women is simply a ritual that defines the boundaries of the tribe, then the real betrayal of secrets and the deaths that result mean little to him, and his own reality becomes real to him only by being "anthropologized," as Helen Vendler puts it. The poet stands at a distance and queasily observes, without real engagement or moral responsibility. In a sense, he fiddles while Rome burns.

Heaney acknowledges the partial truth of these accusations, even in "Punishment" itself. Heaney as Irishman is a kind of typical Pharisee. Casting the "stones of silence" means that he would have stood by and not intervened when others stoned to death the woman taken in adultery: already an implicit condemnation both of himself for disapproving and not intervening, and of the Irish for doing what even the Pharisees did not do in the presence of Christ. In the Gospel account, of course, there is no stoning of the woman. The one who *is* stoned, early in *Acts*, is Stephen, the first martyr (and the eponym of James Joyce), and the one who casts "the stones of silence" by holding the coats and approving of the deed is Saul, who in time will praise the strength of the weak and the wisdom of the foolish. Heaney feels the anguish of self-discovery, of moral weakness, but at the same moment he also feels the redemptive poetic energy in the sudden coalescence of images that makes the poem possible: he has seen the "little adulteress" of the peat bog alive, weeping, handcuffed to the railings in Belfast. The pleasure of this startling recognition shines through the poem, however he restrains it with ambivalence. Blake claimed that Milton, as a true poet, was of the devil's party without knowing it, but Heaney clearly knows that his real sympathy, *as poet*, is with this "little adulteress." The poem very nearly makes her a saint of the pleasure-seeking imagination, a Persephone released at last from her ugly moral Hades. When he recognizes his own queasy twist of silent consent to her death, he does two things: he breaks his silence by writing the poem, and he makes her the "poor scapegoat" for himself; in other words, for a kind of betrayal.

Poetic pleasure takes the poet into a deep sympathy with those who, in their passionate addictions, step over the lines. His comic poem "An Afterwards" imagines him as another Dante consigned to the ninth circle of hell, where the poets, all betrayers of kin and country, are embedded in ice. When his wife makes her circuit, all he wants to know is "who wears the bays / in our green land above." But "Aided and abetted by Virgil's wife," she disavows all knowledge of poets and poetry and asks instead,

> "Why could you not have, oftener, in our years
> Unclenched, and come down laughing from your room
> And walked the twilight with me and your children—
> Like that one evening of elder bloom
> And hay, when the wild roses were fading?" (*Ground* 166)

What private, ambitious intensity has kept him so occupied that he can so neglect the natural pleasures of his own family, his own children? He is like the Irish airman of Yeats who disregards the complexity of allegiances because the "lonely impulse of delight" drives him into the clouds. Even when he writes the words of his wife's accusation, he gives the *poem* the feel of closely attended art unclenching—as if to say that even his wife's fury against him needs his art for its force, especially the soft-voiced metrical relaxation of her line, "And walked the twilight with me and your children." Surely there is some forgiveness if even the poet's accusers need him? And he gives her some lines that somewhat ameliorate his crime, though they end with a powerful indictment, softened in turn by his having said it for her: "You weren't the worst. You aspired to a kind, / Indifferent, faults-on-both-sides tact. / You left us first, and then those books, behind."'

Heaney recognizes that tribal and familial shame, within limits a powerful, positive force *of* limits, can also hold one in a position that serves neither
one's own interests nor those of one's people. The shame is transformed by
imagination. By its nature, the tribe will claim that the poet *owes* it his talents
and that he must subordinate to it "the grand elementary principle" of his
art. Its weapon against him will be shame. Letting the girl in "Punishment"
die for the tribe, he writes in ambiguous praise of her bold passion. The
ending of the poem reflects the poet's shame before her (since he does not
intervene), before civilization (since he rejects it for his own tribal idiom),
and before the tribe (since he sees the universality of love), but he accepts the
shame as fertile for poetry, which has its own governance and which, in its
way, redeems them all.

This shame is precisely what he means in *The Government of the Tongue* by his
phrase, "the embarrassment of the poet because of the artfulness of his art."
But "Punishment" is also an insistence: better embarrassment than the loss of
freedom. Moreover, a poem so energetically divided upon itself, with continuously ramifying tensions continuously harmonized in the poetic structure, is
the achievement of an intuition of balanced governance glimpsed through the
"timeless formal pleasure" of the poetry. Heaney writes that "the order of art
becomes an achievement intimating a possible order beyond itself, although
its relation to that further order remains promissory rather than obligatory"
(*Government* 94). If the poet had yielded to full participation in the Irish
moment instead of seeking to bring its archetypes close, he would have given
up his power to transform it. Despite the pressures brought to bear on him,
not least from his own cultural conscience, Heaney has worked to uphold the
preeminence of poetic pleasure as "a premonition of harmonies desired and
not inexpensively achieved" (*Government* 94).

N OT inexpensively: that is, poets and pilgrims do not come to such
harmonies without prayer and fasting. In the title poem of *Station
Island* (1984), Heaney makes himself "a fasted pilgrim, / light-headed" in an

encounter both with the Irish dead and with the huge overarching presence of Dante. As he explains in a note, "'Station Island' is set upon an island of that name in Lough Derg in Co. Donegal. For centuries it has been the site of a pilgrimage which involves fasting, praying and going barefoot around the 'beds'—stone circles believed to be the remaining foundations of early monastic buildings" (*Selected Poems* 241). The very choice to "do the station" suggests a deliberate renunciation of pleasure in its ordinary sense, a midlife coming to terms with the dead, those who have gone beyond or ahead into a being as shades. In his stations, he meets his significant dead: the "sabbath breaker" Simon Sweeney; William Carleton, who wrote about his experiences on the island 150 years earlier; teachers and murdered friends; and in the eighth of twelve sections, the second cousin, Colum McCartney, whose murder Heaney had written about in his poem "The Strand at Lough Beg" (*Ground* 145), originally published in a 1979 collection. Colum, a "bleeding, pale-faced boy, plastered in mud," is particularly troubling, because he quietly accuses Heaney of not showing enough agitation when he first heard of the murder. Heaney tries to defend himself by saying how he was struck dumb by it:

> 'I kept seeing a grey stretch of Lough Beg
> and the strand empty at daybreak.
> I felt like the bottom of a dried-up lake.' (*Ground* 239)

But like Carson and others who attack Heaney's avoidance and the "timid circumspect involvement" he accuses himself of in the previous section, cousin Colum will have none of it:

> 'You saw that, and you wrote that—not the fact.
> You confused evasion and artistic tact.
> The Protestant who shot me through the head
> I accuse directly, but indirectly, you
> who now atone perhaps upon this bed
> for the way you whitewashed ugliness and drew
> the lovely blinds of the *Purgatorio*
> and saccharined my death with morning dew.' (*Ground* 239)

The last three lines refer to the end of "The Strand at Lough Beg," where Heaney imagines greeting his cousin on the beach of Purgatory and reprising the scene in which Virgil washes Dante clean of the filth of Hell.[5] From the fasted perspective of "Station Island," Heaney finds this earlier Dantean trope saccharine and unearned, and he corrects it by bringing Colum's death and his own self-criticism into a strong, vernacular explicitness more in keeping with Dante's entirely unsentimental practice.

This poetic self-purgation calls to mind something that Carleton interrupts Heaney to say, enigmatically, at the end of Section Two: "'All this is like a trout kept in a spring / or maggots sown in wounds— / another life that cleans our element'" (*Ground* 228). Maggots "sown in wounds" eat the decaying flesh and prevent gangrene—if imagination can stand the remedy. Does Carleton mean by "all this" that doing the station and facing the dead, facing "the fact" of Colum's actual circumstances, will paradoxically clean the wound? "Another life that cleans our element" might also be, given the context, the "inflow of God into the soul" that St. John of the Cross describes. He speaks of two "nights" in his famous mystical poem and commentary on it, *The Dark Night*. The night of the senses—a deprivation of pleasure—comes to those beginners who think they are most enjoying God's favor:

> He leaves them in such dryness that they not only fail to receive satisfaction and pleasure from their spiritual exercises and works, as they formerly did, but also find these exercises distasteful and bitter.... As these souls do not get satisfaction or consolation from the things of God, they do not get any out of creatures either. Since God puts a soul in this dark night in order to dry up and purge its sensory appetite, He does not allow it to find sweetness or delight in anything. (312-13)

Pleasure, physical or spiritual (in the poet's case, the "personal Helicon"), dries up and gives nothing. If "the grand elementary principle of pleasure" no longer operates, as it ceased to do for the great Romantics, what will replace it?[6] Wordsworth's resigned consolations "In the soothing thoughts that spring / Out of human suffering" seem rather provincial beside the poetic and mystical tradition of the West—St. Augustine, Dante, and St. John of the

Cross—about the spiritual meaning and transformation of the aridity and loss of pleasure that comes at mid-life, especially to the man whose work is language. Unlike Wordsworth, Heaney deliberately invokes it, both in the pilgrimage itself and in the Dantean form of his poem. He seems very much aware that the terrible second night, the "dark night of the soul," is literally "another life that cleans our element":

> This dark night is an inflow of God into the soul, which purges it of its habitual ignorances and imperfections, natural and spiritual, and which the contemplatives call infused contemplation or mystical theology.... Insofar as infused contemplation is loving wisdom of God, it produces two principal effects in the soul: it prepares the soul for the union with God through love by both purging and illumining it.
>
> Yet a doubt arises: Why, if it is a divine light (for it illumines and purges a person of his ignorances), does the soul call it a dark night? In answer to this there are two reasons.... First, because of the height of the divine wisdom which exceeds the capacity of the soul. Second, because of the soul's baseness and impurity; and on this account it is painful, afflictive, and also dark for the soul. (335)

This inflow, in other words, will be felt as the most painful self-awareness, an unavoidable clarity about one's actual motives and weaknesses. In this light, Heaney's self-accusations in the poem can be regarded as a liberating public confession about what he is to be as a poet, since his "doing the station" is primarily a pilgrimage to clarify his sacred vocation. Still, one can ask whether Heaney actually does suggest that he has experienced a purging "inflow of God," or whether he uses this religious frame of reference as a complex homage to the central Catholic tradition in which he personally does not believe. It is entirely possible that Heaney understands and honors the formal exercises whose motivating faith has left him. On the other hand, his real question is what kind of penance is due before the aridity ends, the spring clears, the pleasures return, and the "premonition of harmonies desired and not inexpensively achieved" breaks through his imagination?

In Section XI of "Station Island," Heaney's confessor tells him to "'Read poems as prayers...and for your penance / translate me something by Juan de la Cruz'" (*Ground* 243). Heaney chooses "Cantar del alma que se huelga de conoscar a Dios por fe" ("Song of the Soul that Rejoices in Knowing God through Faith"), a poem whose central image is a fountain. The section closes with his translation, and the refrain calls into presence Heaney's awareness of what "the night" means to St. John of the Cross:

> How well I know that fountain, filling, running,
> although it is the night.
> ....
> So pellucid it never can be muddied,
> and I know that all light radiates from it
> although it is the night.
> ....
> This eternal fountain hides and splashes
> within this living bread that is life to us
> although it is the night.
>
> Hear it calling out to every creature.
> And they drink these waters, although it is dark there
> because it is the night.
>
> I am repining for this living fountain.
> Within this bread of life I see it plain
> although it is the night. (*Ground* 243-44)

The Eucharistic imagery of this ending needs to be understood in terms of Heaney's penance to "translate" Juan de la Cruz. To translate here, it hardly needs saying, means not just to put St. John of the Cross into English, but to find his own meaning in choosing this poem and these words. He chooses the fountain: the living water that Christ promises to the woman at the well, and for Heaney, what he was looking for when "As a child they could not keep [him] from wells" ("Personal Helicon"). These are also the waters of Frost's "Directive," where one can "drink and be whole again beyond confusion." In the original context of St. John of the Cross, to find this fountain "although it is the night" means to be able to discern by faith the source of eternal refreshment in the "darkness" of the sacrament and the obscurity of earthly forms. For Heaney, this sacramental faith "although it is the night" translates into a poetic faith (the trout-cleaned spring). The pilgrimage and its encounters have not made things easy in this regard. A young priest whom Heaney had known when he was a boy, a missionary who died in the rain forest, asks Heaney,

> 'What possessed you?
> I at least was young and unaware
>
> that what I thought was chosen was convention.
> But all this you were clear of you walked into
> over again. And the god has, as they say, withdrawn.' (*Ground* 231)

Poetic faith, then, means recognizing and voicing all the objections, but also witnessing to the complex analogical gesture of all creatures toward the poet disposed to "seeing things"; it means recognizing a metaphorical convertibility in which bread is also water is also God.

Is this poetic faith to be understood as the religious faith of Dante or St. John of the Cross? Not necessarily, however much one longs here for Heaney to step beyond Matthew Arnold's substitution of poetry for religion. He gains access to the larger *made* worlds of the poetic tradition, but one had somehow hoped for more of a breakthrough; one had wanted access to a larger metaphysical world, and perhaps the sadness of the poem, from Heaney's perspective as well as the reader's, is that this genuine transcendence remains just beyond the "windowpane of literature." His last encounter, in this regard, is highly ambiguous. When the boat from Station Island leaves him at the jetty near the parking lot, the man who grips his hand seems blind, and Heaney cannot tell whether he is there "to guide / or to be guided." Then he recognizes the voice "eddying with the vowels of all rivers": James Joyce.

In itself, the appearance of Joyce at the end of Heaney's "doing the station" is an extremely complex trope. All through the sequence, "familiar ghosts" have asked Heaney what he was about and warned him not to fall for it. Patrick Kavanagh, after mocking Heaney for slavishly repeating what he'd written about in 1942, even gives as a parting shot, "'In my own day / the odd one came here on the hunt for women'" (176). In this respect, Joyce can hardly be taken as the devil of the piece, the tempter who greets the returning pilgrim. Far from it. Joyce immediately puts Heaney on the defensive, not so much by calling the whole pilgrimage into question as by telling him that it is not enough:

> ...suddenly he hit a litter basket
>
> with his stick, saying, 'Your obligation
> is not discharged by any common rite.
> What you must do must be done on your own.
>
> The main thing is to write
> for the joy of it. Cultivate a work-lust
> that imagines its haven like your hands at night
>
> dreaming the sun in the sunspot of a breast.
> You are fasted now, light-headed, dangerous.
> Take off from here. And don't be so earnest,
>
> so ready for the sackcloth and the ashes.
> Let go, let fly, forget.
> You've listened long enough. Now strike your note.' (*Ground* 245)

At first glance, Joyce might seem to suggest that Heaney is merely (and belatedly) reiterating the movement of *A Portrait of the Artist as a Young Man*, but he also recognizes that the impulse might have its own reasons: the sense of "obligation" or vocation.

Obligation to what? Primarily to a pleasure from which other considerations have been removed: "the joy of it," the almost sexual desire to write. Joyce warns him about becoming too embroiled in Irish questions ("That subject people stuff"), regardless of the pressures put on him, and, in effect, urges him to stop being like that young missionary of Section IV "doomed to the decent thing" (172). Artistic liberty is the recommendation of Joyce:

> 'You lose more of yourself than you redeem
> doing the decent thing. Keep at a tangent.
> When they make the circle wide, it's time to swim

out on your own and fill the element
with signatures on your own frequency,
echo soundings, searches, probes, allurements,

elver-gleams in the dark of the whole sea.' (*Ground* 245-46)[7]

Poetry matters, from this perspective, because it risks an encounter with the dangerous powers outside its own cultural boundaries. In the opening lecture of his October 1986 series at the University of Kent's Eliot College, Heaney made this point explicitly:

> Poetry's special status among the literary arts derives from the audience's readiness to concede to it [an inspired] efficacy and resource. The poet is credited with a power to open unexpected and unedited communications between our nature and the nature of the reality we inhabit.
>
> The oldest evidence for this attitude appears in the Greek notion that when a lyric poet gives voice, 'it is a god that speaks.' (*Government* 93)

The joy of it is the surprising clarification of life for which the poet momentarily becomes the vehicle. This gift ceases to be offered if the poet is *primarily* concerned with what is expected and edited, with convention, "the decent thing." Heaney has a discernible hunger for orthodoxy, a desire to "get himself in with all the establishments," as Fr. O'Connell put it, but he feels it as the kind of temptation that the older Wordsworth should have resisted and did not. One does not sense in him the defiance and independence that characterized Joyce, but more a kind of permission being granted to his gift. The voice of the god and the "unedited communications," those "elver-gleams in the dark of the whole sea," come from a "fasted, light-headed, dangerous" poet such as Juan de la Cruz was and Heaney aspires to be.

WHEN he writes of "signatures on [his] own frequency," Heaney is remembering the radio of his childhood. Eleven years after the publication of "Station Island," accepting the Nobel Prize for Literature in Stockholm, he begins and ends his speech ("Crediting Poetry") with the image of leaning close to the wireless. Hearing the different accents and languages coming through the set from all over Europe became a first image of the "whole sea" in the sense that he means it here, and the polyphony also prepared for the "echo soundings, searches, probes, allurements" that his poetry would become.[8] Like Augustine's *Confessions*, Dante's *Inferno* and *Purgatorio*, Wordsworth's *Prelude* and Joyce's *A Portrait of the Artist as a Young Man*, "Station Island" is a confessional autobiography of preparation, a kind of promissory note on the great things to follow. "Crediting Poetry" especially alludes, I think, to the last two sections of this poem:

> for years I was bowed to the desk like some monk bowed over his prie-dieu, some dutiful contemplative pivoting his understanding in an attempt to bear his portion of the weight of the world, knowing himself incapable of heroic virtue or redemptive effect, but constrained by his obedience to his rule to repeat the effort and the posture. Blowing up sparks for a meagre heat. Forgetting faith, straining towards good works.... Then finally and happily, and not in obedience to the dolorous circumstances of my native place but in despite of them, I straightened up. (423)

The image of Joyce as "the downpour loosed its screens round his straight walk" is also the picture of Seamus Heaney straightening up and beginning to write "for the joy of it." Joyce's benediction sweeps away overly dutiful considerations of an audience and gives Heaney the freedom, not so much to do as Joyce had done, but to move in his own true direction.

⎯⎯ And what might that be? "I began a few years ago to try to make space in my reckoning and imagining for the marvelous as well as for the murderous" (423). Helen Vendler sees the beginning of this turn at the time of Heaney's mother's death in 1984, especially as Heaney commemorates her loss in the sonnet sequence, "Clearances," published in *The Haw Lantern* (1987). Her loss becomes associated for him with the chestnut tree, planted at his birth, that grew in their yard, since cut down. Like his mother, "Its heft and hush become a bright nowhere, / A soul ramifying and forever / Silent, beyond silence listened for" (*Ground* 290). Heaney's 1991 volume *Seeing Things* further articulates the possibilities of "the marvelous" first intuited in "Station

Island" and experienced through his mother's death. It begins with a translation from *Aeneid* VI, in which the Sybil gives her instructions about the underworld to Aeneas, and ends with a translation of Canto III of the *Inferno*, when Virgil explains who the souls on the riverbank are and how to deal with Charon. Framed by the continuity and difference between Virgil and Dante, by translation and influence, the book is a meditation on the difficult, marvelous entrance into "seeing things." It is a book of return (as in the sequence called "Glanmore Revisited") and of marking out new boundaries, remarking new kinds of openness. In "Fosterling," midway through the volume and just before the long sequence called "Squarings," Heaney acknowledges a "lightening" with its double sense (more light, less weight) that accompanies his new willingness to give "credit"—a witting avoidance of the heavy word "belief"—to other kinds of realities: "Me waiting until I was nearly fifty / To credit marvels." (*Ground* 331)

What kinds of marvels these are might best be seen in the title poem, "Seeing Things." Marvels of water, first of all: not the "clotted water" of frog-spawn, but a water charged with spiritual transparency. Each of the poem's three sections moves toward a moment of lightening in which something else, not necessarily from outside, seems to flow into perception. The first section of the poem is set in Inishbofin, an island in the Atlantic off Galway where Cromwell once had a kind of concentration camp for Catholic priests during his attempt to eradicate Catholicism from Ireland. Like Station Island, Inishbofin gives a Dantean polysemy to Heaney's poem, since its historical ruins predict, cause, and commemorate contemporary Irish religious divisions. But the poem also imagines the island as a past being left behind, a point of embarkation, like the mouth of the Tiber for the Italian souls in *Purgatorio*:

> Inishbofin on a Sunday morning.
> Sunlight, turfsmoke, seagulls, boatslip, diesel.
> One by one we were being handed down
> Into a boat that dipped and shilly-shallied
> Scaresomely every time. We sat tight

On short cross-benches, in nervous twos and threes,
Obedient, newly close, nobody speaking
Except the boatmen, as the gunwales sank
And seemed they might ship water any minute.
The sea was very calm but even so,
When the engine kicked and our ferryman
Swayed for balance, reaching for the tiller,
I panicked at the shiftiness and heft
Of the craft itself. What guaranteed us—
That quick response and buoyancy and swim—
Kept me in agony. (*Ground* 316)

This childlike fear of the unstable boat glides into the ancient terror of entering a world of shadows, unsubstantial bodies. This ferry's predecessors are Charon's boat that sinks almost to the gunwales when Aeneas steps into it (*Aeneid* VI), Phlegyas' little ferry on the Styx, which responds similarly to Dante (*Inferno* VIII), the quick, light craft that brings the newly dead souls to Mt. Purgatory (*Purgatorio* II), and the reader's "little bark" of *Paradiso* II. Unlike Aeneas or Dante, however, Heaney is not the only one with a body. The poem is about the predicament of shared weight, when everyone (to pinch the cliché) is in the same boat, the "nervous twos and threes" strangely, because so naturally, like the "two or three" of the Gospels to whom the presence of Christ is promised. Like everyone else, Heaney panics at "the craft itself" (with a play on his own "craft") because something in the "quick response and buoyancy and swim" of it—its spiritual lightness—is what it feels like to "credit marvels." The crossing requires a natural trust that points beyond itself to something more buoyant and wonderful. Familiar descriptions of belief and communion seem too heavy and contrived.

In effect, Heaney is having to reinvent a way of talking about the real co-presence of different levels of being and meaning. Homer could describe an event—the death of Sarpedon or Achilles dragging the body of Hektor around Patroklos' tomb—by giving the same action a phenomenological nearness and, at the same time, a mountaintop view from the perspective of the gods, who could see into greater contexts of space and time. Similarly,

Dante could establish it as axiomatic that any person or scene that the pilgrim encountered in the poem was divinely written in advance, so that the pilgrim always walked through a bountiful, exfoliating text.[9]

Heaney, by contrast, is, like every other poet of modernity, the cultural heir of what Paul Evdokimov calls "the triumph of pure semiology, the victory of the sign over the symbol, of the 'geometric spirit' over the 'spirit of finesse'" (Evdokimov 171). He walks through a world without presence, a semiological world of information. The poet has to overcome a philosophical predisposition that now exists in the language itself in order to texture it and achieve unexpected refractions. Still, given the abstractly materialist bias of the language that he works with, it is considerably easier for the poet to lade the page with heavy frog-spawn (the wonder of the particular) than to do convincingly what Evdokimov says that the liturgical icon does: "'de-thingifies,' dematerializes, and lightens reality but does not disintegrate it" (221). Poetic access to the "marvelous" that might be encountered in real circumstances (and Heaney does not *simply* mean the surprise of metaphor) requires considerable finesse. Characteristically, Heaney goes by water:

> All the time
> As we went sailing evenly across
> The deep, still, seeable-down-into water,
> It was as if I looked from another boat
> Sailing through air, far up, and could see
> How riskily we fared into the morning
> And loved in vain our bare, bowed, numbered heads. (*Ground* 316)

The actual view down through the water to the shadow of the boat far below gives way to the "as if" that suddenly floats him far above, clear water dematerialized into clear air, in an access of what Victor Turner calls "subjunctivity."[10] Vision suddenly doubles, he sees as a god sees, and he feels a detached impulse of love. There is a kind of gesture in the last line, a downward wave, as if from a Vatican apartment, of understanding, fellow-feeling, general absolution, helplessness. Why "in vain"? For the same reason that Zeus's love of Sarpedon is in vain—because mortals are mortal. The risks of our freedom and the vulnerabilities of our "bare, bowed, numbered heads" cannot be obviated. With the word "numbered," Heaney manages to suggest, at the same instant, a nightmare regime of hyper-rational horror that enumerates its victims and a God who has numbered the hairs on the head of each of his children. Further, he suggests that these two realities might both be fully present at the same time.

In the shorter second part of "Seeing Things," Heaney describes the "carved stone" water of the Jordan on the facade of a cathedral, where John baptizes Jesus: "Lines / Hard and thin and sinuous represent / The flowing river" (*Ground* 316-17). The marvel in this scene does not lie in an allegorical signifying, a semiological function by which the water "stands for" the already-accepted death of Christ, but in the way that the stone is transubstantiated into water:

> And yet in that utter visibility
> The stone's alive with what's invisible:
> Waterweed, stirred sand-grains hurrying off,
> The shadowy, unshadowed stream itself.
> All afternoon, heat wavered on the steps
> And the air we stood up to our eyes in wavered
> Like the zigzag hieroglyph for life itself. (*Ground* 317)

In this poem, "what's invisible" is a higher level of meaning: the reality of water, the irresistible, dematerialized experience of real water that flows miraculously in living stone. On the "steps," literally the steps of the cathedral and figuratively the means of spiritual ascent, the heat wavers like the stone lines that represent the river, the air heats into water, the water is what those present stand up to "[their] eyes" in, a wavering light, as though their eyes were just at the surface of this baptismal river. The reality of water is not disintegrated, but seeing itself is transubstantiated." Like the poets in the terrace of lust in *Purgatorio*, Heaney stands in a kind of living fire that is also water, air, life. "Seeing things" again seems to be the point. As Dante's baptism of the eyes in *Paradiso* XXX represents the ultimate reversal of mortal sight into divine seeing, Heaney's deciphering of the hieroglyph is a turn, however

momentary, that enables him to see the very air "alive with what's invisible."
Again, it seems to be a "lightening" into the serious poetic pleasure of vision
or *"Claritas"*—the "dry-eyed Latin word," as he calls it, that announces
the section.[12]

"Seeing Things" ends with a wry fairy tale. Beginning the third section
with "Once upon a time," Heaney describes a meeting with his "undrowned
father," closes the last line with a syntactically stressed "happily ever after," and
somehow avoids both mere cleverness and disguised sentimentality. This last
part of the poem remembers a time when his father came back from almost
being drowned after the horse had reared and the whole potato-spraying rig,
horse and all, had tilted over the bank and into the river, "hoofs, chains, shafts,
cartwheels, barrel / and tackle, all tumbling off the world," sweeping his hat
with them. The present perspective after his father's death makes him remember that earlier scene, when his father seemed almost to have survived himself
already, as if it were already in that earlier time a miraculous return. Memory
itself offers more than a fading, three-times-ungraspable image of the dead.
Instead, his father's image, coming to him now in recollection, has the "promissory" quality to which he alludes in "The Government of the Tongue":

> But when he came back, I was inside the house
> And saw him out the window, scatter-eyed
> And daunted, strange without his hat,
> His step unguided, his ghosthood immanent. (*Ground* 317)

Without his things, Heaney's father wanders back like the rich man who has
passed through the eye of a needle. Not "imminent" but "immanent," this
"ghosthood" is not the father's imitation of old Hamlet, but his spiritual
existence surfacing, an unexpected, minor pentecost of one. The disastrous
loss of his equipment strangely, and, in Heaney's memory, blessedly, gives
them a moment when they break through their differences and meet on the
same plane, in the I-Thou *communitas* that fairy tales always long for:

> That afternoon
> I saw him face to face, he came to me
> With his damp footprints out of the river,

And there was nothing between us there
That might not still be happily ever after. (*Ground* 317)

The sense of the last two lines, straightened out and robbed of their twisting negatives and wry diffidence, might be, "what was between us there can still be there forever," but the syntax of "That might not still be happily ever after," posed against the complex ambiguity of "there was nothing between us there," keeps the meaning spinning at the end of its wound-up cord. What comes across with increasing *claritas*, however, is the child's unprejudiced view of this numinous yet entirely human encounter. The "undrowned" father comes "with his damp footprints out of the river" (like someone baptized) to meet him "face to face," directly and personally, as one cannot meet God in this life. On that level, nothing could ever be between them, not even death.

To describe such a memory in terms of "pleasure" seems irrelevant, but it is not trivial to describe *the effect of the poem* in those terms. When Heaney praises Christopher Marlowe's "Hero and Leander" for its fresh language and untroubled eroticism in his essay "Extending the Alphabet," he writes, "An exuberant rhythm, a display of metrical virtuosity, some rising intellectual ground successfully surmounted—experiencing things like these gratifies and furthers the range of the mind's and the body's pleasures, and helps the reader to obey the old command: *nosce teipsum.* Know thyself" (*Redress* 37). Like Marlowe among the Elizabethans, Heaney has been trying to "extend the alphabet" of contemporary English into a range of pleasures that will help the reader to know himself. He scorns no poetic gratification, no revelation. But the pleasures of his poems are hardly the sensuous ones that characterize "Hero and Leander"; the "redress of poetry" in our own time lies in a different direction. At the end of "Squarings," Heaney writes, "Strange how things in the offing, once they're sensed, / Convert to things foreknown," and he goes on, playing off clichés with an almost Elizabethan *sprezzatura*, "Seventh heaven may be / The whole truth of a sixth sense come to pass" (102).[13] The bent of contemporary thought—its "alphabet"—is to ignore both sixth senses and seventh heavens, but Heaney tries to reground such experiences (in good Thomist fashion) by showing that they arise from, not in defiance of, sensation. "Sink every impulse like a bolt," he writes in a poem that might be the *ars poetica* of "Squarings": "Secure / The bastion of sensation. Do not waver / Into language. Do not waver in it" (*Ground* 333).

The American paperback edition of Heaney's most recent book, *The Spirit Level*, has a photograph of a carpenter's level: the trapped bubble of air showing midway in the water, between the markings, above the brass and weathered wood. Late in the book, Heaney's poem "The Errand" suggests that he got both the title and a level spirit out of a riddling play of wits with his father:

'On you go now! Run, son, like the devil
And tell your mother to try
To find me a bubble for the spirit level
And a new knot for this tie.'

But still he was glad, I know, when I stood my ground,
Putting it up to him
With a smile that trumped his smile and his fool's errand,
Waiting for the next move in the game. (*Ground* 404)

The game of wits requires fathers to find out whether their sons are fools and sons to expect the tests to keep getting harder. Part of the game here, I think, lies in recognizing that "a bubble for the spirit level / And a new knot for this tie" are both images for the formal achievement of poetry. Hugh Kenner has written in *The Pound Era* about knots as a figure of poetic form, a way of binding energies into patterns. By calling his book *The Spirit Level*, Heaney's move (if it is not a "fool's errand" for critics) is to focus attention on the trapped bubble of air and what it does. Released, the air is nothing, indistinguishable. But held inside the tube of glass, it reveals the perpendicular to the pull of gravity, the perfect tangent to the earth's sphere, and becomes in its balance a metaphor for the revelatory artifice of poetry.

The poem that opens *The Spirit Level*, "The Rain Stick," concentrates on the pure pleasure of this revelatory artifice. It is an emblematic poem for

Heaney, because in this native-American object made from a stalk of dried cactus, obviously from the desert and probably sacred in its original uses, he finds the ultimate "dematerializing" of his major symbol:

> Upend the rain stick and what happens next
> Is a music that you never would have known
> To listen for. In a cactus stalk
>
> Downpour, sluice-rush, spillage and backwash
> Come flowing through. You stand there like a pipe
> Being played by water, you shake it again lightly
>
> And diminuendo runs through all its scales
> Like a gutter stopping trickling. And now here comes
> A sprinkle of drops out of the freshened leaves,
>
> Then subtle little wets off grass and daisies;
> Then glitter-drizzle, almost-breaths of air.
> Upend the stick again. What happens next
>
> Is undiminished for having happened once,
> Twice, ten, a thousand times before.
> Who cares if all the music that transpires
>
> Is the fall of grit or dry seeds through a cactus?
> You are like a rich man entering heaven
> Through the ear of a raindrop. Listen now again. (*Ground* 371)

Does pleasure lead the mind astray, if "grit or dry seeds" can turn into "glitter-drizzle," despite the disclaimers of the reason? Delightfully, paradoxically, the water-music transpires from the driest things, combined by a wise art. One's reaction is strangely like what Coleridge describes as the motive force behind pursuing, of all things, chemistry: "The serious complacency which is afforded by the sense of truth, utility, permanence, and progression, blends with and ennobles the exhilarating surprise and the pleasurable sting of curiosity, which accompany the propounding and the solving of an Enigma." Solving the enigma of the rain stick, like devising an experiment that reveals what is elemental in all matter, involves "the sense of a principle of connection given by the mind, and sanctioned by the correspondency of nature. Hence the strong hold which in all ages chemistry has had on the imagination....we find poetry, as it were, substantiated and realized in nature: yea, nature itself disclosed to us,...as at once the poet and the poem!" ("The Charm of Chemistry"). In his late poems, I would argue, Heaney begins resurrecting himself as a naturalist on a higher level, as art serves to reveal nature's less obvious moves. His mood, in this regard, is like Shakespeare's in *The Tempest* or *The Winter's Tale*. In *The Winter's Tale*, for example, when Perdita expresses her distaste for any art that "improves" nature, Polixenes responds,

> Yet Nature is made better by no mean
> But Nature makes that mean; so over that art,
> Which you say adds to Nature, is an art
> That Nature makes. (IV, iv, 89-92)

From this perspective, the capacity of art to improve nature lends greater credit to the marvelous active nature *from which* one works, rather than simply the passive one *to which* one does clever things in the modern technological spirit. "Waiting for the next move in the game" in the larger sense means crediting a "further order" that poetry itself helps to reveal. The relation of achieved poetic form to that order "remains promissory rather than obligatory" (*Government* 94). Poetry does not attempt to stake out and systematize this metaphysical presence in a way that makes it assert its claims and preempt human freedom. In Heaney's lyric achievements, at least, there is a strong Keatsian negative capability, a steady ability to "remain in uncertainties, mysteries, doubts, without any irritable grasping after fact and reason." The lyric enterprise becomes a matter of finding a new bubble for the spirit level, getting just enough of what one can sense "in the offing" within the form, balanced between the lines.

I have sometimes felt toward Heaney what many have felt toward Wordsworth: that his best work has the air of perpetual promise, as though it were the "prelude" to something evermore about to be. At present, conclusions about his career are premature, but I strongly suspect that he will not

become an epic poet in his old age, much as he gestures toward Virgil or
Dante or the Beowulf poet. One of the reasons for Heaney's popularity,
however, might be his lack of pretension in the line of supreme fictions. He
finds himself in the position of Frost, who speaks of the poem as a "momentary stay against confusion." Yet he is also a great deal more hopeful than
Frost, and he clearly credits, more than Frost ever did, the high spiritual
claims of a poetic tradition from Aeschylus to Dante in which he has found
himself, as it were, at home in a greater Mossbawn. He has stood for what
poetry actually is, in its deep teaching pleasure, regardless of what pressures
toward the uses of his gifts might be brought upon him—and they have been
greater pressures than any American poet since Eliot has faced. One of his
greatest strengths is precisely what Keats means by calling it *negative* capability, a power to resist what would kill the essential poetry by attempting a
conceptual clarity alien to the imagination.

In "Postscript," the poem that closes both *The Spirit Level* and *Opened Ground*,
he speaks directly of the futility of thinking that one can foreclose on intuition. Writing in a casual imperative mood ("And sometime make the time"),
he tells the reader to drive out west "In September or October, when the wind
/ And the light are working off each other" along the Flaggy Shore of County
Clare. He imagines a moment when the ocean on one side "is wild / With
foam and glitter," while on the other side, the slate-grey surface of an inland
lake "is lit / By the earthed lightning of a flock of swans, / Their feathers
roughed and ruffling, white on white." Helen Vendler writes of this as an
"ecstatic moment" when "the wild and settled parts of being do not forget
each other, when the ocean is the partner of the lake, and when wind and light,
strength and clarity, contest for presence" (Vendler 26). I would add that in
this ecstatic moment, as in the last poem of "Squarings," "things in the offing,
once they're sensed, / Convert to things foreknown." The swans embody and
personify inwardly that wild revelatory outer openness, and the perceiver
passing between them is, for an instant, the pure medium of conversion:

> Useless to think you'll park and capture it
> More thoroughly. You are neither here nor there,

A hurry through which known and strange things pass
As big soft buffetings come at the car sideways
And catch the heart off guard and blow it open. (*Ground* 411)

Again, "pleasure" hardly seems an adequate word for what Heaney means to bring to his reader here, but in another sense it is the least pretentious one. What should we be now? he asks. Not those who stop and conscientiously photograph the swans and the whitecaps, but what we actually find ourselves being: "A hurry through which known and strange things pass." Perhaps we can ask in tranquility, as the poem does, what it means to *be*, rather than to be *in*, a hurry, what it says that the preposition has dropped away and that we have become this unmediated urgency to be somewhere else or to get something done, and what might be the implications of the "big soft buffetings" that seem to want to blow open, not the car, but the heart. The poem and the book entitled *Opened Ground* end with a kind of gentle violence, characteristic of Heaney, on the word "open": an ecstatic release of what has been trapped like a bubble in the interior, a new inflow from outside the self, a poised and alert "waiting for the next move in the game."

3.
Recasting Paradise

ARLIER in the same year that Tom Wolfe rolled out *A Man in Full*, Toni Morrison published her first novel since winning the Nobel Prize in 1993. Like Wolfe's novel, *Paradise* received mixed reviews. To those who admired Morrison, the book's serious merits were a relief, because they demonstrated that her gifts had survived the glare of global fame. To her detractors, the question was not whether the book was "literature"—at least not in the sense that opposed literature to journalism—but whether the public definition of literature was not being governed by social agendas. The book critic for *National Review*, for example, found the praise for the novel to be clear evidence of a liberal wish to affirm even incoherence if it was by an African-American:

> If ever there was an occasion to psychoanalyze white liberals, this is it. That black people praise Toni Morrison poses no problem; there's nothing wrong with boosterism. And Mrs. Morrison probably owes her Nobel Prize to it.... But whites? Modern liberalism is an alternative morality system where racism is one of the Seven Deadly Sins. So lionizing a black woman writer gives proof of your virtue. But lionizing a black woman writer who isn't much good—now that' s one thrill on top of another. (Klinghoffer 30)

Deriding the "foaming prose" of John Leonard's praise in *The Nation*, the reviewer finds the novel confusingly written and thinly plotted. There must be *another reason* besides its literary merit for all this undue adulation. What could the reason be, he asks, if not "white liberalism"? For this reviewer, Toni Morrison has as little claim to merit as the Mapplethorpe-like artist Wilson Lapeth that Wolfe satirizes in *A Man in Full*, and her reputation owes everything to liberal social agendas.

As an "external good," according to Aristotle, honor points back to the distributive justice of those bestowing it, and "boosterism" does in fact come powerfully into play. If the formal merit of a work—its claim to be "literature"—ceases to be the real criterion of judgment, then versions of interestedness become the only thing at issue. With his adolescent insolence, this reviewer, for example, hopes to amuse his conservative readers by boldly taking down a "Nobel-prize-winning author," an icon of campus correctness—feminist and black. The possible merits or complexities of the work have to be skimmed over if not dismissed in advance, because the real point is to claim that her honors stem from the "alternative morality system" of modern liberalism, rather than from the achievements of her fiction. To my mind, even this reviewer might be right if he were discussing Alice Walker, to whom Morrison is often unjustly tied. But Toni Morrison's work must be taken more seriously. Impatient with "race" as a supposed ontology, powerfully intelligent, Morrison does not promote the "black experience" so much as she questions its meaning and locates it thoughtfully within an American literary tradition that prominently includes Hawthorne, Melville, Faulkner, and Flannery O'Connor. Like them, she subjects the stories that people tell themselves (and enforce on others) to a clarifying judgment. But Morrison unquestionably invites politicized criticism as well. In her critical writings, the supple language of her novels yields without irony to sentences as tipsy with jargon as this one: "For excellent reasons of state—because European sources of cultural hegemony were dispersed but not yet valorized in the new country—the process of organizing American coherence through a distancing Africanism became the operative mode of a new cultural hegemony"

(*Playing in the Dark* 8). She writes highly polemical introductions to books that come from the heart of the race-class-gender obsessions of the followers of Foucault, Jameson, and the new historicists: Race-*ing Justice, En*-Gendering Power: *Essays on Anita Hill, Clarence Thomas, and the Construction of Social Reality* or *Birth of a Nation'Hood: Gaze, Script, and Spectacle in the O.J. Simpson Case.* In October 1998, she defended Bill Clinton in *The New Yorker* by arguing that he was inscribed with the cultural markers of "blackness" in the sense that race is a socially constructed reality, and that he was therefore, in effect, "the first black president." His white Southern attackers pursued him, she thought, with a relentlessness typical of "pollution behaviors" (as the anthropologists say) on the hot boundaries of cultural self-definitions.

Morrison comes across in her essays with the humorously elegant hauteur and scathing impatience of someone who at once sees through apparently innocent comments and gestures to the invidious assumptions beneath them. She highlights the kinds of significant details that might fascinate an anthropologist trying to learn the caste system of a foreign culture, but that seem heavy with her contempt in our own. For example, she analyzes the ways that Clarence Thomas, like Friday in *Robinson Crusoe*, was caught in a gift-relation to the dominant white culture. She particularly concentrates on the more or less unconscious ways that whites used Thomas to enforce racial demarcations. For example, Sen. Danforth introduced Clarence Thomas at the hearings by praising the nominee's big laugh. Morrison comments, "For whites who require it, [laughter] is the gesture of accommodation and obedience needed to open discussion with a black person and certainly to continue it" (Race-*ing* xiii). What she writes about the Thomas and Anita Hill hearings also fits her readings of O. J. Simpson and Bill Clinton: "As is almost always the case, the site of the exorcism of critical national issues was situated in the miasma of black life and inscribed on the bodies of black people" (Race-*ing* x). Summarizing the results of the Simpson trial, she draws very close to the central concerns of her own fiction, and she deplores what she sees as the "official story" that results from the Simpson trial, comparing it to D. W. Griffith's racist film, *Birth of a Nation*:

> [Simpson] is not an individual who underwent and was acquitted from a
> murder trial. He has become the whole race needing correction, incarcera-
> tion, censoring, silencing; the race that needs its civil rights disassembled;
> the race that is sign and symbol of domestic violence; the race that has
> made trial by jury a luxury rather than a right and placed affirmative ac-
> tion legislation in even greater jeopardy. This is the consequence and func-
> tion of official stories: to impose the will of a dominant culture. It is *Birth*
> *of a Nation* writ large—menacingly and pointedly for the 'hood. (*Birth* xxviii)

One wants to say, "But this is so different from the tone of her fiction."

But so astute is Morrison at discerning racial markers that she anticipates
this "white" response to her anger in the ironic way that she begins
her essay on Simpson. Substitute the feminine pronoun, and it becomes a
commentary on the reaction of her white readers to her polemics: "We have
been deceived. We thought he loved us. Now we know that everything was
false. Each purposeful gesture, the welcoming smile, the instant understanding of how we felt and what we needed. Even before we knew what was in our
best interests, he seemed to anticipate and execute it right on cue. He gentled
us toward our finer instincts; toward the medicine that would cure us; toward
the rest we needed" (vii). She makes one aware that responses to her fiction are
"racially inflected" and that to read her sympathetically without regard to her
"blackness" is an illusion, dangerously prey to the stereotypes, say, of black
mothering that Flannery O' Connor invokes satirically in "The Artificial
Nigger." Morrison's analysis shows that, for white Americans, the realization
that a black person is not necessarily the saint he or she seemed usually involves a total reversal in judgment: "contemporary 'readers' of the Simpson
case have been encouraged to move from a previous assessment of Mr. Simpson
as an affable athlete/spokesperson to a judgment of him as a wild dog" (*Birth*
viii). She does not invoke Freud's essay, "The Antithetical Meanings of Primal Words," but her point is very much the same: that "black" for a white
American is a "primal word" capable of bearing meanings exactly opposite to
each other. Blackness is deeply and antithetically embedded or "inscribed" in

the American psyche both as nurture and as threat. Morrison's point with Simpson has less to do with *his* guilt or innocence than with the way that white contempt for his release on the "race card" demonstrates a general judgment: that black people are so used to playing on the privileges of victimhood that they recklessly undermine the American system of justice.

Morrison's interest in these large public debates cannot be separated from her concerns *as a novelist* with the power of narratives. She makes constant reference, for example, to Melville's extraordinary novella, *Benito Cereno*, in trying to understand the contemporary reaction to prominent, educated "black" men, such as Clarence Thomas, O. J. Simpson and, if one accepts her argument, Bill Clinton, who consume American attention for months or even years because of the issues at stake in judging their actions and telling a story about them. As with the Dreyfus case in the nineteenth century, their trials enact a "social drama" (Victor Turner's term) in which large contemporary obsessions—in this case, race and gender—cross each other in extraordinarily revealing ways. Tom Wolfe misses the point in *A Man in Full* when he has the black Georgia Tech football star Fareek Fanon (whose name ironically echoes that of Frantz Fanon, Afro-Caribbean author of *The Wretched of the Earth*), allegedly rape the daughter of one of Atlanta's most prominent white businessmen. For Wolfe, the galvanizing contradiction is what happens when the big-money interests of college athletics come into conflict with Southern racial anxieties, but that issue ceased to be the decisive one decades ago (probably when Bear Bryant first coached black players at Alabama). Wolfe himself seems to lose interest in the "rape." But what if the young woman had been the highly educated daughter of Atlanta's ambitious black mayor? What if a sexual violation by an athlete from a poor neighborhood of Atlanta had *contradicted* her education and her father's class aspirations?

Social dramas, as Turner shows, become the central conflicts of literature, and the poetic ways of framing them (the official stories) then influence subsequent social dramas. To the extent that they reveal inner contradictions—what Faulkner calls the heart in conflict with itself—these confrontations of opposing interests remain permanently revealing despite the passage of the particular issues. No one now spends a great deal of time worrying about the conflict between divinely granted legitimacy and effective political rule as it emerges in *Richard II.* "The divine right of kings" seems transparently ideological, especially to a nation that began with a break from the English monarchy. But the deeper conflict between a sense of privileged chosenness, absolutely *a priori*, and a political climate of war and harsh calculation retains a permanent fascination in the play. The politically despised Richard becomes increasingly sympathetic in his humiliation and imprisonment, because Shakespeare finds in him a universal appeal to a sense of inner anointing and spiritual dignity.

So, I think, Morrison finds universal qualities with her subjects, because she chooses, not Us-vs.-Them, but Us-vs.-Us situations. John Ellis, in his recent book *Literature Lost*, misses the point when he writes that Morrison "seems now to limit her writing to group grievances of race-gender-class issues, which results in a poverty of content that will make her work seem badly dated within a few decades and that will bring contempt on the Nobel committee that so foolishly allowed its mental horizons to be narrowed by the fads of our time" (234). Ellis implies that for Morrison, as for those who follow the intellectual fashion in which "power is now the most basic factor in human motivation," all subtlety of motivation vanishes and "one central factor displaces and undermines the multiplicity of other motivations that we used to think so important: love, loyalty, fulfillment, ambition, achievement, friendship, intellectual curiosity, and so on" (9). But these latter motivations above all characterize Morrison's fictional worlds, in deeply moving ways. I am led to wonder whether Ellis confuses the jargon of critical fashion with the real content of American social dramas still being played out over slavery, the sexes, and oligarchic distinctions of class. These dramas stem from the nature of our regime, because its conspicuous commitment to the democratic principles of liberty and equality leads it to natural contradictions.

Rather than "group grievances of race-gender-class issues," Morrison concerns herself with revealing especially the self-contradictions. In *Beloved*, for example, she explores what happens when a black mother, whose children would be taken away from her under slavery and who now faces recapture by her former slave master, kills her own child and thus claims an ownership over the child's life. Her action violently underscores self-ownership and simultaneously contradicts it, as abortion does in contemporary feminism. Sethe is instantly and harshly condemned by the community of former slaves around her. *Beloved* is a matter of "group grievance" in the sense that Exodus is Israel's group grievance against Egypt. Slavery is the backdrop, the memory, the threat, but the drama played out is one that stems from contradictory, tragic reactions—as in Exodus—when the promise of freedom is both offered and deferred. And not black reactions, as though "black" really did, in some secret depth, mean something other than "human": the reactions of humanity in these conditions.

I F *Paradise*, unlike *A Man in Full*, addresses contemporary reality but achieves the standing of literature, it must do so in a way that performs a kind of alchemy with immediate politics and finds a ground of deep reconciliations. One hopes for elicitings and satisfactions of the whole desiring imagination that no one, including its author, could have anticipated in advance. In this novel, Morrison explores the attempt to found a township where race will not be the dominant experience and people will not have to think about being black. The complications arise from two anti-Utopian difficulties: that the pilgrims who originally set out from the South toward the new promise of Oklahoma were rejected by other all-black towns, and that the original settlement lost its defining energy by the late 1940s and needed re-founding. The twins instrumental in the town's second founding, Deacon and Steward Morgan,

> have never forgotten the message or the specifics of any story, especially
> the controlling one told to them by their grandfather—the man who put
> the word in the Oven's black mouth. A story that explained why neither
> the founders of Haven nor their descendants could tolerate anybody but
> themselves. On the journey from Mississippi and two Louisiana parishes
> to Oklahoma, the one hundred and fifty-eight freedmen were unwelcome
> on each grain of soil from Yazoo to Fort Smith. (13)

This controlling story echoes and, to use Morrison's word, "inflects" the Exodus story and its central place in the American imagination, from John Winthrop to Martin Luther King Jr.

The fact that there is already a story before this story (as always for novelists) is the paradox of beginnings to which Morrison points. Nothing is simply new, simply itself. Everything is complicated in advance, before it exists, by the inescapability of repetition. The original exodus of freedmen to found Haven, Oklahoma, in 1890 repeats not only the Biblical story, but the Puritan one, and the re-founding of the community in 1949—a town named Ruby, Oklahoma, after the first woman to die in it—repeats them all. In all ancient or modern American experiments in purity, including the foundings of Israel and New England, the condition escaped and excluded also frames the community's existence and therefore governs its internal decisions. A curious doubling sets in—twins, mirrored situations, the doubled desire of adulteries or idolatries, a split in the nucleus of place. As Boston had Merry Mount with its maypole nearby, not to mention Anne Hutchinson in its very midst, Ruby has antinomian impulses in its young people, as well as a double, a former convent nearby that has become a refuge for women escaping from various troubles. In 1973, threatened by Ruby's internal dissolution, the founders locate the source of all their problems in this *other.* They redefine themselves and their communal righteousness by an act of violence against the women of the convent, most of whom are black. By exploring this division within "blackness"—the masculine, corporate, Protestant, and largely theocratic town against the feminine, communal convent, tinged by contemporary antinomianism and the lingering otherness of Catholicism, with its accommodations of paganism—Morrison shows that race is an *imposed* issue, and she brings the "black experience" into a real, if belated, accord with the complexities of other American beginnings. The real question, she shows, has always been the one that Leo Strauss asks at the end of one of his essays, "Quid sit deus?" What is God, or better, what might God be? As she points out in her 1996 Jefferson Lecture, one of the reasons that "definitions of the period we are living in have prefixes pointing backwards:

post-modern, post structuralist, post colonial, post Cold War" is that "passionate, deeply held religious belief is associated with ignorance at best, violent intolerance at its worst" and that the loss of the idea of eternal life means that the hunger for eternity has to glut itself on the "billions of years gone by."

Morrison goes on to say in the Jefferson Lecture that "serious ethical debates and probings are being conducted" in contemporary literature, debates and probings that re-introduce religious belief and the possibility of a future "that is about to take its first unfettered breath." The literary mode of knowledge, it bears repeating, is not historical but imaginative, and the first test of its strength, its own inner ethics, lies in achieved form. The laws of articulation that govern the largest level can also be found in the smallest parts, in the diction of its sentences and the shape of its paragraphs (like the repeating irregularities of fractals). The part manifests the nature of the whole, because form—from the sphering of water in dust, to the exuberant intensity of a hound running after a dodging rabbit, to the massive act of language in a novel—means an active singularity of self-reference. It becomes visible as meaning because a completed internal ordering reveals a simple distinctness of line at the boundaries. Martin Heidegger writes that "A boundary is not that at which something stops but, as the Greeks recognized, the boundary is that from which something *begins its presencing*" (*An Introduction to Metaphysics* 154, emphasis in original). In a work of literature, every sentence is at once the interior and the boundary that manifests the completeness of the whole. Every scene informs and is informed by every other. In *A Man in Full*, Wolfe is concerned with vividness, from the stallion's mating scene to "drinking ambrosia" in Charlie Croker's analogy for his wife's way of listening to a lecture. He is not worried about the fineness and inner plausibility of perception, sentence by sentence, and his emphasis ultimately shows itself in the vivid but cartoonish character of the whole book. Morrison, on the other hand, is concerned about the art of her book, and she fully expects her serious readers not just to read the text but to reread it, following the clues of its deliberate obscurities. A striking metaphor early in

Paradise—the beam of a flashlight on the floor as a "frond of light"—is a fractal of Morrison's style. Two men from Ruby, a father and son (who later prove to be Harper and Menus Jury), explore the former chapel of the convent in search of the women they have come to kill:

> The father walks the aisle checking the pews right and left. He runs a frond of light from his Black & Decker under each seat. The knee rests are turned up. At the altar he pauses. One window of pale yellow floats above him in the dimness. Things look uncleaned. He steps to a tray of small glasses positioned on the wall to see if any food offerings remains there. Except for grime and spider webbing, the red glasses are empty. Maybe they are not for food but for money. Or trash? There is a gum wrapper in the dirtiest one. Doublemint.
>
> He shakes his head and joins his son back at the altar. The son points. The father beams the wall below the yellow window where, just barely, the sun announces. The outline of a huge cross comes into view. Clean as new paint is the space where there used to be a Jesus. (11-12)

"A *frond* of light" is striking in this scene because it exactly captures the way the directed beam bends along the floor under the pews. Morrison could have passed over the description ("a beam of light") or she could have made it more obviously aggressive (a "stab," a "probe," even a "tentacle"), but instead the light becomes supple and growing, quite against the intention, one feels, of the man with the Black & Decker.

Is the description just, given the context? If Morrison entertains the metaphor, but the man through whose eyes we read and judge the chapel would never imagine such a comparison, then it is out of place. "Clean as new paint" seems perfectly in keeping, but what about that "frond of light" he runs under the pews? To take a single metaphor so seriously might seem to imply some vast legal system of criticism that reaches down into the privacy of individual sentences to interrogate the usual suspects, but it is really a matter of discovering the laws that the fiction itself establishes, discovering an internal pleasure of connection, if it is there to find. In *Paradise*, it is. The "frond of light" is striking in its context because it comes directly from the experience of the building that the men have already had. The convent was originally a mansion built by an embezzler who decorated it according to his own decadent taste: faucets and soap dishes in the shape of genitalia, bathtubs on the backs of mermaids, and so on. The nuns who took it over after his arrest tried to remove the sexual paraphernalia and convert the place into a school for Arapaho girls, but the building was hard to convert. In the first few pages of the novel, Morrison sets up the problems of this complex overlay: the communal on the private, the religious on the criminal, the Catholic on the pagan. The men who enter the convent on their killing mission, protecting their own communal attempt at a repetition that renews the origin, find a fertile Dionysian nature that keeps breaking through the ascetic removals: "Christ and His mother glow in niches trimmed in grapevines. The Sisters of the Sacred Cross chipped away all the nymphs, but curves of their marble hair still strangle grape leaves and tease the fruit" (4).

By the time the father and son arrive at the chapel, a motif has been established: intentions of moral restraint are overwhelmed by the same kinds of luxuriance as the "wanton ringlets" of Eve's hair in *Paradise Lost* or the plants that grow across the paths of the Miltonic garden. They realize that Reverend Pulliam, the most Calvinist of Ruby's preachers, was right all along: "graven idols were worshipped here. Tiny men and women in white dresses and capes of gold stand on little shelves cut into niches in the wall. Holding a baby or gesturing, their blank faces fake innocence" (9). Father and son think that the bowls for holy water on either side of the doorway are for food offerings to the idols. In this context, the flashlight beam, meant to expose hidden things like the eye of God, becomes a *"frond* of light." The understated ambiguity (Apollonian as Dionysian, intellective as vegetative) confirms the men's general judgment. All the details add up for the Jury men. If "the knee rests are turned up," it is because no one kneels and prays. The new women—the third distinct "culture" in the same building—have added their own pagan rejection of Christian restraint to the already dubious overlay of Catholic worship on the Dionysiac energies of sex. If the glasses on the wall do not contain the food offerings to idols, they show habits of neglect at the very least, and the wadded wrapper says all they need to know about gum-chewing in church. And the brand name stands without comment: "Doublemint." A little piece of throwaway cultural trash? The '70's television ads ("Double your pleasure, double your fun") always used twins gamboling in ecstasies of *poshlust*—a comic reminder of Deacon and Steward Morgan, the stern prime movers of Ruby, not to mention the themes of doubling throughout the novel. The little piece of trash, probably left by gum-popping Gigi, the most overtly sexual of the women, is a metonym of the convent's dangerous pleasures that once drew men sneaking out of town.

Why "Mint"? The plant reference picks up "frond," first of all, but mint is particularly appropriate. Every gardener discovers how invasive and ineradicable it is, and the men are there to weed out the convent's influence. The word "mint" itself is double, two different words with the same spelling. One—the aromatic plant—goes back to Old English and Old High German, but the other derives from the Latin *Moneta*, an epithet of Juno, in whose temple money (once sacred and feminine) was coined. Mint and money have the same root. Mint's double is money, both money and mint multiply and take over; one of Ruby's twins is a banker, the other a farmer who sold out to oil interests to make money—and so on. Fronds of meaning run through the novel. The car that Mavis's twin infants suffocate in is "mint green." When Patricia Best, Ruby's genealogist and historian, stands outside in the cold burning the narratives and speculations she has spent years accumulating, the weather detail that precedes her act is "The lemon mint had shriveled"; when Deacon Morgan first looks into the eyes of the novel's major character, Consolata Sosa, he says, "Your eyes are like mint leaves." The word "Doublemint" itself recurs several times in the penultimate section of the novel, when the white woman shot in the first sentence of the book is dying.

What does it mean that the Jury men see the "outline of a huge cross" that appears on the chapel wall? Later in the novel Morrison contrasts the ways that two of Ruby's preachers, Senior Pulliam and Richard Misner, interpret Christian love, and she centers the difference on the relation of love to the cross. For Reverend Pulliam, who does not mention the cross explicitly in his sermon at the novel's only wedding, love is entirely divine, difficult to accept and capable of being expressed only after a long apprenticeship, undeserved by anyone, yet needing to be earned "by practice and careful contemplation" (141). Reverend Misner hears Pulliam's words as a hurtful reference to the family quarrels that have preceded this wedding. Wanting to convey a message of love to reconcile their estranged families and rebuke Pulliam for his interpretation of God, he holds up a bare cross before the congregation. Without speaking, he stands before them for a long time, offering it to be understood, hoping that it will be interpreted as saying what he cannot trust himself to articulate:

> See what was certainly the first sign any human anywhere had made: the vertical line; the horizontal one. Even as children, they drew it with their fingers in snow, sand or mud.... The circle was not first, nor was the parallel or the triangle. It was this mark, this, that lay underneath every other. This mark, rendered in the placement of facial features. This mark of a standing human figure poised to embrace. Remove it, as Pulliam had done, and Christianity was like any and every religion in the world: a population of supplicants begging respite from begrudging authority;...the weak negotiating a doomed trek through the wilderness.... But with [this sign], in the religion in which this sign was paramount and fundamental, well, life was a whole other matter. (146)

Even as he thinks these things, Misner is imagining a black Jesus on the cross, God's divine solidarity with "the other death row felons," and an absolute repudiation of the big-business idea of man's relations with heaven: "See how this official murder out of hundreds marked the difference; moved the relationship between God and man from CEO and supplicant to one on one?"

Those in the congregation interpret the proffered cross, however, in radically differing ways, none of them as Misner hopes. It terrifies the bride Arnette, opens a "rent" in her heart, and exposes her recognition that her new husband is marrying her without love. For Billie Delia Best, Arnette's maid of honor, it elicits the truth about the town's condemnation of her for being light-skinned. For Steward Morgan, the cross bears no meaning in itself: "he had seen...military crosses spread for miles; crosses on fire in Negroes' yards, crosses tattooed on the forearms of dedicated killers" (154). Steward, one of the town's twin founders, is a man heavily invested in the official story of its beginnings (a trek through the wilderness) and implacably harsh in his judgment of anyone who disputes its meaning. When he concludes that a cross is "no better than its bearer," he contradicts himself, because in the instances he thinks of, the cross is *his* ironic moral commentary on the deeds of the one using it. At the same time, the cross is a judgment of love on him. It judges the bearer, simultaneously judges the one judging the bearer, yet judges neither, since it offers to both a sacrificial absence of judgment. A highly charged "attractor" of meanings, the cross is both a sign used in official stories and a judgment on their partiality. Everyone with a cause—and an official story that promotes it—wants to believe that the whole authority of the cultural symbol's meaning lies with his or her own view of righteousness.

Although this crossed wedding at the center of the novel follows the scene of the Jury father and son exploring the Convent chapel, it precedes it by two years in the novel's internal chronology, and it is meant to inform a rereading of the novel's opening passages. The scene of the Jury men in the chapel ends with their ominous study of the *absence* of the crucifix: "The father beams the wall below the yellow window where, just barely, the sun announces. The outline of a huge cross comes into view. Clean as new paint is the space where there used to be a Jesus." The instant interpretation hardly needs comment. Much as they worry about the idolatry of the rest of the chapel, the two men also believe that the women have profanely removed Jesus from His place. The nuns were "Sisters of the Sacred Cross," the Convent was named "Christ the King," and these new women have carted off the very cross that gave the place its meaning. But on other levels, more complicated interpretations suggest themselves. Up above, just barely, the sun "announces" without announcing any *thing* in particular, as though the relation between the source of light and the earth that it makes visible, between the idea of the good and its images, between God and creation, had become strangely intransitive. The whole scene, with its complex symbol of an absence still present as a Derridean "trace" (Morrison named the main character of *Jazz* "Joe Trace"), is full of implicit references to postmodern concerns and the supposed removal of Christianity from the culture of the West. But to remove "a Jesus" also leaves a huge cross on the wall, "clean as new paint." This revelation of a "clean" cross could also describe the historical aftermath of the Nietzschean "death of God"—a removal that reveals the cross cleaned of cultural detritus and "official stories" about God. Perhaps the vitality of contemporary culture does not lie in being "post"-religious, but in reopening the question of what the cross might mean.

M ORRISON'S calling is not to make the kind of art that induces contemplative disinterestedness. Neither, on the other hand, does she write novels that angrily demand immediate action. Like Dostoevsky or Faulkner, she engages the contemporary social drama with her fiction, and she tests dominant ideas by showing what happens when they unfold in plausible human action. Form in her novels is not the conversion of action into inertness, like what happens in freeze tag, but almost the opposite: what happens when something paralyzed comes back to life and motion, like a woman rediscovering her powers of attraction. Art, in other words, has to risk something, like Denver in *Beloved*, the young woman who must leave her self-absorbed household full of old obsessions in order to help it; she has to "step off the porch" into a social and political world that might hurt her. Unlike many contemporary novelists, Morrison seems to me almost primordially moved by beauty; beauty pulls her through the long labor, and the achieved form does nothing if it cannot *act* in the world and move others.

Morrison's opinions, in other words, are strongly valenced and clearly discernible, but not insistent. In the tensions of *Paradise*, her deeper sympathies clearly lie with the community of women, not with the Puritan experiment of the townsmen of Ruby. What happens in this novel is what happens over and over in America: the legal or official community finds itself at odds with a cult that exists outside the law, acting according to its own mandates in ways that pose an extraordinary inner threat to the regular community. As long as the women at the Convent were nuns who owed their allegiance to the Catholic Church, they posed no threat to Ruby. But this new cult of women represents a particularly feminine pollution that suddenly begins to appear *on the inside* of Ruby. The largely male "official story" (the Disallowing by the light-skinned Negroes of Fairly, Oklahoma; the emissary of God who appeared to the Founder in a vision and led him to the site that became Haven; the communal Oven with its disputed motto, *Beware the Furrow of His Brow*) inevitably intersects the stories of the women in the Convent, and the shootings represent the collision or crossing, one might say, of social or political history and a realm of imagination that history will not allow to remain intact. Two distinct and "gendered" ways of approaching contingency and rejection emerge to confront each other, each represented by a number of figures but perhaps best embodied in a pair of former lovers: Deacon Morgan and Consolata Sosa. Morrison mythologizes the central attraction and repulsion of Deek and Connie, illicit on both sides, and resolves the conflict between the town and the convent by ending the novel in a way that does not allow outside law ("white law") to judge the attack.

An early reviewer who generally admired *Paradise* found fault with the ending for being "magically correct." It is true that Morrison seems trendiest when she describes Connie's tutelage of the other women in what look like techniques of guided self-help, and certainly the novel seems least plausible by the standards of modern realism in the sections dealing with Consolata's second sight, her spiritual gifts of healing, and the miraculous escape of the women at the end—after apparently being shot and killed. Morrison risks seeming fashionably New Age, but her real point is a recovery—or more accurately, a discovery—of the sacred character of the world. It hardly takes a zealot to recognize that modern medicine strangely makes the body an "other" to be treated as an entirely material entity. She is clearly drawn toward medicine that does not murder to dissect, and the form that her sympathy takes is a wry exploration of traditional midwives who know "what direction the knife under the mattress should point" (271), herbal medicines, healings that require a deep imaginative engagement of the other person. She lends credence to art and "magic" in their opposition to the collusion of materialist science and Realpolitik—the kind of credence that Shakespeare also lent. The tensions of magic and science that fascinated the Renaissance imagination in *Dr. Faustus* and *The Tempest* have returned on the other side of modernity in the magical realism of Latin American fiction and its infusion into American culture, and like Rudolfo Anaya in *Bless Me, Ultima*, his novel about a *curandera* on the ethical boundary between orthodox Catholicism and a "practicing" of magical arts, Morrison centers her novel on a woman who exists vividly on racial and cultural margins, attempting to understand the ethics of her gifts.

In Anaya's novel, the tensions exist in the male narrator, who must choose between Ultima and the priesthood, but in Morrison's black unofficial mother superior-*curandera*, the conflicts are her own. Within the novel, something is personally at stake for Morrison in the movement from Patricia Best, a woman treated as marginal all her life because of the lighter color that distinguishes her from the deep coal-black (Eight-rock) of Ruby's founding families, to Consolata Sosa. From her place on the sidelines, Pat Best becomes the historian and chronicler of the families of Ruby, a figure like the mixed-blood teacher Lady Jones in *Beloved* (Denver's teacher), who mediates between cultures. Pat burns her manuscripts in despair at the end of the chapter just before Consolata's section begins. It is as though Morrison were moving between two modes of being a novelist: one the chronicler and interpreter of social history, the other the "wise woman," the living memory and healer and source of consolation, the one whose gifts involve "stepping in" to the other, finding the light, and leading the other into a more intimate kind of self-knowledge. Between safe Pat Best and risky Consolata Sosa, she chooses Consolata.

Already thoroughly "creolized" in the isolation of Oklahoma with her blackness, her green eyes, and her European past, Consolata was originally a street child in Lisbon, brought to the Convent by Mary Magna, the Mother Superior, when she was still a child of nine, and she has spent her life as a servant for the Convent. "For thirty years she offered her body and her soul to God's Son and His Mother as completely as if she had taken the veil herself," until her affair with Deacon Morgan: "And those thirty years of surrender to the living God cracked like a pullet's egg when she met the living man" (225). Even then, she does not so much reject her Christianity as she divinizes Deacon and brings such supernatural heat to her love that it my-thologizes everything. In the place they meet are the "two fig trees growing into each other" (230) that Gigi had originally stopped in Ruby to find. Deacon finally breaks off their affair when Consolata bites his lip and hums over the blood she licks from it—an act that revolts him. When she thinks of making a haven for them in the cellar of the Convent, he thinks of imprison-ment and "a woman bent on eating him like a meal" (239). Her impulses, no matter how they are tutored otherwise, never succeed in separating the spirit from the life of the body, and her sexual desires have a clear continuity with her religious ones: "Romance stretched to the breaking point broke, expos-ing a simple mindless transfer. From Christ, to whom one gave total surren-der and then swallowed the idea of His flesh, to a living man. Shame. Shame without blame. Consolata virtually crawled back to the little chapel" (240).

What makes the account so disconcerting, both for Deacon Morgan and Morrison's readers ("She simply bent the knees she had been so happy to open and said, 'Dear Lord, I didn't want to eat him. I just wanted to go home.'"), is the almost invisible boundary between sex and spiritual union. Unlike Protestantism, the Catholic tradition has always kept the Gospel trope of the Bridegroom alive, both in the idea of the nun as the bride of Christ and in the intensities of the mystical tradition; I think of St. Bernard of Clairvaux's extended meditations on the *Song of Songs*, Dante's spiritual and erotic ascent toward Beatrice, St. Teresa of Avila's account of the angel pierc-ing her heart with an arrow (and Bernini's intensely erotic statue of it), or the charged poems of St. John of the Cross. Orthodoxy, for its part, has the extraordinary figure of St. Mary of Egypt, whose frankly described physical lusts became a passion for Christ in the desert after her conversion. Although

Protestant preachers have a long literary history of transgression, from Arthur Dimmesdale to Faulkner's Rev. Whitfield, Protestantism generally draws back in suspicion and propriety from the sacramental identification of the body or the material world with spiritual efficacy—for example, in its rejection of the Eucharist as the real presence of Christ. This suspicion underlies Deacon Morgan's revulsion when Consolata bites him. However mindlessly, the erotic desire to consume the other (in order to be completely one) and the lifelong habit of "swallowing the idea of His flesh" converge for her in her act, but what converges for him is a fear of the all-consuming desire of women and the suspicion of Catholic idolatry. She has an erotic intensity that goes beyond the clarity of sin being sin. She would worship him, make him the meal in a candlelit shrine, keep him in the basement, boxed out of daylight like Christ in the tabernacle.

Consolata's erotic intensities, rejected but not forgotten by Deacon, prepare her for a more dangerous threshold between body and spirit. Just at the time of her menopause, her transition out of natural fertility, she encounters Lone DuPres, who has been gifted from childhood with second sight and who has acted for years, before being supplanted by the hospital in a nearby town, as the midwife of Ruby. At the age of fifty, Consolata is "midwifed" into her gifts by Lone. She discovers that she is able to "step in" or "see in" and bring someone back from death. She does this the first time just after a wreck in which one of Deacon's sons is dying. Finding him covered with blood, she effortlessly follows Lone's instructions to "go inside him" and "wake him up":

> Inside the boy she saw a pinpoint of light receding. Pulling up energy that felt like fear, she stared at it until it widened. Then more, more, so air could come seeping, at first, then rushing rushing in. Although it hurt like the devil to look at it, she concentrated as though the lungs in need were her own.
>
> Scout opened his eyes, groaned and sat up. . . .
>
> Weeks passed before Lone returned to put her mind at ease about the boy's recovery.

"You gifted. I knew it from the start."

Consolata turned her lips down and crossed herself, whispering, "Ave Maria, gratia plena." The exhilaration was gone now, and the thing seemed nasty to her. Like devilment. Like evil craft. Something it would mortify her to tell Mary Magna, Jesus or the Virgin. She hadn't known what she was doing; she was under a spell. Lone's spell. And told her so.

"Don't be a fool. God don't make mistakes. Despising His gift, now, that is a mistake. You calling Him a fool, like you?" (245-46)

Each "stepping in" means that Consolata has to stare into the "pinpoint of light" and strengthen it. She guiltily keeps Mary Magna alive long past the time of her natural death, taking the old nun's body between her knees as though she were giving birth to her: "so intense were the steppings in, Mary Magna glowed like a lamp till her very last breath in Consolata's arms" (247).

Her use of her gifts, however, burns away the natural green of her eyes and fills her with guilt. After losing the woman who had given her life its meaning, alcoholic, longing for death, drinking the embezzler's wine and avoiding the sun, she stays in the cellar of the Convent because she cannot bear ordinary daylight, until she finally ascends with a question for the dead. Sitting in an old chair in the garden, she addresses the mother superior:

"Non sum dignus," she whispered. "But tell me. Where is the rest of days, the aisle of thyme, the scent of veronica you promised? The cream and honey you said I had earned? The happiness that comes of well-done chores, the serenity duty grants us, the blessings of good works? Was what I did for love of you so terrible?"

Mary Magna had nothing to say. Consolata listened to the refusing silence, more wondering than annoyed by the sky, in plumage now, gold and blue-green, strutting like requited love on the horizon. She was afraid of dying alone, ungrieved in unholy ground, but knew that was precisely what lay before her. How she longed for the good death. "I'll miss You," she told Him. "I really will." The skylight wavered.

A man approached. Medium height, light step, he came right on up
the drive. He wore a cowboy hat that hid his features, but Consolata couldn't
have seen them anyway. (251)

This is one of three appearances by mysterious strangers to the people
associated with Ruby: the man who led Big Papa to Haven in 1890, a young
man who repeatedly appears to Dovey Morgan in her garden, and this one
who addresses Connie alone and remains invisible to the others. A kind of
Hermes figure, he remains ambiguous. Is he, as the men of Ruby would
believe, the demonic replacement of Jesus, summoned by her despair? Or is
this the "You" that Consolata thought she was giving up for good—a cool,
green-eyed Jesus in a cowboy hat, a man like her with a kind of creole flavor
to his language, her soul's lover and male twin?

This moment in the novel has the comic cast of Huck Finn's decision,
when he finally defies his conscience to help free Jim: "All right, then, I'll
go to hell." I think that Morrison imagines in this figure, not so much a new
age incarnation (a Rastafarian savior) as a surprisingly literal interpretation
of what has been there in the Gospels for twenty centuries: a Jesus at ease
beyond death and the fixity of the cross, a figure of the resurrected body
who humorously and ironically transcends the old moral valences of
embodiment and appears to his friends in uncanny but unspectacular ways.
This is the Jesus who accompanied the travelers on the road to Emmaus and
revealed Himself to them in the breaking of bread (Luke 24), the one who
ate fish with the disciples on the shores of the Sea of Tiberias (John 21).
Morrison leaves him ambiguous, but it is clear that his appearance begins the
last phase of Consolata's work at the Convent, the one that makes the women
most unacceptable to Ruby: the work of the "templates" in the cellar.

When Consolata first takes charge of the women after long being a
"play mother who could be hugged or walked out on, depending on the
whim of the child," she takes them down into the cellar, where she has each
undress and lie down, and each finds "the position she could tolerate on the
cold, uncompromising floor" (263). Consolata paints the silhouette of each
body, and the women lie, with an increasingly "acute distress," inside what

they have chosen, while Connie begins to tell stories of paradise, "Of scented cathedrals made of gold where gods and goddesses sat in the pews with the congregation. Of carnations tall as trees. Dwarfs with diamonds for teeth. Snakes aroused by poetry and bells" (263-64). Some of the early reviews of *Paradise* found the Convent sections of the novel to be sentimental feminism, and almost no one, at least in the first year of its reception, found much to praise about the way that Morrison handles the women in the cellar. They begin with "loud dreaming," a communal talking-out of the traumas of their pasts. For example, Mavis is a mother from New Jersey whose infant twins suffocated when she left them in her husband Frank's "mint green Cadillac" while she went into the grocery store to get hot dogs (instead of the Spam she had at home) to keep Frank happy. In the "loud dreaming" they do in the templates, all the women "enter the heat in the Cadillac, feel the smack of cold air in the Higgledy Piggledy. They know their tennis shoes are unlaced and that a bra strap annoys each time it slips from the shoulder. The Armour package is sticky. They inhale the perfume of sleeping infants and feel parent-cozy although they notice one's head is turned awkwardly" (264).

From the talking, they go on to fill in the templates, to paint substitute bodies with ornate details and fantastic additions: "Life, real and intense, shifted to down there in limited pools of light in air smoky from kerosene lamps and candle wax" (264). Every obsessive detail gets revisited and questioned. The others ask Seneca, who was abandoned as a child by a woman she thought was her sister, "Are you sure she was your sister? Maybe she was your mother. Why? Because a mother might, but no sister would do such a thing" (265). The descriptions of the decorated templates sound like meditations in the mode of Frida Kahlo's painful art: "careful etchings of body parts and memorabilia occupied them. Yellow barrettes, red peonies, a green cross on a field of white. A majestic penis pierced with a Cupid's bow. Rose of Sharon petals, Lorna Doones" (265). As Kahlo's art owes a great deal to the Mexican-Catholic traditions of making *ex voto* images of body parts, so there are Catholic traditions of mutilated women well-represented in the Convent's own collection of saints' images, such as one of St.

Catherine of Siena holding up her severed breasts on a platter (74, 286). The problem is that St. Catherine here is like "Cortez" in Keats' "Chapman's Homer" sonnet: it was St. Agatha, one of the saints of the early church, not St. Catherine of Siena, who suffered this sexual mutilation. But there are reasons, most of them having to do with feminism, but some with the discipline of the Desert Fathers, for Morrison's emphasis of Catherine. Rudolph Bell's 1985 book *Holy Anorexia* prominently features Catherine, and the subject of food and women's bodies in the Middle Ages occupies the New Historicist studies of Caroline Walker Bynum. The reasons for the contemporary attention that she has attracted can be gleaned from this 1913 entry in the Catholic Encyclopedia:

> At the age of seven she consecrated her virginity to Christ; in her sixteenth year she took the habit of the Dominican Tertiaries, and renewed the life of the anchorites of the desert in a little room in her father's house. After three years of celestial visitations and familiar conversation with Christ, she underwent the mystical experience known as the "spiritual espousals," probably during the carnival of 1366. She now rejoined her family, began to tend the sick, especially those afflicted with the most repulsive diseases, to serve the poor, and to labour for the conversion of sinners. Though always suffering terrible physical pain, living for long intervals on practically no food save the Blessed Sacrament, she was ever radiantly happy and full of practical wisdom no less than the highest spiritual insight. All her contemporaries bear witness to her extraordinary personal charm, which prevailed over the continual persecution to which she was subjected even by the friars of her own order and by her sisters in religion.

Morrison does not denigrate these impulses. The women in Morrison's Convent, who voluntarily cut off all their hair, are virtual anchorites: "With Consolata in charge, like a new and revised Reverend Mother, feeding them bloodless food and water alone to quench their thirst, they altered" (265). Like Joan of Arc, St. Catherine also broke the mold of feminine expectations, since she shook the masculine world of politics by working tirelessly to have the

Pope moved back to Rome from Avignon, and she miraculously learned to write, later composing her famous *Dialogue.*

Images of mutilation and desire, like the illuminations in the *Très Riches Heures* of the Duc de Berry, play out something less than art. Yet it is more than Jungian "active imagination," whose intent is "healing the psyche by re-establishing it in the metaxy from which it had fallen into the disease of literalism," according to James Hillman in *Healing Fictions.* "This return to the middle realm of fiction, of myth carries one into conversational familiarity with the cosmos one *inhabits*" (80). Still, it is less than art, for obvious reasons: the cellar looks to the invading men from Ruby more demonic than anything else—"The devil's bedroom, bathroom, and his nasty playpen" (17), a place of "defilement and violence and perversions beyond imagination. Lovingly drawn filth carpets the stone floor" (287). Morrison herself does not reproduce the whole grotesquerie of the images so much as she suggests it: a fertile proliferation of self-understanding, like that of medieval illuminations, that defies the "letter" of the templates. At the same time, it is more than the injunction "Know Thyself," even though its end result is to make these women "sociable and connected when they spoke to you" yet "calmly themselves" (266). When Consolata introduces this discipline, she tells the other women, "'I will teach you what you are hungry for,'" and she instructs them that if there is somewhere else where someone who loves them is waiting, then they should leave the Convent. "'If not, stay here and follow me. Someone could want to meet you" (262). She tells them that flesh and spirit must not be separated: "Hear me, listen. Never break them in two. Never put one over the other. Eve is Mary's mother. Mary is the daughter of Eve" (263).

Consolata's is not so much a course of Platonic (or new age) self-understanding as it is the de-familiarized vocation of preparing to be surprised, as Consolata was, by the beloved of a transcendent desire. Despite what the men from Ruby think, the templates on the cellar floor are paradoxically where the women work through what the cross is: a template of desire's encounter with the harsh rejection of the self. Even the silhouette recalls the first template of the novel: "The outline of a huge cross comes into view." Like a "new and revised" cross, the deliberately abstract-sounding templates are personal acknowledgments of the death that makes everyone a trace. In being filled in and re-imagined without self-censorship, however, each becomes a way of transcending the fixity of the self, escaping from history as mere repetition, conquering death through acceptance, and liberating the transfigured body.

M ORRISON's conflation of Agatha and Catherine, however, remains troubling. When Gigi discovers the image of a woman offering her breasts on a plate, Morrison describes "A knocked-down look, cast-up begging eyes, arms outstretched holding up her present on a platter to a lord. Gigi tiptoed over and leaned close to see who was the woman with the I-give-up face. 'St. Catherine of Siena' was engraved on a small plaque in the gilt frame" (74). In this novel of palimpsests and layers of contradictory purpose in the same place, is the frame on the wrong picture? If the nuns themselves have made the mistake of confusing one of the most dynamic and powerful women in the history of the West with young, humiliated St. Agatha, then is the point that the gestures of Catherine's self-starvation and Agatha's sexual mutilation by men are ultimately the same in the official church? Does the church (like the men of Ruby) deny women their flesh and make them internalize and perform upon themselves—as they always will—the punishment for the male mistrust of the world's body? In that case, Morrison's vision is merely fashionable, and her writing is predictably driven by group grievances, including a mockery of the men from Ruby "Fondling their weapons" as they enter the Convent. The question of *Paradise* is whether it breaks new ground and adds something to our self-understanding that a novel like *A Man in Full* does not, or whether its resolutions are merely a fashionable hitching of African-American and feminist agendas to magical realism. Morrison's point at the end of the novel is not condemnation so much as it is the inevitable and wryly comic crossing of the disciplines of freedom. *Paradise* moves toward a tragic ending, the murder of the Convent women by the men of Ruby, and two women at least are clearly killed: the "white girl" (hard to identify but associated in my mind most clearly with Gigi) and Consolata herself, whom Steward Morgan shoots between the eyes. Yet when Roger Best, the undertaker, goes out to the Convent to collect the bodies, he finds "No bodies. Nothing. Even the Cadillac was gone" (292). In this ending, both the men and the women escape from the frame of law, and the last few pages of the novel have a gravely joyful spiritual lightness.

Morrison's real interest lies in a temporal eschatology—a "composted" Christianity (to use Mary Douglas' term), a doubling of God back into the world. Fiction takes on the responsibility of this vision, and Morrison's novel becomes like the ship in Consolata's vision on the last page, when her own dreamed black mother superior-singer takes on the final point of view: "Piedade looks to see what has come. Another ship, perhaps, but different, heading to port, crew and passengers, lost and saved, atremble, for they have been disconsolate for some time. Now they will rest before shouldering the endless work they were created to do down here in Paradise" (318). Her real interest lies in this anagogical vision, though it might take some time for the racial and feminist dimensions of the novel to come into the right perspective. She sets the novel in the late 1960s and the 1970s, ending it in the Bicentennial year, to suggest the throes of an old order coming to an end and a new, more substantially hopeful one, coming to birth. The flaws of the novel stem from a kind of urgency to make the worlds of Ruby and the Convent as polyphonic as possible. In the many voices and perspectives that she grants (and I have perhaps unduly emphasized Consolata's), Morrison ends up having to give overly quick signatures to the development of her characters. For example, Menus Jury is a Vietnam veteran who drinks too much after Ruby refused him the white bride he wanted to bring home. Gigi has a memory of seeing a small black boy shot during a riot or demonstration, but the nature of the occasion remains undeveloped and less than convincing for someone as sexually obsessed as she is at the beginning of the novel. Steward Morgan, Deacon's twin, remains somehow unsatisfying, to my mind, a little too much of a black John Wayne, and other characters such as "Luther" have to be summed up in the knowing references of the other characters. The scenes with the templates perhaps too much resemble the middle section of *Beloved* when "124 was loud," and Consolata's teaching in some ways reprises that of Baby Suggs. But in this novel, the difficulty Morrison faces is in bringing the religious sensibility to bear, not on intense private consciousness, but on the act of living together for which it is a crucial bond. She succeeds imperfectly, she is too obvious with her opinions and her fashionable knowingness, but she nevertheless breaks into that space of the religious imagination which has always been the birthright of poetry.

When Morrison claims in her Jefferson Lecture that at the heart of literary form, serious ethical debates and probings are taking place, she somewhat understates the case. Literature is the mode of testing out the official stories that can become versions of what Tocqueville calls "majority tyranny." Its forms are ways of prying open assumptions, finding what lies behind the "rage for order," making it more difficult to assign anyone a predetermined voice or standard position. Perhaps the finest means of examining social and philosophical constructs is to submit them to the test of formal plausibility in human action. Literature gauges the deepest beliefs that hold us, and at its best it can provide a transforming experience of realities beyond those we had premised for ourselves. *Paradise* is not Dantean in achievement, certainly, but it affords glimpses that have nothing to do with fashion, literary or otherwise. Morrison's strangely plausible ending marks something new, I think, in the American imagination, despite approaches to it in the late fiction of Caroline Gordon and William Faulkner: the tone of inhabiting the daylight American world in the resurrected body, beyond the "inflections" of race, class, and gender, when a reunited mother and daughter eating grits and drinking fresh orange juice at Jennie's Country Inn can take on the pure gravity of presence.

4.

Othello and the
Marriages of Politics

W HEN the news of Nicole Brown Simpson's murder broke one afternoon in June of 1994, I was teaching in a summer institute on tragedy and comedy at L.S.U., where the lecture and seminar that morning, by exotic coincidence, had been on *Othello*. In the next day's seminar, a participant from Ghana kept expressing his astonishment at the parallels between Shakespeare's tragedy and the contemporary event; it was not a matter of similarity simply, but something deeper and more personal, as though awakening the tragic paradigm in his own imagination had somehow elicited its real re-enactment. Simpson *was* Othello to him, a character saturated with déja vu, an Americanized dream-version of himself, still exotic and African, in a Venice-like America. For him, and for those of us listening to him, the categorical membrane between literature and news, archetype and stereotype, psyche and outer event, seemed about to dissolve.

Although this play based on an inter-racial, cross-cultural marriage has always been a magnet for the problems of American politics and culture, for the past several decades its force has been particularly strong, and since Simpson's arrest, it has been virtually impossible to discuss it without referring to the Simpson trial. Like Othello's, Simpson's most obvious motive for killing his wife was jealous rage, and where is the story of the prominent black man who turns murderous more powerfully enshrined than in Shakespeare's play, at the center of the "Western canon"? Yet Toni Morrison, in her introduction to *Birth of a Nation'Hood*, does not even mention *Othello*. Other essayists take up the play only to dismiss the parallel. For example, Morrison's co-editor Claudia Brodsky Lacour writes:

> The Simpson trial has been readily identified with *Othello*, but its drama lay elsewhere, for no one can read or view *Othello* and believe the root of evil lay not with Iago, or that Othello and Desdemona did not love each other, or that their "mixed" marriage was blasphemy. Too many white husbands murder too many white wives, and cause the ruin of too many white lovers and daughters in Shakespeare (and in the everyday history of the world), and they do so for more ignominious reasons than carefully fomented jealousy, for the tragedy of Desdemona to offer anything but another thoughtless cliché in relation to our nation's consuming spectacle. (401)

But Lacour's dismissal is puzzling. One prominent strain of commentary finds Othello and Desdemona unwise in their elopement and ripe for Iago's abuse, despite their love for each other. What can lie behind Lacour's assertion that "too many white husbands murder too many white wives" in Shakespeare for anyone to take racial difference seriously in *Othello*? Is there another instance of wife-murder in Shakespeare, much less a number great enough to keep the differences of Othello and Desdemona from having a bearing on the murder? I cannot think of even one.

In the Latin American tradition, critics routinely blame *The Tempest* for imagining indigenous people as "Caliban." It is surprising that Morrison, Lacour, and the other commentators on the Simpson phenomenon seem not to hold *Othello* responsible for the "official story" of Simpson's trial— especially if Allan Bloom's account of *Othello* in "Cosmopolitan Man and the Political Community" is correct. Bloom argues that the play draws upon and fosters prejudices already current in 1604:

> To the untutored English audience, the Moor was a stranger bringing from his dark continent mysteries, dangers, and a new religion. Shakespeare, in

making a Moor his hero, runs counter to an established pattern of thought. He must make special efforts to convince us of Othello's nobility and superior humanity. But in so doing he does not intend enlightenment, as Lessing does in *Nathan the Wise*. For Shakespeare's Moor, after making all the detours of civilized man and manifesting an unexpected depth, returns at the end to the barbarism that the audience originally expected. The first, primitive prejudice against Othello seems to find justification in the conclusion. (43)

Morrison maintains her silence on *Othello*. Although she does not explain her omission, as Lacour does, one can speculate that she is more concerned with American than with English Renaissance "Africanism," influential as Shakespeare might have been, and for these purposes, she is better served by the works that she does examine, Melville's *Benito Cereno* and D. W. Griffith's racist classic, *Birth of a Nation*.

But the real reason, in Morrison's case, was probably that the official, cultural power of *Othello* had already been exposed, with more satisfying subtlety, in the Clarence Thomas hearings—on which Morrison had edited her previous book, Race-*ing Justice, En-*Gender*ing Power : Essays on Anita Hill, Clarence Thomas, and the Construction of Social Reality*. Sen. Alan Simpson attacked Anita Hill by quoting the lines, "Good name in man and woman, dear my lord, / Is the immediate jewel of their souls." His obvious meaning was that Anita Hill was assaulting the good name of Clarence Thomas—but why did his quotation have to come from *Othello*? The allusion sparked essays about the uses of Shakespeare, and with reason: the lines about "good name" are lifted from Iago's seduction of Othello into a jealousy based on Desdemona's "unnatural" choice of a black husband. Anita Hill becomes the Iago of the piece, and Clarence Thomas's identification of himself with whites, including his marriage to a white woman, becomes the extraordinarily rich subtext of her sexual accusations. In the cultural ironies that surrounded naming a black man to the Supreme Court under a conservative Republican administration, Hill could not simply be accusing Thomas of sexual harassment. This white Simpson's *Othello* reference reveals how many cultural questions about Shakespeare's place in what Morrison calls the "official story" were already seething in the confirmation hearings, well before the murder of Nicole Brown Simpson.

This kind of engagement between permanent texts and real events is intoxicating. It enables critics to break the formal membrane of the fiction and exercise powers of literary interpretation on the whole cultural context in which a particular work is being quoted or interpreted. In American social dramas as intense as those of the early 1990s, the political *use* of a "canon-ized" play about a high-minded but impolitic marriage across racial lines provides prime opportunities for commentary about received understand-ings. Cultural potencies can be played against each other, ironies of misread-ing unmasked and imbued with dark import. On the one hand, the play as a formal construct dissolves into another force in the operation of what is *really* interesting: power. On the other hand, everyone involved is suddenly caught in the birdlime of textuality, like characters in a play who can be treated as constructs of language.

When one considers the academic pressure to write about what is writ-ten about what is written, the endless proliferation of readings and theories, the stirrings of portentousness and pretension; when one contemplates the sheer bureaucratic effort that it takes to sustain the fiction that all these things must be said; when one thinks of the advancement into tenure, promotion, and perhaps, in a very few cases, academic fame that depend on them, it might be bracing to remember Ecclesiastes: *Vanity of vanities*. At one time, a remark like Sen. Simpson's would have been dismissed as relying with embarrassing inappropriateness on *Bartlett's Quotations*, and the senator (a term used with mockery, as coincidence would have it, by Iago himself) would have been recognized as another of those who begin a sentence with "As Shakespeare says...." Shakespeare's play would have been held by the educated as a thing apart from its rhetorical abuses: think of the way a Sen. Simpson would have fared in Jane Austen, for example. But if the very description "the educated" is held by the enlightened to be an invidious distinction that preserves certain relations of power (an opinion that greatly enhances their own power), then the useful difference between the best interpretation of a play and the cultural uses to which the play might be put threatens to disappear. The play *is* its cultural uses, in this view. The formal textuality of it—the fact that *Othello* contains the same lines to which one could turn in the time of Oliver Cromwell or Abraham Lincoln—becomes less a stabilizing corrective than an opportunity to change the valence of its influence. Stephen Greenblatt has argued that Shakespeare's plays offer "no central, unwavering authorial presence" (254), and one has only to compare Shakespeare to Milton's "egotistical sublime" to see what he means. But to speak of form in *Othello* is not to try to extract something pure (and dead, like Desdemona) from the messy contingencies, not to try to make an argument for the autonomy of the text, but to try to apprehend the live field in which meanings become active, the culturally contingent self-sufficiency of the whole, the provisional completion of forces in language that originally grow upon a particular time and place.

Anyone who chooses to write about *Othello* means to do something with it. The question is how one confronts its indwelling intentionality of language. Does the interpretation mean to wonder at it, as though one came upon it from flat and arid surroundings, like Ayer's Rock? To tease out a publishable new twist? To think through a particular "teaching" discovered in the text? Or does interpretation always promote another end—political, philosophic, or religious—for which the work is usefully illustrative? Framing this question is a still larger and older one: is literature itself primarily a mode of knowledge or a means of persuasion? If the latter, then literature is understood always to stem from a prior rhetorical end that determines the way it presents its images, characters, and actions. For example, let us say that the historical Shakespeare wanted to promote the obedience of daughters and discourage marriages between unequals. In that case, *Othello* should be read as an amplified version of its source story, because Disdemona in Giraldi Cinthio's *Hecatommithi* says to her friend: "Much I fear that I shall prove a warning to young girls not to marry against the wishes of their parents, and that the Italian ladies may learn from me not to wed a man whom nature and habitude of life estrange from us" (179). This didactic dimension would then be disguised (if not actually weakened) by the text's generosity toward Othello and Desdemona in giving one a vivid grandeur and the other an unquestionably faithful nature as they move toward their tragic ends. Or perhaps Shakespeare had no design on his audience, but despite his real sympathies for Othello and Desdemona, he *had* to serve prevailing opinion, whether he wanted to or not, by the very act of writing plays for the public stage. Perhaps he felt himself limited on one side by the possibility of censorship, on the other by the marketability of his play. Since the public would not accept a happy ending for the marriage of an aging Moor and a white Venetian teenager, he wrote a tragedy and "persuaded" his audience to accept disaster as the only possible outcome, although the implicit structures of power were in fact persuading both playwright and audience in advance.

If Shakespeare meant to put a stop to unequal marriages, he must have been as bitter after several months as Gulliver exclaiming to his Cousin Sympson (a name that seems oddly to recur), "I should never have attempted so absurd a project as that of reforming the Yahoo race in this kingdom." If, on the other hand, literature is a mode of knowledge, part of whose nature is to work through and with all these other influences, then the rhetorical occasion informing the past-tense historical Shakespeare and his intentions ceases to be crucial. Rather, the audience, like the playwright, is enjoined to the same artistic justice that Othello requests at the end of the play: "Nothing extenuate, / Nor set down aught in malice." The play formally advocates only the *habitus* of imaginative justice.

I T is no accident that two of the most prominent and influential contemporary schools of political commentary have begun by reinterpreting the particular anxieties of *Othello*. In *Shakespeare's Politics* (1964), the book in which the influence of Leo Strauss first made itself felt in literary study, Allan Bloom argues that Iago is the catalyst but by no means the cause of the tragedy. Bloom's chapter dismantles the pretensions of a universal religion of love and ends with praise for Iago's wife Emilia, who represents an alternative to both modern materialist despair and the unstable claims of love: classical political philosophy. Stephen Greenblatt's last chapter in *Renaissance Self-Fashioning* (1980), the book that inaugurated the New Historicism, interprets the improvisations of power in *Othello*. Greenblatt compares the ways that Europeans improvised upon the beliefs of tribes in the new world to the way that Iago improvises upon the sexual anxieties of Othello. He goes on to make claims about Shakespeare's disquieting (Desdemona-like) affirmations of the structures of Elizabethan and Jacobean power. Both Bloom and Greenblatt give brilliant readings, without question, readings that introduce into one's own familiarity with the action a strangeness, an otherness, as though one were finding out that a spouse or close friend had a hidden life. Both are attracted to this play because of a certain historical and political dimension—Bloom because of the play's reflection both on the supposed openness of commercial republics and the supposed inclusiveness of Christianity, Greenblatt because of what it supremely exemplifies about "self-fashioning" in the Renaissance. Both Bloom and Greenblatt have designs on the play in their different bids for cultural influence. The play matters a great deal for what they attempt to do, and matters in an entirely different way than it does for Claudia Brodsky Lacour or Alan Simpson. Yet each of them, to my mind, distorts the play, and to the extent that each achieves cultural influence, each ultimately fosters this characteristic distortion.

Greenblatt's reading of *Othello* culminates his examination of the self-fashioned character of such distinctive Renaissance men as Thomas More, Tyndale, Wyatt, Spenser, and Marlowe. Greenblatt himself has found it ironic that his work, which has exercised its influence far beyond Renaissance studies, has not been known by the term he chose—a "cultural poetics," drawing upon the work of such anthropologists and theorists of culture as Clifford Geertz, Mary Douglas, and Victor Turner. Greenblatt meant to show that poetic texts and the cultures in which they occur have, as it were, a single circulatory system: "Social actions are themselves always embedded in systems of public signification, always grasped, even by their makers, in acts of interpretation, while the words that constitute the works of literature that we discuss here are by their very nature the manifest assurance of a similar embeddedness" (5). Yet the response to his work settled on describing it the school of thought for which he was in part responsible as the "New Historicism," a term that he once used much more casually. Nevertheless "New Historicism," better than "cultural poetics," catches something of the novel gloom of Greenblatt's approach. By echoing "New Criticism," the term "New Historicism" suggests that no work can be read iconically, without constant reference to its context, and that the New Critical weapons of close reading and interpretation now serve a thoroughgoing recognition that there is no possible autonomy, no possible transcendence, especially in one's own "free choices." In his epilogue to *Renaissance Self-Fashioning*, Greenblatt says that when he began the book, he meant to analyze what seemed to him the remarkable shaping power that these Renaissance men had over their own lives: "I saw the power and the freedom it implied as an important element in my own sense of myself" (256). What is unsaid, but almost said, is that he had conceived of writing the book as his corresponding act of self-fashioning power and freedom. Strongly implied as well is an insight into the motives of power (or "empowerment") that move academics toward certain figures, certain works. What he had thought would be liberating, however, proved quite otherwise:

> indeed, the human subject itself began to seem remarkably unfree, the ideological product of the relations of power in a particular society. Whenever I focused sharply upon a moment of apparently autonomous self-fashioning, I found not an epiphany of identity freely chosen but a cultural artifact. If there remained traces of free choice, the choice was among possibilities whose range was strictly delineated by the social and ideological systems in force...." (256)

Still more to the point, he found that his sense of control over his own identity was certainly an illusion, yet "to let go of one's stubborn hold upon selfhood, even selfhood conceived as a fiction, is to die" (257). He closes the book with a kind of ironic testimony, both personal and profoundly impersonal in his own terms. He has come to believe that the self with which he feels and needs is itself a cultural construct, yet, he writes, "I want to bear witness at the close to my overwhelming need to sustain the illusion that I am the principal maker of my own identity" (257).

Greenblatt's reading of *Othello* is necessarily affected by these conclusions about his freedom. He concentrates brilliantly on Iago's improvisations, on Othello's narrative construction of himself, and on Desdemona's troubling and apparently excessive love of her husband—troubling and excessive because Iago works with a longstanding Christian tradition that lust between partners even within marriage constitutes adultery: a husband could be "too familiar" with his own wife. The genius of Iago's improvisation is that it reveals Desdemona as an adulteress in the very fervor with which she loves her husband. The exuberance of her innocence constitutes her guilt. Greenblatt's reading moves with such revelatory force that it entirely justifies his lengthy detours from the text, not only into the Spanish improvisations upon the beliefs of the Lucayans in the New World, but also into medieval and Renaissance views of pleasure in marriage. When he returns to the murder of Desdemona, his argument has become altogether compelling:

> Othello's identity is entirely caught up in the narrative structure that drives him to turn Desdemona into a being incapable of pleasure, a piece of "monumental alabaster," so that he will at least be able to love her without the taint of adultery:
>
> > Be thus, when thou art dead, and I will kill thee,
> > And love thee after.   (5.2.18-19)
>
> It is as if Othello had found in a necrophilic fantasy the secret solution to the intolerable demands of the rigorist sexual ethic, and the revelation that Cassio has not slept with Desdemona leads only to a doubling of this solution, for the adulterous sexual pleasure that Othello had projected upon his lieutenant now rebounds upon himself. (252)

Greenblatt is right when he argues that "pleasure itself becomes for Othello pollution, a defilement of his property in Desdemona and in himself" (251); and it is true that "beneath his cynical modernity and professed self-love Iago reproduces in himself the same psychic structure" (251).

What Greenblatt does not remark on in this psychic structure, however, is the extent to which this "rigorist sexual ethic" comes into effect only when a much more profound anxiety has already been evoked. Iago's first profane burst of self-exposition to Roderigo centers on the fact that Cassio—Cassio, a mathematician, a "fellow almost damned in a fair wife," a "counter-caster" who knows as little about actual battle as a spinster—was chosen as lieutenant over him. Despite his own more substantial qualifications, "he, sir, had th' election." Given the play's heated rhetoric of sexual anxiety and his own concern with self-fashioning, Greenblatt understandably concentrates on Iago and Othello rather than this unobjectionable lieutenant who seems perfectly adapted to Venetian society. Yet it seems foreordained that Greenblatt, thinking in a loop of psychological and cultural causality, never sufficiently admits the possibility of real transcendent causes. Like Iago—and eventually Othello—Greenblatt grounds all religious concerns in the "rigorist" suspicion of pleasure and sees Cassio only as the recipient of others' projections. But the world of *Othello*, beyond its bragging and bluster, is one in which identity finds itself moved, with fear and trembling, through events mysteriously penetrated by divine intention.

The Ur-anxiety in *Othello* concerns preferment or election. Calvin's emphasis on double predestination introduced a monstrous dread into the common imagination of Shakespeare's milieu, but the world of the play need not be specifically Calvinist. In a military career and in love, in business ventures as in one's eternal destiny, salvation lies in "preferment and affection," and neither in the "old gradation" that Iago claims to prefer, nor in merit per se. Merit, in fact, might stem from being preferred, much as one might want causality to work in the other direction. In this regard, the dominant factor in *Othello* is not the sexual ethic that Othello and Iago might share, but the more profound worry about being the preferred one selected from many, the *chosen*. Cassio captures one's attention, not because he has a critically neglected depth of psychological structure, but because, from the beginning of the play to the end, regardless of Iago's attempts and his own moral weaknesses, he is undoubtedly the chosen. "He hath a daily beauty in his life," Iago admits late in the play, "that makes me ugly." Through the sequence of abuses to which Iago subjects him, Cassio reveals an unexpected *gravitas* and moves toward yet another preferment—as lord governor of Cyprus. For those who actually live with him, no one so occupies their obsessed attention as this courteous Florentine, upon whom—for the audience of the play—no slander or salacious suggestion will stick. The greatest passions of improvisation and narrative self-fashioning rage precisely around Michael Cassio, the one already chosen, always to be chosen.

In this language of election, the tendency is powerfully to mystify preferment. Iago attempts, at every stage, to demystify anything having to do with being chosen or blessed. When Iago first begins to convince Roderigo of Desdemona's passion for Cassio, Roderigo says that he cannot believe it of her, because "She is full of most blessed condition." Iago scornfully retorts, "Blessed, fig's end! The wine she drinks is made of grapes." "Fig's end" refers to the obscene Italian gesture that Iago no doubt makes as he says it. Its genital suggestiveness—and the *naturalness* of the analogy to fruit—shock both Roderigo and the audience. In his interpretation, bodily need and a rhetorical haze of sexual desire explain everything about so-called blessedness. Everything "blessed" relates to the physical body, not to any imagined infusion from a divine source. The wine she drinks, in other words, is not God's blood—"'S' blood'" ("by God's blood") is his first word in the play—transubstantiated, but the physical grape rotted into intoxicating fermentation. Like Callimaco in Machiavelli's *Mandragola*, who first poses as a doctor and examines the urine of the woman he wants to seduce, Iago approaches the aura of feminine beauty with a ferociously reductive rhetoric of *physis* that dispels its effects on him and gives him a contemptuous power over sexual attraction. In the same way, he treats preferment, not as mysterious or graced, but as the result of discernible causes. He recognizes that, as Cassio has been chosen to be lieutenant for specific, comprehensible reasons, so Othello has been preferred by Desdemona to all the "wealthy curled darlings" of Venice—not miraculously, as though out of unmerited grace—but for particular reasons that he can exploit. Desdemona chose Othello, he reasons, not because she was spiritually able to transcend all their differences to see his true merit, but because she was a credulous girl, ready for sexual adventure, who loved what happened to her imagination when the exotic Moor was "bragging and telling fantastical lies."

Greenblatt's interpretation, without explicitly saying so, vindicates Desdemona by finding her capable of eroticizing everything. Her paradoxical capacity to free her passion, instead of constraining it, through conventional forms and to find greater intensities of pleasure in obedience to Othello than in the assertion of her own will becomes for Greenblatt the mark of her freedom and her tragic misinterpretation. More disquieting in her submissions than in her defiance, she ultimately becomes Greenblatt's paradigm for Shakespeare's own embrace of "the social and ideological systems in force" in England: "In Shakespeare's narrative art, liberation from the massive power structures that determine social and psychic reality is glimpsed in an excessive aesthetic delight, an erotic embrace of those very structures—the embrace of a Desdemona whose love is more deeply unsettling than even a Iago's empathy" (254).

Allan Bloom's reading of the play, also a brilliant one, begins from a very different perspective. To Bloom, schooled in classical political philosophy, Desdemona's love stems from a dangerous fascination with otherness and demonstrates Shakespeare's strong suspicion of a state like Venice whose regime necessarily allows such openness to the outsider.[1] Bloom cites with approval the opinion of the Earl of Shaftsbury that "the marriage of Othello and Desdemona is a mismatch, a monstrous union founded on the lying pretensions of a charlatan and the unhealthy imagination of a misguided young girl" (36). In Plato's *Laws*, the Athenian stranger imagining the regime of the Cretan city being founded by his interlocutor Klinias, lays it down as a principle that there will be as little trade with outsiders, as little innovation in games, and as little variance in musical forms as possible, and that there will be no travel at all even for the male citizens until after their fortieth year. Needless to say, the women neither travel nor meet "extravagant and wheeling strangers" in the family home. Drawing upon this ancient understanding of what makes a vital and lasting regime, Bloom emphasizes both the older, more traditional understanding of arranged marriages that would have been present to Shakespeare's audience and the non-liberal suspicion of "the barbarism of those who lay beyond one's own borders" (41) that would also have informed their lively self-estimate.

> Each city has its manners and its gods; the very life of the city depends on this particularism: to live, it must defend its ancestral ways which is a combination of human accidents and special institutions adapted to the here and now. Good citizenship implies a devotion to those ways; a universality, a cosmopolitanism that devoted itself to the essence of man as he is eternally, would destroy those roots of affection which are necessary to political life. (46)

He means to cut sharply and shockingly across modern sentiments about marriage and toleration that he strongly associates with "the Romantic tradition" (43). But he also means to do considerably more than that, particularly in exploring (largely by way of suggestion and the apparatus of the "secret teaching") what he considers Shakespeare's real point: that *Othello* is a play about faith, and that Othello himself might be the God of Christianity.

A good Straussian secret teaching, as Leo Strauss explains in "Persecution and the Art of Writing," will always have built into it what certain administrations call "deniability." Part of Bloom's elusiveness, admittedly, lies in the text he chooses for all his citations: the Furness variorum edition published in 1886. Line numbers crucial to an understanding of his extremely significant notes thus have to be traced back to an edition that Borges, perhaps, had on his bookshelf, but that the rest of us might have more difficulty locating. Some of Bloom's points lie very much on the surface, however, although they are turned to a different facet than the one he really wants to show. For example, once he has established that a "cosmopolitanism" devoted to the essence of man instead of his political particularity would "destroy those roots of affection which are necessary to political life," then he need only add a page or two later, apparently in praise of Othello, that

"The local—the political, in the ancient sense—does not weigh so heavily on a man in the Christian context" (48). Moreover, drawing upon what he knows to be the prevailing opinion in America, he can seem to praise the very things that he is dispraising: "The [Christian] faith provides a cosmopolitanism which is not limited by the accident of birth, the peculiarity of education, or the difference in social position. The importance of Othello's Christianity, both for his own sense of dignity and purpose and for the possibility of his stepping over boundaries that would otherwise have been insuperable, cannot be overestimated" (48). Such phrases as "not limited by" seem to support the opinion that all boundaries need to be crossed by a universal toleration, all accidents and peculiarities overcome, whereas Bloom's real view stems from a classical critique of this position.

Nowhere is this critique sharper than in his analysis of love, the passion obviously as central to Christianity as it is to the play. However disingenuously, Bloom argues that, for those of us in the Biblical tradition of Shakespeare's audience, the jealousy of the Old Testament God "unconsciously affects our perception of those who suffer it. Shakespeare's Othello does act out on the human scene a god's role; he is a universal stranger, a leader who can command and punish wherever he goes" (53). If Othello is jealous like the Old Testament God, if he acts a god's role in being the stranger in any city, and if he embodies a cosmopolitanism of faith that destroys the local attachments at the root of politics, then Bloom's description of Othello in love should be applied to the Old Testament God in love—that is, the Old Testament God just at the point of becoming the New Testament God:

> Othello, though radically dependent, represents himself as completely independent; and the myth of his independence seems to be less for his own benefit than for the sake of those who made him. They could not trust him if they knew him to be their own creation.... All might have succeeded, there might have been no revelation of Othello's true situation, if he had not gone one step too far in the direction of his conquest of Venice. That step was his falling in love with Desdemona and marrying her. In Desdemona, he had chosen the fairest flower of one of the best families in Venice. In marrying her, he seemed to prove that he was fully

lovable in Venice by Venetians, that he had fully naturalized himself. In the manner of his wooing, he continues the masquerade that not he but Desdemona is the one who needs; she is the lover, and he the beloved. He is still the independent being to whom others come because of his qualities. But Iago knows that this is not true. It is his awareness of Othello's absolute dependence on Desdemona, of which Othello himself is totally unaware, that allows Iago to bring about the destruction which he plots. (50-51)

Bloom's reading of Othello's situation parallels a Machiavellian interpretation of Christianity. (Nietzsche might have held the same opinion, but he would be considered irresponsible in expressing it explicitly.) Gods, in this view, are human inventions that should serve specific, local purposes—that is, political purposes in the ancient sense—in much the same way that Othello serves a purpose for the Venetians. The problem lies in the Incarnation. As Bloom remarks in an endnote, "Shakespeare draws out the parallel [between Othello and the Old Testament God] in presenting the relationship between Othello and Desdemona as spiritual, with the physical motivations appearing as the great sin. Immediately before declaring his jealousy, the God of the Old Testament specifies the meaning of infidelity: the worship of physical objects—all that paganism implied (Exodus 20:4-6; cp. IV.i.137)" (71, n31). In other words, Desdemona appears as Mary, Othello as the apparently independent but in fact extraordinarily needy god, and the whole relation between the universal stranger and the maiden as having to deny that it is actually sexually idolatrous and pagan in Old Testament terms, precisely to the extent that it involves the body. Bloom is altogether conscious that this suggestion will be blasphemous to Christians. In discussing Iago, Bloom uses without quotation marks the sentence, "I am not what I am" (63), that Iago uses in describing himself to Roderigo. Bloom thus identifies himself both with Iago and with the Devil: "Iago is clearly the Devil. He says so himself and is often so called. But in the case where God is not perfect, the Devil's negativity may be a source of liberation, an aid to the discovery of the truth" (62). In this rather extraordinary praise for Iago, the erstwhile villain begins to emerge as the true philosopher:

He speaks out for a freedom which none of the others recognize. Iago
wishes to live his own life free from the domination of other men, and
especially of other men's thoughts. He realizes that true tyranny is not
imposed by force, but imposes itself on the minds of men. For Iago, man
can free himself only by thought. He has thought through the emptiness
of most beliefs and will not live in subordination to them. He cannot
found his life on self-deception, as Othello does. (63)

Yet Bloom ultimately finds Iago lacking because his private freedom "is
compatible with the basest and most arbitrary ends" (66), and his use of the
beliefs of others would, "grafted onto the thought of a political man" (like
Machiavelli) would result in "a severe, punishing morality" because, believing
that men are by nature bad, "he must believe in the use of force, deceit, and
terror to make them conform" (65).

The alternative to Iago's essentially private and mean-spirited selfishness
is, unexpectedly, Emilia: "Iago, otherwise so clear-sighted, fails to see one
thing. He cannot foresee that Emilia would be willing to die for the truth.
The possibility of a simple, unadorned passion for nothing but truth is not
within his ken" (66). Bloom's reading of the play finds it ultimately didactic,
in this sense: neither love, Christian or erotic, nor the modern philosophy of
selfishly power-based improvisation and interpretation can be trusted. The
truth comes through Emilia, who judges the marriage a "most filthy bargain"
yet defends Desdemona's fidelity, condemns her husband for his web of
deceit, and dies on behalf of the truth, like Socrates. Not so much the
common sense of Emilia but her noble passion for the truth turns out to be
the play's powerful analogue for classical political philosophy, in this reading.
Bloom ends the chapter by asking, "Would not a life expressing such a passion be both noble and, by its very nature, free of deception?" (66). In order
to advocate this classical position, the Shakespeare of Bloom's interpretation
has to reject Christianity's claims and let the nature of things reassert the
necessary boundaries. Othello's suicide significantly follows upon Emilia's
revelation of his true situation.

Although Bloom anticipates Greenblatt by two decades in suggesting
that the very physicality of Desdemona constitutes her infidelity, his

argument is far more radical than Greenblatt's. Bloom's Shakespeare actively dismantles "the massive power structures that determine social and psychic reality," the ones that Greenblatt thinks Shakespeare disquietingly embraces; moreover, Bloom's Shakespeare provides a figure of real autonomy and, I suppose, "self-fashioning," in Emilia. For Allan Bloom, "Shakespeare is, in the final accounting, very hard" (63). He resists the dangerous charms of tragic emotion and recommends instead the kind of restraint to which Jane Austen's Mr. Knightley would advise the "imaginist," Emma Woodhouse. At the moment of greatest tragic revelation, when a kind of rift opens in the being of the West and one encounters the ontological anguish of its contradictions, the point for Bloom is Emilia's core insistence on her responsibility to the truth. The difficulty with this reading, however, is that, for all his compelling insight, Bloom ends up seeming a little too youthfully swaggering in his assertions (I am not what I am), a little too Romantically engaged, so to speak, by his Nietzschean capacity to bear "very hard" kinds of truth, a little too delighted in the anticipated effects of his closer-than-thou readings. He has to end up skirting the actual emotional appeal of the end of the play, when Desdemona dies innocently and Othello recognizes his great crime. He has to bottle the abyss of Othello's unbearable self-condemnation in a "teaching" something like this: if God had been as wise as Socrates, the West would have been spared that most tyrannical of allurements, the abyss of post-Christian nihilism.

Greenblatt's mode of questioning has entered the contemporary academic mainstream of thought distantly shaped by Marx, Nietzsche, and Freud: it is analysis in terms of determinant conditions, including the subjective condition of will to power, brought to bear on the text, not as a form with fictional closure, but as an open linguistic symptom. The New Historicism that followed Greenblatt's lead found all sorts of cultural contexts—always in terms of power—that at once restored a kind of living circulation to the reference of the language and in effect attached critical leeches to the skin of the texts. Bloom's approach tends, with less condescension toward the formal text, nevertheless to foster the kinds of cold-blooded readings that treat Shakespeare's plays as expositions of political philosophy. Readers in this Straussian school have added, often brilliantly, a valuable, undoubtedly valid dimension to criticism of Shakespeare, but they have just as frequently missed implications that might stem from the interior of faith— not necessarily religion, but "that willing suspension of disbelief that constitutes poetic faith," in Coleridge's famous phrase.

In his drive to reveal a Shakespeare about whom "we sense that he has both intellectual clarity and vigorous passions and that the two do not undermine each other in him," Bloom hopes to "recapture the fullness of life" lost in a split between "abstract science on the one hand and unrefined passions on the other" (12). Yet Bloom's reading concentrates almost entirely on an abstracting intellectual clarity that undermines the vigorous passions that evidently move the plays.[2] Bloom's approach to Shakespeare rightly restores the honor to Shakespeare as a thinker, but it also does him a major disservice by implying Shakespeare has a rhetorical argument to make, that in being "very hard," he charts out his teaching in advance, and that he molds the speeches to his thesis. Seamus Heaney quotes a passage from Frost's essay "The Figure a Poem Makes" that seems as apt for *Othello* as for "Mending Wall" or "Home-Burial": the true poem "can never lose its sense of a meaning that once unfolded by surprise as it went" (*Government* 93).

The surprise in *Othello* begins with the phenomenon, not of choosing, but of being either chosen or rejected, and the response of the characters has less to do with "the improvisation of power" than with the imagination seeking the new form that must accompany new fortunes. Once again, I turn to the question of Cassio. Like his marriage to Desdemona, Othello's choice of lieutenant reflects one of Shakespeare's most powerful insights about the self as an image given from outside, especially the self that already feels itself to be the *xenos* or outsider. Many critics, Bloom among them, have noted that Othello would traditionally be associated by his race and culture with the enemies of Christian Europe.[3] Although he has converted to Christianity, he not only keeps the looks and manners of the stranger, but he uses them to great advantage in his dealings with the Venetians, because his difference, bringing an air of domesticated barbarian menace, is his chief selling point. Venice has literally bought his persona, because he is not only a mercenary soldier in the hire of the Senate, but the general of their troops. The senators, if Brabantio is any indication, seem to enjoy his robust, exotic manner and his stories. Although it seems strange that someone who seems so supremely confident at the beginning of the play has such a need to have his persona "bought," Othello is in a sense a celebrity, a star recognizable everywhere. In a very real way, he is always acting and therefore always needs an audience to validate his role. When Brabantio's men come to arrest him at the beginning of the play, he conceives of himself as someone being watched, like an actor onstage: "Were it my cue to fight, I should have known it / without a prompter" (1.2.82-83). Like an actor who cannot escape his role as the *xenos* and warrior, he eventually has to have his persona "bought" even in order to exist for himself. What inevitably raises questions, however, is to what extent Desdemona—the sought-after golden girl, pursued by all "the wealthy curled darlings" of the nation—has not so much bought as staked her life on this exotic persona, accepting him in a way that he could never have anticipated: whole-heartedly, sincerely, with an absolute love that both ratifies his preferment and leaves him extremely vulnerable.

Like *Medea*, which also deals with sexual jealousy, *Othello* is a tragedy about the stranger, the *xenos* or foreigner, who tries to become a part of his adopted city by marrying into it. Like Medea, Othello is exotic and associated with witchcraft; unlike Medea, he is not really rejected and he does not devise evil on his own. The "witchcraft" of the *xenos* is displaced onto Iago, who turns it against Othello himself for believing that he has really been accepted. In Iago's estimation, Othello's choice of Cassio, like Desdemona's choice of Othello, brings something indigestible and unreal into the military world that he inhabits, an elegant illusion that he feels a compulsion to demystify and deconstruct. He takes up a kind of intelligence discarded by Othello in the flush of his erotic success in order to demonstrate the necessity of being ruthlessly self-serving and mistrustful on the enemy's ground. As the *xenos* who has been welcomed into the city, Othello has a counter-cultural or antinomian knowledge that he can potentially use (as it might be argued he has used his life story with Brabantio) against the supposed allies who will never really accept him past the point of his usefulness to them. Yet in his marriage to Desdemona this *xenos*-intelligence is now a reality of himself that he denies. When his denial also leads him to choose Cassio at almost the same time, Iago compulsively takes up this rejected dimension. His compulsion obviously has nothing to do with justice toward the whole truth; it is all about interpretation as power, and the hunger for power stems from the prior condition of being passed over, of not being the chosen.

Milton, whose Satan first separates himself and his angels from the host when the Son is preferred to him, might have learned something of the dynamics of Satanic envy from reading this play. Harold Bloom, in fact, writes that "Satan (as Milton did not wish to know) is the legitimate son of Iago, begot by Shakespeare upon Milton's Muse" (434). Iago's envy stems, as this second Bloom says, from a "sickening loss of being at rejection" (435) when Othello prefers Cassio to him as lieutenant, probably because Cassio could better maintain the difference between peace and war than Iago (434). But Iago's envy is also concerned with Othello's Christianity. At some point in the past, Othello has converted, and in becoming Christian he has accepted his preferment on three counts, closely related in his own mind: by Venice, God, and Desdemona. If his conversion were merely political, as it might very well be otherwise and as Iago would surely approve and understand, then his acceptance by Venice would be, in effect, part of a contractual arrangement like the arrangement made with Shylock at the end of *The Merchant of Venice*. But if it is *sincere*, if he accepts as a miraculous "grace" the unexpected and unmerited love of Desdemona, then Iago must necessarily feel rejected. The association between Desdemona and grace, erotic love and Christian acceptance, is doubtless powerful. Cassio tells the Cyprians that Othello has "achieved a maid / That paragons description and wild fame" (2.1.61-62), "the divine Desdemona" (2.1.73). Iago later describes her divinity more contemptuously:

> And then for her
> To win the Moor—were't to renounce his baptism,

All seals and symbols of redeemed sin—
His soul is so enfettered to her love
That she may make, unmake, do what she list,
Even as her appetite shall play the god
With his weak function. (2.3.342-48)

What others take as her divinity, he must also, but one of Greenblatt's strongest arguments is that Othello is undoubtedly sincere when he tells the Venetian senators that he desires to take Desdemona to Cyprus "not / To please the palate of [his] appetite" (1.3.256-57) but to honor her own wishes. A sincerely converted Othello, for whom Desdemona is the seal and symbol of redeemed sin, rejects his "dark self," the Satanic old man and stranger-to-grace that his visible appearance—"the Moor"—suggests to the Venetians, and in rejecting sin casts it, in effect, into Iago. The unrecognized displacement of evil onto the "ancient" reflects the hidden workings of this conversion: theologically, Iago becomes the rejected tempter, returning in another guise; psychologically, he truly becomes "honest Iago," who embodies Othello's inner stirrings of suspicion and unbelief, not to mention his "magic," that are consciously denied.

Even Iago has to admit that "The Moor is of a free and open nature"— though of course Iago goes on to qualify it with the comment that Othello "thinks men honest that but seem to be so." Othello has a golden amplitude and nobility that Desdemona obviously loves. He makes the world she inhabits larger in scope, more bountifully possible, less concerned about social niceties and appearances. She elopes with Othello, one suspects, largely for the outright thrill of it, because escaping from her father's house in the middle of the night to get married seems to her entirely in keeping with the kind of adventure she associates with him. But for her father, waked and profanely informed of the elopement by Iago and Roderigo, this same deed has the smack of evil arts and the worst kinds of moral corruption. Two images of Othello—images that affect the way he exists to himself and the reasons that he chose Cassio—are already at work in the first scenes of the play, Desdemona's and her father's. To understand what is at stake in these images, one needs to look at the first lines of the play and follow a series of displacements.

One infers that Iago has been taking money from Roderigo to act as a go-between to help him woo Desdemona, whom Roderigo wants to marry. On the same night, Iago and Roderigo both find out that Desdemona has eloped with Othello. Roderigo thinks that Iago must have known about it, but Iago protests—I think truthfully—that he did not, even though this admission of ignorance casts him in a bad light. When it comes to Othello's confidence, he says, Cassio has it, not himself. In the speech explaining why he hates the Moor (1.1.38-62), he tells Roderigo that Othello chose Cassio as his lieutenant, even though Iago had seniority and more field experience as a soldier. In justifying his continued service to Othello, Iago has some strange lines:

> It is as sure as you are Roderigo,
> Were I the Moor, I would not be Iago.
> In following him, I follow but myself. (1.1.53-55)

Is he saying, "If I were you, I wouldn't be me"? On one level, such a statement seems stupidly true; on another level, a piece of advice—*you don't want to be me, believe* me. But what does he mean, "Were I the Moor, I would not be Iago"? The first sense is stupidly true; the second seems to be something like this: *If I had the advantages of rank and favor that the Moor has, I wouldn't have to be scrounging around the way I'm doing now.* But there is also a third possible sense: *If I were Othello, I would make the decision, as he has done, to "be" Cassio and not Iago, in the sense that the lieutenant represents his superior.* "In following him, I follow but myself"? Level one: *the only reason I stay with him is that I am serving my own ends.* Level two: *Othello is Iago, I am Othello—the xenos, the perpetual outsider—and since I have been displaced by Cassio,* "I am not what I am" (62). Complicated as this "explanation" is—and it is meant to befuddle both Roderigo and audience—it contains important clues to Iago's sense of not being the chosen or the elect. Where he saw himself, Cassio now is, the *chosen* of Othello ("he, sir, had th'election").

When Allan Bloom writes that "Iago wishes to live his own life free from the domination of other men, and especially of other men's thoughts," he romanticizes him as the post-Christian philosopher, without sufficiently acknowledging the level of outraged *belief* in Iago, from which he can never be free. It is not enough to say that Othello himself was Iago's god and that Iago is now an atheist; Othello's choice of Cassio manifests a deeper and always prior non-election in Iago; it reveals but does not cause a metaphysical decentering as the subject (not object) of choice. His own "I am" lacks the deep, inner anointing that would give him the peace to *be*, and this lack—his already *not* being chosen in this inner sense—paradoxically causes him not to be chosen by others such as Othello. Being passed over constitutes a kind of revelation, and through it, a kind of freedom like that of the poet with "negative capability," since he no longer has any restraining pieties. Harold Bloom admires the energy and freedom of Iago, who "shines equally as nihilistic death-of-God theologue and as advanced dramatic poet" (436); for Iago, he writes, "the death of belief becomes the birth of invention" (438). But this delighted invention stems, not from the Nietzschean freedom to occupy the space once imagined for "God," and not from what Harold Bloom calls "ontotheological absence," but, like the freedom of Grendel or Milton's Satan or Victor Frankenstein's monster, from the sense of a present blessing specifically denied to *him*. His freedom, in other words, has nothing to do with the absence of *belief*, unless one takes Othello as God. But Othello is not only not God, but, as Iago immediately sets out to show, he is also not the chosen—certainly not the chosen of the *father* in the play, not blessed as the son on whom favor rests, in this regard—and in that denied election lies Iago's opportunity for revenge.

Iago's plot begins more or less spontaneously when he and Roderigo wake Brabantio by shouting at him from the street. Using images of bestial and demonic sex—"an old black ram is tupping your white ewe" (1.1.85-86) and "the devil will make a grandsire of you" (88) and "your daughter and the Moor are making the beast with two backs" (113-14)—Iago poisons Brabantio's view of the marriage and sets up his belief that Othello must have won his daughter by using "chains of magic," "foul charms," "arts inhibited and out of warrant" (cf. 1.2.61-80). Brabantio, as we soon discover, has heard Othello's stories, and reference to such magic perhaps played a part in them, as they do later in the play, when Othello frightens Desdemona by telling her that the lost handkerchief had "magic in the web of it" (3.4.69). Part of his exotic appeal and danger, in other words, has to do with the suggestion that he has unusual powers because of his commerce with arts unknown to Venetian—European, white, Christian—society. Brabantio holds this image of himself up to him: far from being the beloved chosen son, Othello is the barbarian, the *xenos* who has used his evil intelligence to overcome the rational desire of his daughter. Brabantio presents this Othello before the Senate largely on the basis of what seem to him evident inferences from nature: "For nature so prepost'rously to err, / Being not deficient, blind, or lame of sense, / Sans witchcraft could not" (1.3.62ff). He exclaims, thinking that he knows his daughter, "she, in spite of nature, / Of years, of country, credit, everything, / To fall in love with what she feared to look on!" (96-98). He refers to "all things of sense" and "all rules of nature" to back him up in his supposition that Desdemona would never have fallen in love with Othello naturally. In making this argument, he makes Othello see the estimation in which the Venetians really hold him and the basis on which they have really chosen him as general: despite their favor and friendship, they think of him as a dangerous, ill-favored foreigner, good to send against enemies, entertaining to hear stories from, but certainly not the man for one's daughter.

For his part, Othello does not seem surprised or disconcerted in the least by this view of himself. Why should he? His career has been well-served until this moment, I suspect, by his intelligent use of the effect of his warlike looks and rough splendor on refined Europeans. Not rattled in the least, he goes on to give his famous speech about the real magic he used on Desdemona: his stories about his life. "She loved me for the dangers I had passed," he concludes, "And I loved her that she did pity them. / This only is the witchcraft I have used. / Here comes the lady. Let her witness it." His confidence stems, in large part, from the image of himself that Desdemona gives him, one that she presents to her broken-hearted father and the whole Senate in this scene, yet from this very image it is clear that in no way could Othello ever become the chosen son of Brabantio, who bitterly feels in Desdemona's election of the man she rather oddly calls "the Moor" his own absolute rejection. When the Duke wants to send Othello immediately to Cyprus to fight against the Turks—those others that Othello seems particularly well-qualified to match—Desdemona pleads to be allowed to go with him:

> That I [did] love the Moor to live with him,
> My downright violence, and storm of fortunes,
> May trumpet to the world. My heart's subdued
> Even to the very quality of my lord.
> I saw Othello's visage in his mind,
> And to his honors and his valiant parts
> Did I my soul and fortunes consecrate.
> So that, dear lords, if I be left behind,
> A moth of peace, and he go to the war,
> The rites for why I love him are bereft me,
> And I a heavy interim shall support
> By his dear absence. Let me go with him. (1.3.243-54)

What does it mean to say, "I saw Othello's visage in his mind"? Not *her* mind, in other words: *his*. In one plausible interpretation, she simply means that she loves his mind, not his outer looks. But she means more than that. She means that she saw the visage, the self-image, that Othello holds in his mind. She sees his image of himself, a kind of ideal face that he presents to her imagination, the one out of which he lives his true life and that makes him able to be accepted for himself. She saw, in effect, his noble "I am." This stirring and revealing speech, more than any other, tells us how thoroughly and in what sense Desdemona has "bought" Othello's noble persona. These lines constitute her defense against the charge of unnaturalness and her defiant explanation—if the Senators wanted one—for her elopement. Her nocturnal wedding was not meant to be furtively guilty, but military, an unexpected night assault on the polite conventions that she has found so stultifying. Her "downright violence and storm of fortunes" are her means of taking this warrior on his own terms, and her wedding "trumpets" her love to the world. It is a speech so moving—so unguardedly *erotic*—that Othello feels it necessary in the next lines to say that the reason he wants her to come with him is not "to comply with heat"(258) or sexual passion, "But to be free and bounteous to her mind" (260). He recognizes that she loves him in part because he can liberate her from Venice, and he wants to keep her unexpected, still almost unbelievable, love very much, indeed, far too much, as Iago sees.

"I saw Othello's visage in his mind," Desdemona tells the senators. Again, on one level, it is his own face as she sees it through his language of honor, the kind of face that will not hide but "must be found" because, as Othello tells Iago when the Venetians come to arrest him, "My parts, my title, and my perfect soul / Shall manifest me rightly" (1.2.29-31). His absolved conscience and his high self-estimate manifest the visage that Desdemona sees. On another level, the visage in Othello's mind is not Othello's at all. As the foreigner, Othello can play on his difference to good effect, but he also needs to present a diplomatically acceptable face to Venice so that he can have an insider's acceptance, at least in his representative.[4] One should, I think, imagine Iago and Cassio, neither of whom has a speaking part but both of whom are present, during this exchange of accusations and explanations. Cassio is handsome, urbane, polite, sincere, diplomatic; Iago is plain. Why did Othello choose Cassio over Iago? Because Othello does not need someone honest—I use the word everyone else uses about Iago—but someone courteous. Othello's personal aims are diplomatic, not military, directed toward the Venetians, not the Turks. Othello wants Cassio as his lieutenant for some of the same reasons that he wants Desdemona as his wife: Cassio, like Desdemona, presents him to himself and to others in the mirror of his best desire.[5] In this respect, Cassio's face is the visage he has in his mind. When Desdemona sees Cassio, she recognizes what Othello thinks of himself. She would not want him to be Cassio, but on the other hand, she understands him through Cassio, who is so much more like her. Cassio stands for his taste, his discernment, his chosenness. In this strong representative sense, even to Desdemona herself, Cassio is Othello, as Iago could never have been. He mediates between the lovers, in effect; he interprets Othello to Desdemona and gives his exotic looks an ameliorating introduction, as he later does on Cyprus, when he disposes the Cyprians very favorably to a couple very recently called unnatural in Venice.

By the end of this scene in the senate, Iago has intuited almost every-thing he needs to know, especially about the place of Cassio. He knows that the means of his approach must be to "abuse Othello's ears / That he is too familiar with his wife" (1.3.386-87). The "he," Greenblatt argues, is intention-ally ambiguous: it can mean either Cassio, whom Iago has mentioned a few lines earlier, or Othello himself. Greenblatt's argument follows up the latter possibility. But I suggest that there is more to Cassio's familiarity than mere fiction. Cassio may be the necessary mediator between Othello and Desdemona, the necessary interpreter of each to the other. Cassio is dis-missed, as it were, in mid-consummation, on the night that they all arrive in Cyprus, after the destruction of the Turkish fleet by a storm at sea—the first night that Othello spends with Desdemona. After Iago uses the general mood that night to get Cassio into a drunken brawl, first with Roderigo, then with Montano, Othello comes down (like Brabantio waked in the middle of the night) to discover that his acceptable visage, his other self, Cassio, has already dishonored him by this explosion of violent unrestraint. Iago cannot under-stand what happened: "Friends all, but now, even now, / In quarter and in terms like bride and groom / Devesting them for bed..." (2.3.178-80). He introduces into Othello's imagination, just at this moment of being undercut and exposed in his choice of lieutenant, another comparison: "bride and groom / Devesting them for bed." As Cassio turned out to be, the sug-gestion is, so Desdemona will also. Cassio's unrestrained drunken behavior interprets Desdemona to Othello, as though there were some analogue to "Cassio high in oath," something that "till tonight"[Othello] "ne'er might say before" (234-35). As soon as he says, "Cassio, I love thee; / But never more be officer of mine" (2.3.247-48), Desdemona enters to see the lieuten-ant in the first blush of his dismissal. One feels a sense of disquieting repeti-tion, a doubling and splitting of identity in this scene: Othello finding himself, not as the one eloping, but as the figure of authority, the "father" called from his bed like Brabantio; Desdemona again not indoors, but out on the street to share the excitement ("the rites for why I love him"), no doubt somewhat in deshabillé; his lieutenant, who had the election, revealing an unsuspected and dangerous lack of self-control; Othello himself being exposed as weak in his judgment of his most important subordinate besides his wife ("I fear the trust Othello puts in him," Iago says coyly at 2.3.123). Feeling all these things, especially a chagrin at seeing his young wife out in the street fresh from the bedroom, Othello displaces his anxieties onto Cassio—"I'll make thee an example," he tells his former lieutenant (2.3.250)— and takes Desdemona back to bed (251).

It will take only a hint, the barest nudge, to convince Othello that Cassio is in fact "too familiar with" Desdemona. When Iago tells Cassio that the sure way to get back in Othello's good graces is by having Desdemona intercede with her husband, he guarantees himself a predictable occasion when he can walk up with Othello and see Cassio leaving her. All he has to say is, "Ha, I like not that" (3.3.34)—and everything unfolds. In Act III, scene iii, Othello goes from a man who feels himself unbelievably blessed in his marriage to a man consumed with jealousy who has contracted Cassio's murder and plots his wife's death. At a crucial point early in Act III, we discover for the first time—just as Iago does—that Cassio was the go-between for Othello and Desdemona. This fact, more than any other, reveals to Iago himself the nature of Cassio's importance as a necessary mediator, his already intimate place between them. Making her plea for Cassio as she promised him, Desdemona is also pleading, little as she might know it, for the return of the visage he made it possible for her to see in Othello:

> Tell me, Othello. I wonder in my soul
> What you would ask me that I should deny
> Or stand so mamm'ring on. What? Michael Cassio,
> That came awooing with you, and so many a time,
> When I have spoke of you dispraisingly,
> Hath ta'en your part—to have so much to do
> To bring him in? By'r Lady, I could do much— (3.3.68-74)

Obviously, Desdemona means to remind Othello that Cassio visited her often to plead for the Moor as Iago was supposed to have done (but did not) with Roderigo. What Cassio has been as the diplomatic liaison between Othello and the Senate has also been true of his role with Desdemona. He "hath ta'en your part," she tells him. He has defended Othello in his absence, no doubt, when Cassio would be called on to exercise his skills of persuasion. But "ta'en your part" is also a stage metaphor; one actor takes another actor's part in a play, not necessarily with great good will. Othello thinks in stage metaphors, probably because he must always be concerned with self-presentation; back in Act I, as we have seen, he tells the men who are drawing their swords, "Were it my cue to fight, I should have known it / Without a prompter." Desdemona here reminds him that Cassio has played the part of Othello and knows the role.

This knowledge galvanizes Iago, who immediately uses it in one of his most spectacular improvisations:

> *Othello.* Excellent wretch! Perdition catch my soul
>   But I do love thee. And when I love thee not,
>   Chaos is come again.
> *Iago.* My noble lord—
> *Othello.*   What dost thou say, Iago?
> *Iago.* Did Michael Cassio, when you wooed my lady,
>   Know of your love?
> *Othello.* He did, from first to last. Why dost thou ask?
> *Iago.* But for a satisfaction of my thought,
>   No further harm.
> *Othello.*   Why of thy thought, Iago?
> *Iago.* I did not think he had been acquainted with her.
> *Othello.* O, yes, and went between us very oft.
> *Iago.* Indeed?   (3.3.90-101)

The fact is, Iago did *not* know that Cassio "had been acquainted with her." It explains everything. For one thing, it reveals to him that Cassio has a considerable capacity for deceit himself and that he won his position as lieutenant because of his success as a go-between. Would Iago have succeeded at the same task? Almost certainly not. Yet Cassio not only woos Desdemona effectively, he also manages to look entirely uninvolved. Early in the play, when the party with Brabantio meets the party who have come from the Senate to find Othello, Cassio comes to the inn with the summons from the senators, and, although he knew of Othello's love for Desdemona "from first to last," he acts ignorant of the wedding. He entirely deceives Iago about his involvement:

> *Cassio.* Ancient, what makes he here?
> *Iago.* Faith, he tonight hath boarded a land carack.
>   If it prove lawful prize, he's made forever.
> *Cassio.* I do not understand.
> *Iago.*   He's married.
> *Cassio.*   To who? (1.2.48-51)

Iago knows that Othello would be impressed by Cassio's capacity to play the innocent and therefore must now be particularly distressed to find Cassio so violently intemperate. But, as Iago recognizes, the same line of argument applies exactly to Desdemona, and he can exploit this capacity for smooth deceit as a cultural quality that Othello would not have access to: the subtle art of the insider, the kind of thing that an outsider senses but cannot quite penetrate—a whole complex system of manners that seem to be one thing, but are in fact highly coded. Desdemona, Iago can suggest, is one of the most adept at this art, a prodigy even by Venetian standards. Within a hundred lines, Iago is saying to Othello,

> Look to your wife; observe her well with Cassio;
> Wear your eyes thus, not jealous nor secure.
> I would not have your free and noble nature
> Out of self-bounty be abused. Look to't.
> I know our country disposition well:
> In Venice they do let heaven see the pranks
> They dare not show their husbands; their best conscience
> Is not to leave't undone, but kept unknown.
> *Othello.* Dost thou say so?
> *Iago.* She did deceive her father, marrying you;
>   And when she seemed to shake and fear your looks,
>   She loved them most.
> *Othello.*   And so she did.

Nothing that Iago brings to bear on Othello, including the evidence of the handkerchief, can be more convincing in itself than this bedrock truth: Desdemona deceived her father. The last thing that Brabantio said to Othello was, "Look to her Moor, if thou hast eyes to see. / She hath deceived her father, and may thee" (1.3.287-88). The experience of the old man already displaced in her affections now rings in his ears.

Othello wants to be a Christian and a Venetian; he wants to be married, as he is, to the darling of Venice and to be the general of the army, but to have these things as he wants to have them, he has to forget his difference. This forgetting means that he must actively *adopt* the imagination of the other. If Desdemona loves him, then he has no doubts about himself, and he does not ask questions. But suppose that someone makes him ask questions, and he realizes that she loves him, not for what he wants to be, but for what he is? Suppose she loves him with a strong erotic charge, a downright violence, precisely because he is not Venetian at all, but a man who brings the spaces of a larger and more exciting world to her and whose very looks are part of his appeal? A few lines later, as he first takes in the "unnaturalness" of this preference, he makes what seems to me the crucial turn. Seeing himself *unsympathetically* as Desdemona might see him, he unconsciously adopts the position of Brabantio:

> *Othello.* I do not think but Desdemona's honest.
> *Iago.* Long live she so. And long live you to think so.
> *Othello.* And yet, *how nature erring from itself*— (3.3.225-27; my emphasis)

"Nature" here means the normal and plausible. Once he has this opening, Iago fills in the details as though he were continuing Brabantio's earlier objections:

> *Iago.* Ay, there's the point, as (to be bold with you)
>   Not to affect many proposed matches
>   Of her own clime, complexion, and degree,
>   Whereto we see in all things nature tends—
>   Foh! one may smell in such a will most rank,
>   Foul disproportions, thoughts unnatural.
>   But pardon me, I do not in position

> Distinctly speak of her; though I may fear
> Her will, recoiling to her better judgment,
> May fall to match you with her country forms,
> And happily repent. (3.3.228-38)

"Nature" means the "better judgment" after the storm of passion has passed. No one satisfies the "country forms" or natural appearances better than Cassio. The fact that he took the part of Othello and represented him as normal and plausible was the very point of choosing him.

What happens in this exchange is a terrible violence of displacement. Othello recognizes a kind of staged quality to his whole life and has to say, "I am not what I am." Where he has been, even in his own imagination, Cassio now is, and the understudy now has the part—in fact, it seems, he has really had it all along. Cassio has always been the chosen, even in Othello's greatest intimacy with Desdemona. Instead of being able to see himself in the esteem of Cassio and Desdemona, Othello now recoils from himself as the monstrous outsider whom they have been able to use effectively in compassing their own ends, for the very reason that he had trusted them as insiders in compassing his own. Once love has made him vulnerable, his doubt makes him entirely adopt the imagination of the condemning father, and he finds himself discarded, with no place to *be* from, no source but a rejected one.

Everything in the world of the play—except, ironically, Desdemona—confirms this rejection. When Lodovico comes from Venice, his news is that Othello is being relieved as commander of Cyprus. By whom? By Cassio, who in this too has "ta'en his part" and displaced him, simply because he is the one on whom election "naturally" lights. Both Othello and the others, including Desdemona, take this move by the Senate as a belated attempt to appease Brabantio now that the danger from the Turks has passed. Obviously, if her choice of Othello had ever rested on the approbation of Venice, Desdemona would never have engaged in the "storm of fortunes" that accompanied her elopement, but Othello interprets one removal in terms of the other and publically strikes her (4.1.235-44) as the embodiment of everything fickle and hypocritical about Venice. When he attempts to tell Desdemona in private what he feels, the imagery of his speech is wrenching:

> But, alas, to make me
> The fixed figure for the time of scorn
> To point his slow and moving finger at.
> Yet could I bear that too, well, very well.
> But there where I have garnered up my heart,
> Where either I must live or bear no life,
> The fountain from the which my current runs
> Or else dries up—to be discarded thence,
> Or keep it as a cistern for foul toads
> To knot and gender in—   (4.2.52-61)

Othello imagines his own inmost interiority—"there where I have garnered up my heart"—as radically in Desdemona's possession; he has given it away, like the storehouse and spring that gives a besieged city its source of sustenance. Hers is the fountain—both sexual (Othello describes her hand as "Hot, hot, and moist," 3.4.39) and spiritual—from which he can be discarded. His own "I am" is now a current running from Desdemona's Venetian love, and his only recourse if he is "discarded thence" is to harden into the role for which Venice actually chose him—the "thing" with the "sooty bosom." If she has rejected him, what can Desdemona be in his imagination but the "cunning whore of Venice" who would marry the monster "Othello"? What can he do but kill her if his tormented identity has no place to be *from* except a supersubtle embodiment of his adopted city, one who is also its betrayer?

The tragedy that Shakespeare seizes upon lies in the terrible uncertainty of identity that emerges, in this modern context, between being chosen in Christian love and being chosen in erotic passion. If Othello takes the Gospels and St. Paul seriously, there are no distinctions in Christ according to race or culture or sex, and Desdemona's disregard of his appearance can therefore be understood as profoundly Christian. She herself has a strong faith and a clarity of conscience that coexist with her powerful erotic love for Othello and her capacity to deceive her father. Othello's own Christianity obviously depends upon an idea of himself as included, despite his difference. What he has to put aside to believe this, however, is a natural skepticism about whether he is really being accepted—but more than that a knowledge of otherness that comes with being an outsider. The outsider sees the forms of a society—its subtle ways of self-definition and exclusion—in many ways better than those who are in it. Because of his Christianity, embodied for him in the pure grace of Desdemona loving him, Othello has set aside both his skepticism and his outsider knowledge. Iago's sentence, "I am not what I am," is often noted to be the reverse of what God calls Himself in Exodus 3:14, "I Am who Am," or as Harold Bloom argues, it "deliberately repeals St. Paul's 'By the grace of God I am what I am'" (435). In other words, if Othello is *included*, Iago takes up the part of the ultimately excluded one, as Allan Bloom says, the Devil beyond all grace, and deliberately partakes in the evil metaphysical freedom of the unchosen. He brings Othello into the same decentered space that he inhabits, but Othello, very much unlike Iago, has a soul large enough to recognize that it is radically inadequate even to its own being and therefore to become vulnerable to the need of being completed by another. Capable of love, Othello opens himself to attack. The weakness implicit in love, the same weakness that Allan Bloom indirectly ascribes to the Old Testament God who became Incarnate, leaves Othello subject to manipulation. More even than Mark Antony, it also makes him the figure who reveals the greatness and terror that lie in the contingency of loving. An extraordinary power flows from the capacity to hold the truth of this incompleteness open and unprotected in the great world, visible and invisible. Othello's tragedy is that, being capable of love, he fails, precisely by attempting to close off the anguish of his incompleteness in killing Desdemona— the woman who chose him out of all the world, above all those of her own clime, complexion, and degree, to give her own love. Unlike Othello, she distinguishes between her spouse and God ("we must think that men are not gods," 3.4.148), and between Othello's opinion of her and her own unquestionable love for him. Her death is the crucifixion of Othello's own undifferentiated divinity, from whom he feels himself discarded. He says, after killing her, "Methinks it should be now a huge eclipse / Of sun and moon, and that th' affrighted globe / Should yawn at alteration" (5.2.97-99).

Although Desdemona's death is strangely reminiscent of the offstage suicides (usually by hanging) of women in Greek tragedies, no Greek tragedy brings the most private and intimate space, the bed, into public view, and makes it the actual locus of the action. As the violence of Iago's street brings both Brabantio and Othello out of the bedroom and into the public space, so now his violence makes the bed itself the imaginative focus of the tragedy and implies that the sexual act is the great problematic scene of identity and substitution, not to mention Harold Bloom's "ontotheological absence." In the era of Iago, one seeks knowledge in bed. Instead of moving toward a conclusion in the court or on the battlefield, those places of public performance and contention, the action of *Othello* moves toward an exposed inwardness, a place of unbearable vulnerability and spiritual nakedness. The murder of Desdemona is clearly an erotic consummation that opens a metaphysical abyss. Killing her, Othello completes himself as the inner stranger and anguished Judas who murders, in a sense, because he has been chosen since before time to be the necessary, intimate *xenos* for whom it would have been better never to have been born, the unanointed one, the never-son. Being killed, Desdemona completes "the rites for why [she loves] him" in an insupportable communion between eroticism and self-abnegation, as the Cyprian Aphrodite, ever-virgin, and the Virgin Mary. Even as she pleads for her life, she weeps for Cassio, refusing to believe that he would ever say that he "used" her unlawfully (5.2.71) and recognizing that someone has betrayed him and "undone" her (76), as though the loss of his mediation already meant her destruction. She knows Cassio better than she knows her own husband, yet she chooses Othello and forgives him even past death in the posthumous words she speaks in Emilia's hearing, with a mercy that approaches Cordelia's "No cause, no cause."

For his part, Othello reacts to Emilia's revelations about Iago and the handkerchief with what Greenblatt might call (but does not) a stunning last improvisation. Once Iago has been silenced, the outsider-intelligence that had been displaced onto Iago returns to him. Restored to himself as the actor, Othello recognizes that there is no possible return either to Venice, or, he believes, to the Christianity that Desdemona embodied for him. More than in any other play, erotic love in *Othello* opens onto divine love, and "the Moor" seems, not simply to associate, but to *experience* the love of Desdemona as the love of God. Nothing cynical has touched this love before Iago's insinuations. From the way that Othello speaks and acts, it is emotionally manifest that in Desdemona's love—I am not speaking of sex—he has felt a profound gentleness, an extraordinary *kindness* to him as a person, that reminds one of Queequeg's effect on Ishmael: "I felt a melting in me," says Ishmael. "No more my splintered heart and maddened hand were turned against the wolfish world" (Melville 52). Like the harsh, mocking voice of Mercutio that modifies and validates Romeo's love, Iago so strongly embodies the principle of what Robert Penn Warren calls "impure poetry" that it is all the more crucial to imagine Othello experiencing Christ in the wonder of Desdemona's love, the balm and anointing of her absolute acceptance. I do not mean that she provokes him to catechesis, but that she offers to him a deep, redemptive, self-sacrificial intimacy that breaks open the public self and gives him an access to joy.

Losing Desdemona also means losing God: the experience that she gave him is no less real for now being denied *to him*, and killing Desdemona, even before Emilia comes in with her news, already reminds him of the crucifixion: "Methinks it should be now a huge eclipse/ Of sun and moon, and that th' affrighted globe / Should yawn at alteration." But when he knows of her innocence and looks upon her again, conscious that he has killed her in the very heart of her love for him, that she has sacrificed herself—given her life—for him, the sight plunges him into the most passionate hunger for damnation in literature:

> Where should Othello go?
> Now, how dost thou look now? O ill-starr'd wench!
> Pale as thy smock! when we shall meet at compt,
> This look of thine will hurl my soul from heaven,

And fiends will snatch at it. Cold, cold, my girl!
Even like thy chastity. O cursed slave!
Whip me, ye devils,
From the possession of this heavenly sight!
Blow me about in winds! roast me in sulphur!
Wash me in steep-down gulfs of liquid fire!
O Desdemona! Desdemona! dead! (5.2.272-82)

"Compt" or "Last Judgment" already takes place in his own imagination, like something in an altar piece, and Desdemona's very look of forgiveness, I take it, hurls him from heaven. Having murdered the source of a grace he cannot deny having experienced, having killed Desdemona, in a real sense, *because* he experienced a love, like Christ's, beyond his capacity to merit it, he cannot go on to imagine the forgiveness that both Christ and Desdemona would offer him especially now. His own shame becomes those "steep-down gulfs of liquid fire" that he refuses to escape.

Oddly, against this abyss of his damnation, Othello still speaks in terms of outer honor and recognition. He holds his captors at bay with an apparent attempt to govern the "official story" of his deeds that the Venetians will receive in the "letters" (5.2.336) that those present will write. Like Hamlet's famous advice to the players to "o'erstep not the modesty of nature: for anything so o'erdone is from the purpose of playing," he urges upon them a moderation and fairness: "Speak of me as I am. Nothing extenuate, / Nor set down aught in malice" (338-39). The only worthy account of his tragic jealousy, in other words, will be one that does not skew it rhetorically but tells the truth of it as plainly as possible. What is the truth about Othello? That he kills the highly favored daughter who betrayed her city by eloping with its natural enemy and that he also avenges the murder of this same woman whose love embodied a noble self-sacrifice. His suicide, which he presents to the spectators from Venice and Cyprus as a kind of stage piece, is a staggering feat of estrangement and identity at once. Knowing that he was never unchosen, at least by Desdemona, Othello also sees the necessity for discarding the self so easily persuaded to betray the greatness of love, so unworthy of what he had been given. He is the "one whose hand, / Like the base Judean, threw a pearl away / Richer than all his tribe" (343-44), but he is also, finally, the avenger of Venice and of Desdemona on those like himself:

> And say besides that in Aleppo once,
> Where a malignant and a turbaned Turk
> Beat a Venetian and traduced the state,
> I took by th' throat the circumcised dog
> And smote him—thus. [*He stabs himself.*] (348-52)

In this deed, Othello as he *wishes* to be (the Christian and Venetian) takes by the throat the monstrous other that he supposes he *is* (the cultural "Turk," the murderer who is the enemy of Christianity and the state) and executes him on behalf of Venice. Othello becomes at the end an Iago with nobility, an Iago who feels his own deeds, imagines them otherwise, and dramatizes the end point of what would later become a Lacanian password out of Mallarmé: not only "I am not what I am," but its even more alien corollary, "I is the other."

WITH *Othello*, as with *King Lear* or *Macbeth*, the formal completion of the play has the feel of a great purgation, an enormous self-righting, like the Pequod after the whale's head is cut loose from its side. But does the play have a "teaching," as Straussian critics tend to say? At the end of a six-session class that I once taught on *Othello*, a middle-aged black woman asked more or less the same thing. She wanted to know what, in the end, Shakespeare thought about mixed marriage. I repeated what I had said before, that it would be a mistake to read the play simply in terms of American issues of race. In the action, Othello is a noble general, a convert from an Arab culture, whom Desdemona loves, and, despite everything that Iago says about her, Shakespeare does not call the quality of Desdemona's love into question. But she kept pressing. Granted that there were cultural differences, what would he say, she wanted to know, to a couple like this of mixed race, given what happens in the play? "Don't try it"? Probably, I said. "I thought so," she replied. Her nod seemed to me ambiguous. It could have meant that Shakespeare was now revealed as the problem behind everything from the murder of Martin Luther King Jr. to the trial of O. J. Simpson. It could just as easily have meant that he was hard-headed and wise enough not to be sentimental about transcending such obvious differences. If the latter, then she would have been confirming Allan Bloom's opinion: "Lived over and over again, the love of Desdemona and Othello would end the same way. Yet, no matter how often it happened, each time we would be as shocked and surprised as we were the first time, for the result runs counter to our wish, and our wishes cause us to bury the truth" (63).

For Bloom and for the woman in my class, *Othello* has a teaching: "Don't try it." Unlike Keats, who wrote in a letter to his friend Reynolds, "We hate poetry that has a palpable design upon us—and if we do not agree, seems to put its hand in its breeches pocket" (Noyes 1213), Bloom tries to give *Othello* such a palpable design, as though only such a design could justify it. Bloom would add that included in the teaching is an admonition not to try a universal religion of love, because it will not work with the necessities of politics. From his perspective, Shakespeare wrote the play as a mimetic argument meant to convey a salutary message ("Don't try it") to the less discerning members of his audience and a more difficult teaching to those who followed out the implications. In this regard, the apparently Desdemona-like embrace of "the massive power structures that determine social and psychic reality" is even more subversive than Greenblatt suspects, because it has a much more conscious end in mind.

The Straussian approach shares a great deal with the New Historicism and other versions of literary theory that have emerged in the wake of the New Criticism, at least in one respect: it does not "privilege" poetry in distinguishing it from other kinds of discourse. Shakespeare's poetry is a profound way of thinking about political things, and its thought clearly engages the nature of regimes, such as the English monarchy and the Venetian commercial republic, in ways continuous with the writings of Plato, Aristotle, and Machiavelli. But from the perspective in which literature is a mode of knowledge that finds its completion in the achievement of form, literature must be distinguished from other kinds of writing: what one knows has to take place in the imagination, and the completed play, in all its interrelations, constitutes what one knows, whether one is Shakespeare or his audience. Brian Vickers writes that "The main weakness of many Shakespeare critics writing today is that, intent on practicing the type of interpretation of the school to which they belong, they tend to lose all notion of experiencing or interpreting a play as a whole" (144). To argue from form at the end of *Othello* would seem to require some view of what the whole looks like and some account of how, at the instant of "achieving form," if there is one such instant, the play passes from incompletion into an essential self-containment, a separate ontology beyond the contingencies of its usefulness. Although form can never be so absolute, its reality must nevertheless be acknowledged. For an adequate understanding of the play's teaching, one would need to think in all the registers of feeling, from the delicate self-mocking, self-correcting emotion of foreboding that Desdemona expresses when she tells Emilia about Barbary's "song of 'Willow'": "That song tonight / Will not go from my mind; I have much to do / But to go hang my head all at one side / And sing it like poor Barbary" (4.3.30-33); to Othello's terrible emotional logic over the sleeping Desdemona, "Be thus when thou art dead, and I will kill thee, / And love thee after" (5.2.18-19); to Emilia's last words, "Moor, she was chaste. She loved thee, cruel Moor. / So come my soul to bliss as I speak true" (5.2.246-47). One would need to understand how Cassio comports himself when he says of his "dear general" (5.2.295) after Othello's death, "he was great of heart" (5.2.357). One would have to take into account the irony of Gratiano's first appearance in the play just when Iago has failed to kill Cassio in the street (5.1.38 ff.), and one would also need to guess what the effect of Gratiano's news might have been. As Desdemona's kinsman, he obviously came from Venice to tell the young bride of her father's death of a broken heart (5.2.201-3) and to inform the couple that the old man's fortunes "succeed on" them, as they do upon him at the end of the play (5.2.362-63).

Each new subtlety of register, by adding more complexity, modifies the meaning of the whole. Allan Bloom argues that Emilia has "a simple, unadorned passion for nothing but truth" (66), but her passion is rather obviously for the truth about Desdemona, whom she loves. What effect does it have on Emilia that Desdemona shares with her, so beautifully and unguardedly, her story about Barbary and her brave irony about her own premonitions? Emilia sings "Willow, willow, willow" (5.2.245) as she dies, strong evidence of the way that Desdemona's imagination has pierced her own, in more ways than one. Telling the truth to protect her mistress's name is inextricable from her hope to "come to bliss." Bloom distorts the meaning of the play by failing to take sufficient account of Emilia's love for *someone*, a love sufficient to make her lay down her life for a friend whose absolute fidelity has edified her. Instead, Bloom makes it a passion for "the truth" simply and schematizes it into a Shakespearean endorsement of classical political philosophy as the mean between revelation and Machiavellianism. The elements that he underscores are certainly present, but the "whole" that constitutes the play is inseparable from a movement of intelligent feeling or felt intelligence unfolding in time, and Bloom, wanting Shakespeare to be "very hard," has to ignore the most important influences on the very character on whom his interpretation comes to rest. Oddly, Bloom's particular distortion seems to follow precisely from an idea of the whole, especially from Leo Strauss's description of the perfect book as a work of art. According to Strauss, the idea of the perfect book stems from a Greek philosophic view absolutely opposed to the Biblical view of revelation: "The perfect book is an image or an imitation of that all-comprehensiveness and perfect evidence of knowledge which is aspired to but not reached. The perfect book acts, therefore, as a countercharm to the charm of despair which the never satisfied quest for perfect knowledge necessarily engenders" (224-25). It is as though, taking to heart the idea that a "perfect book" must necessarily be "a countercharm to the charm of despair" and therefore essentially opposed to divine revelation, as Strauss argues, Bloom felt justified in removing from his consideration of the play anything that seems genuinely to arise from Christian faith, as though Shakespeare were strong in imagining Iago but merely satirical in his presentation of Desdemona. Yet the whole, as Bloom conceives of it, seems to me considerably diminished from the amplitude of its actual imagining. Ultimately, his reading reminds me of what Keats writes about the obsession with control that characterizes the writers that, as "moderns," he contrasts to the ancients: "Each of the moderns like an Elector of Hanover governs his petty state, and knows how many straws are swept daily from the causeways in all his dominions and has a continual itching that all the Housewives should have their coppers well scoured" (Noyes 1214).

Played or read over and over again, *Othello* will never register twice in exactly the same way, even though Othello, Desdemona, and Emilia always die, and Cassio will always survive with a "daily beauty in his life" (5.1.19) that has something to do with his chosenness. Since the living form cannot be fixed, always to be attempting to seize upon the "teaching," not to say "fact and reason," is to risk being like Mary Bennet in *Pride and Prejudice*, who has a formidable collection of "extracts" from the books that she reads and "who pique[s] herself on the solidity of her reflections." On the other hand, the difficulty of saying once and for all what the play means ought not to underwrite some endless deconstruction of meaning, but rather to bear testimony to the fact that the fountain from which *Othello*'s current runs is in no danger of drying up.

In my own reading of *Othello*, I have emphasized and no doubt distorted one important dimension of the play: its intense fascination with religious and erotic chosenness and the displacements that accompany it. Meditating on the play, one can sense that Shakespeare foresaw a growing displacement in which everyone would be, to one degree or another, the actor and *xenos*, uncertainly approved, always feeling on the edge of a community that seems impossible quite to define. *Othello* raises to the level of tragedy questions of identity that have become more acute in the centuries since Shakespeare, especially now, when the dissolution of old loyalties and ties to place has accelerated into the universal Venice of "globalization." When great poetry takes on the depth of imagined reality, it becomes virtually prophetic, certainly revelatory. The aim is truth, but truth through the deep and serious pleasure that comes of a doubled accuracy, like the second shot that splits the arrow still trembling dead-center. Criticism of poetry that begins in a suspicion of the pleasure that constitutes its mode of knowledge will always want to validate the work with some rhetorical end, to justify what would otherwise seem fanciful by having it strongly advocate some position. What might it mean in a few years if, instead of turning it to use, one gave its whole action an increasingly intelligent consideration? If the interest of pleasure that accrues on a text like *Othello* were not to be immediately spent but reinvested in an ever more subtle (if asymptotic) apprehension of its form? Would one then come to its teaching? I suspect that especially then the play would not yield a teaching. Rather, it would become manifest as the unstinting teacher of the complex, attentive patience required for neither extenuating justice nor setting down aught in malice.

5.

The Intelligence of Feeling
and the Habit of Art

I N an interview for *Atlantic Monthly*, Peter Davison asked Richard Wilbur what he was most grateful to poetry for, and Wilbur replied, "I enjoy being able to do something with the important feelings of my life. I think that to be inarticulate can be a great suffering, and I'm glad that my loves, and my other feelings, have sometimes found their way into poems that fully express them." Two things struck me about this artlessly honest comment. First is that it is exactly the kind of thing most people would expect a poet to say, because poets, as everybody knows, are beings who not only operate in a finer register than most, but whose capacities with language also allow them to say "what oft was thought, but ne'er so well expressed"; they are allowed to go around, unlike most working people, taking their feelings seriously. The second is that very few people in my experience of academic life have explicitly and seriously spoken of poetry or literature in terms of feelings, as Wilbur has here. Quite the opposite. Literature as it has usually been taught can be analyzed in all kinds of ways, but they always lead away from feelings to meanings—and for good reason. "The feelings," John Crowe Ransom writes, "are grossly inarticulate if we try to abstract them and take their testimony in their own language. Since it is not the intent of the critic to be inarticulate, his discriminations must be among the [literary] objects" ("Criticism as Pure Speculation" 882).

Both the poet and the critic, then, begin with feelings but must be concerned with articulation. When Wilbur says that poetry has allowed him to "do something with the important feelings" of his life, he implies that they would have remained unrealized in themselves had he not found a poetic form for them. The emphasis does not lie on commemorating or preserving these feelings like pressed flowers, but on giving them wit and wakefulness. Understood in this way, feelings *require* expression. If, remaining inarticulate, they cause "great suffering," it follows that their full expression underlies the greatest pleasures of poetry. Reading a good poem should mean being drawn by a language alive in every syllable into the significant emotion that both requires and finds such articulation. One should be brought to self-knowledge in the welcome of a large recognition. Great poetry invites its audience into the feelings of Zeus, Dido, Iago, Cordelia, Ahab, Emma Bovary, or Alyosha Karamazov, and by this generosity—I think of the host's "you shall be he" in George Herbert's great "Love (III)"—articulates, puts in context, and so *forms* the feelings, good and bad, recognizable to all.

In his early essay "Hamlet and His Problems," T. S. Eliot writes that this articulation requires a necessary objectivity: "The only way of expressing emotion in the form of art is by finding an *objective correlative*; in other words, a set of objects, a situation, a chain of events which shall be the formula of that particular emotion; such that when the external facts, which must terminate in sensory experience, are given, the emotion is immediately evoked" (766, emphasis his). It is striking how little Eliot speaks of poetry as the medium of ideas and meanings and how much he attempts to understand poetry in terms of its two major components: "emotions and feelings" ("Tradition and the Individual Talent" 763). As he distinguishes between these terms in his usage, *emotions* are particular states such as sexual jealousy, impatient ambition, or numb grief that color the whole of one's experience; *feelings* are more glancing, less predictable interior breezes and gusts. Very probably in the Harvard background of this famous passage is another one, from the work of William James in *The Principles of Psychology*:

> If we fancy some strong emotion and then try to abstract from our
> consciousness of it all the feelings of its bodily symptoms, we find we
> have nothing left behind, no "mind-stuff" out of which the emotion can
> be constituted, and that a cold and neutral state of intellectual perception
> is all that remains.... What kind of an emotion of fear would be left if the
> feeling neither of quickened heart-beats nor of shallow breathing, neither
> of trembling lips nor of weakened limbs, neither of goose-flesh nor of
> visceral stirrings, were present, it is quite impossible for me to think.
> Can one fancy the state of rage and picture no ebullition in the chest, no
> flushing of the face, no dilatation of the nostrils, no clenching of the
> teeth, no impulse to vigorous action, but in their stead limp muscles, calm
> breathing, and a placid face? (Quoted in Damasio, *Descartes' Error* 129)

When Eliot speaks of the "objective correlative" of an emotion, he means the
images or situations that correspond to or evoke the "bodily symptoms" or
feelings that constitute the knowable existence of the emotion. Yet there are
also feelings that run counter to the emotion or modify it. Eliot uses as his
example the Brunetto Latini section of Dante's *Inferno* (XV), in which the
canto as a whole develops the emotion of Dante's encounter with his teacher,
distressingly discovered in Hell, then unexpectedly ends with the final
simile—"a feeling attaching to an image" ("Tradition" 763)—of Brunetto
running as though he were the winner of a race. One might also think of
Othello over the sleeping Desdemona, governed in what he says and does by
the consuming emotion of jealousy, but also experiencing the feelings—
aesthetic, tactile, strangely erotic and idolatrous—implicit in such lines as
these: "Yet I'll not shed her blood, / Nor scar that whiter skin of hers than
snow, / And smooth as monumental alabaster" (5.2.3-5).

    Antonio Damasio, a neurologist interested in understanding the ways
that reason itself is rooted in emotions and feelings, speaks in physiological
terms of an awareness of changes in one's "body state" as constituting what
we ordinarily call feelings:

> That process of continuous monitoring, that experience of what your
> body is doing *while* thoughts about specific contents roll by, is the essence

of what I call a feeling. If an emotion is a collection of changes in body state connected to particular mental images that have activated a specific brain system, *the essence of feeling an emotion is the experience of such changes in juxtaposition to the mental images that initiated the cycle.* In other works, a feeling depends on the juxtaposition of an image of the body proper to an image of something else, such as the visual image of a face or the auditory image of melody. The substrate of a feeling is completed by the changes in cognitive processes that are simultaneously induced by neurochemical substances.... (*Descartes'* 145-46, his emphasis)

Unseemly as it might be to trace poetry down into "neurochemical substances," what goes on in the experience of literature has to be considered an extremely complex physical process. For example, one immediately intuits, through the language of Othello, the experience of changes in body state passing through his mind. The *whiteness* of Desdemona's skin suggests to him (therefore to us) the mental image of *snow*, and the cognitive processes that juxtapose the paradox of this cold purity to Desdemona's supposed "hot" impurity, as well as his *blackness* (which Iago has made him feel in its damning otherness), also lead Othello (therefore us) to the tactile image of what she will be in her death, when she is cold. Her coldness to the hand will be like the cold smoothness of a statue on a tomb, "smooth as monumental alabaster": the very rhythm and sound of the phrase elicit feelings of exalted inaccessibility, juxtaposed to her warm sleeping presence, her troubling sexual aura, her vulnerability.

Yet where does this complex process go on? Othello is himself fictional, but to the extent that the actor truly takes on the role, his gestures—perhaps even his feelings—will correspond to these images. For the audience witnessing the actor or reading the speech, some such changes must necessarily register bodily—that is, be literal *feelings*, in certain organic ways—to the extent that the context and meaning of the lines truly register. Even quietly reading *Othello* with understanding is very much a bodily experience of emotion, if only on what Damasio calls an "as-if loop" that imitates emotions and feelings without involving the whole exhausting bodily reaction (*Descartes'* 155-58). But the emotion is not personal for either author or audience.

Perhaps because the emotions and feelings arise from Othello's imagined situation and because they would not be modified if one discovered that Shakespeare himself had been jealous at some point instead of merely observing the jealousy of others, Eliot emphasizes that poetry does not express the poet's personal emotions and feelings. He writes that the best criticism needs to concern itself neither with the sincerity of the poet's emotions nor with the poem's merely technical excellence, but with poetry as "an expression of *significant* emotion, emotion which has its life in the poem and not in the history of the poet" ("Hamlet" 787). For Eliot, the personality of a Shakespeare or Dante makes no difference; crucial is that each becomes "a particular medium...in which impressions and experiences combine in peculiar and unexpected ways" ("Hamlet" 786). In one of the most famous and influential statements of the early twentieth century, he goes on to assert that "The emotion of art is impersonal. And the poet cannot reach his impersonality without surrendering himself wholly to the work to be done. And he is not likely to know what is to be done unless he lives in what is not merely the present, but the present moment of the past, unless he is conscious; not of what is dead, but of what is already living" ("Hamlet" 787).

Without at all abandoning the basis of poetry in a medium of feeling, Eliot seeks a means of describing the emotion of art that distinguishes it from the person of the artist. This severing of the poetic work from the biographical personality obviously prepared the way for various kinds of formal criticism (including what became the American New Criticism) that would examine poetry in terms of its effectiveness in providing objective correlatives. But something in the sound of Eliot's statement that "The emotion of art is impersonal" also had a distancing effect, as if it were urging, not a way of *knowing* through the formed emotion of the work, but a rejection of the language of feeling altogether, except perhaps in discussing Aristotelian pity and fear. Some of this effect was a bracing and salutary part of what made the study of literature a *discipline*, but a side effect was an ironic stance toward any expression of emotion. What Robert Penn Warren describes as "Mercutio in the garden"—the witty, ironic critic of the tendency to give the feelings free rein—became not so much a validating tension within art as a critical *habitus*, so much so that even the "emotion of art" began to seem suspect. Well before the "death of the author" and the new vocabularies of post-structural criticism, it began to sound ingenuous—however widespread among general audiences the tendency might be—to speak of literature in terms of "emotions and feelings." Again, no one did more to turn criticism toward the work of art rather than the emotions than Eliot. In distinguishing between Coleridge and Aristotle, Eliot was very much concerned to make it clear that both poetry and its criticism ought to be concerned with the work of art rather than with the feelings:

> But a literary critic should have no emotions except those immediately provoked by a work of art—and these (as I have already hinted) are, when valid, perhaps not to be called emotions at all. Coleridge is apt to take leave of the data of criticism, and arouse the suspicion that he has been diverted into a metaphysical hare-and-hounds. His end does not always appear to be the return to the work of art with improved perception and intensified, because more conscious, enjoyment; his centre of interest changes, his feelings are impure. In the derogatory sense he is more "philo-sophic" than Aristotle. For everything that Aristotle says illuminates the literature which is the occasion for saying it; but Coleridge only now and then. It is one more instance of the pernicious effect of emotion. ("The Perfect Critic," 1920)

Eliot obviously wants to distinguish a classical approach from a Romantic one, and, like T. E. Hulme, he just as obviously associates Romanticism with "the pernicious effect of emotion"; the difficulty with this act of redress is that critics began to treat the literary text without sufficient regard to the fact that the "data of criticism" lie in the work's ongoing flow of intelligent feeling.

The difficulty then became how exactly one should speak of what a poem "says" or what it "teaches," if the satisfying articulation of complex emotion is not an adequate formulation. Fifty or sixty years ago, one of the great gentlemanly disagreements within the New Criticism was whether a poem can be paraphrased. In an essay published in 1941, John Crowe Ransom argues that it can; he settles on saying that "A poem is a *logical structure* having a *local texture*"

("Criticism" 886, his emphasis). His way of discriminating leads to a view, largely in accord with what he understands T. S. Eliot also to say,

> that a poem has a central logic or situation or "paraphrasable core" to which an appropriate interest doubtless attaches, and that in this respect the poem is like a discourse of science behind which lies the sufficient passion.... [A]t the same time, and this is the important thing, that the poem has also a context of lively local details to which other and independent interests attach; and that in this respect it is unlike the discourse of science. ("Criticism" 883)

Ransom carefully avoids describing the "independent interests" that attach to the "lively local details" with anything like the vocabulary of feelings. The very description mildly satirizes the "discourse of science" that speaks as though human beings were mere loci of general forces, but at the same time it demonstrates a wary concern not to undercut the defense of poetry by appearing to advocate unguarded feeling and sentiment.

Both Ransom and Cleanth Brooks are concerned with the more or less predatory abstracting impulse that wants to seize the poem's "meaning" and discard the rest. Ransom, in his paradoxical way, grants the poem a usefulness and at the same time protects its inner pleasures and play of feelings by allowing for a detachable paraphrase. Yet for Brooks, it gives away the crucial thing to argue that the "paraphrasable core" can be separated from the "*irrelevant* local substance or texture" (Ransom, "Criticism" 887, my emphasis), even when Ransom is arguing for an ontological criticism capable of addressing both. In the final chapter of *The Well Wrought Urn* (1947; reprinted in Adams, 1992), Brooks objects to the idea that the poem has any genuinely separable thing that it "says" and attacks Ransom's view as an instance of what he called "the heresy of paraphrase." The word "heresy" suggests that Brooks finds a more than casual connection between the orthodox understanding of the Incarnation and the proper understanding of poetry. It also implies that the critical establishment ought to be conservative and normative in its essential function: as the Church safeguards and extends into the world the full mystery of Christ as both true God and true man, so criticism should protect the mystery of the poem as a kind of hypostatic union in which thought has become one with its embodiment in image and metaphor. Brooks writes that "the reader may well ask: is it not possible to elaborate a summarizing proposition which will 'say,' briefly and in the form of a proposition, what the poem 'says' as a poem, a proposition which will say it fully and will say it exactly, no more and no less? Could not the poet, if he had chosen, have framed such a proposition?" (965). If the poet could have done so, Brooks says, he would not have had to write the poem. "The truth is," says Brooks, "that the apparent irrelevancies which metrical pattern and metaphor introduce do become relevant when we realize that they function in a good poem to modify, qualify, and develop the total attitude which we are to take in coming to terms with the total situation" (966). The paraphrase, in other words, will never be true unless one adds all "the qualifications exerted by the total context" (965), and these qualifications in their totality constitute the poem itself.

Ransom, for his part, uses the idea of irrelevance to distinguish what really matters to us in our particularity from what matters in a general sense. As always, Ransom's language is employed in ironic ways, so that the very way that he speaks, considered beside what he is saying, often shows that he is satirizing the inadequacy of contemporary language about these matters. The modern prejudice, he points out, is toward direct economic and scientific standards of measurement. But these ignore the particulars:

> The fierce drives of the animals, whether human or otherwise, are only towards a *kind* of thing, the indifferent instance of a universal, and not some private and irreplaceable thing. All the nouns at this stage are common nouns. But we, for our curse or our pride, have sentiments; they are directed towards persons and things; and a sentiment is the totality of love and knowledge which we have of an object that is private and unique. This object might have been a simple economic object, yet we have elected to graft upon the economic relation a vast increment of diffuse and *irrelevant* sensibilia, and to keep it there forever, obstructing science and action. ("Forms and Citizens" 36, my emphasis)

In this great essay, "Forms and Citizens," he argues that forms, far from making us less authentic, actually bring about the possibility of individual experience by diverting passion into a consideration of matters that have no direct bearing on the "fierce drives of the animals," whether these formal indirections involve courtship or religious rituals for the dead. Form in poetry actually impedes the poet's direct expression: "It delays and hinders him. In the process of 'composition' the burning passion is submitted to cool and *scarcely relevant* considerations. When it appears finally it may be said to have been treated with an application of sensibility" ("Forms" 40, my emphasis). When Brooks attacks Ransom for emphasizing "irrelevance" in the poem, he does not sufficiently acknowledge, as Ransom does, the ways that "relevance" forces poetry into justifying itself on the basis of the efficient causality emphasized by economic and scientific modernity.

This quarrel, innocent of our many contemporary enlightenments, comes from a period when serious readers were being taught to discipline themselves against the intentional and affective fallacies, among other temptations to self-indulgence. It is true that the Yale branch of New Criticism, in particular, refined itself out of existence with its reluctance to engage the author's biography or the context of the culture, with its insistence on the lyric poem as the "verbal icon," the tensed, ironic index to all literature, and with its emphasis on a method of close reading that, abused, came to resemble cryptography. It is true that poetry after a time no longer seemed to consist of "emotions and feelings" chastened and satisfied by the very act of their complete articulation, but a clever system of checks and balances. But the New Critical training in close reading has never been superseded. Moreover, as Louise Cowan has pointed out, the Southern critics (Ransom, Tate, Warren, and Donald Davidson) were never so interested in a method of reading or an ideology of texts as in the larger cultural place of poetry. (Davidson anticipated and almost certainly influenced Marshall McLuhan in his insistence on the priority of oral poetry to literature—in effect, to "textuality" itself.) In any case, despite all the weathers of suspicion that have eroded the landscape of literary criticism, the central practical concern of this debate half a century ago—the relation of literature's propositional "paraphrasability" to its experiential texture—has by no means been superseded in any milieu where the capacity of literature to teach is taken honestly and seriously. The question remains not *whether* literature can teach but *how* it does so. If it teaches by an articulation and formation of the "emotions and feelings" arising from dramatic situations, then only the whole work as *an experience that the reader or audience undergoes* will ever be adequate; the play or poem or novel is already articulate, and what one says about it can only serve to emphasize and deepen certain dimensions of the experience. If, on the other hand, there is nothing truly paraphrasable about the work, then it is difficult to understand how poetry is more philosophic than history, as Aristotle claims, or how experience itself can ever teach anything, for that matter, since no two circumstances will ever be exactly the same.

T HIS question came forcibly to mind during a colloquium in Seattle on the novels of Jane Austen, when our discussion leader asked in the final session how we would characterize Austen's social philosophy, assuming that Austen's work could be taken as the articulation of a consistent philosophic view. Abstracting from the three novels under discussion—*Pride and Prejudice, Emma*, and *Persuasion*—it seems to me plausible to argue that Austen understands a good marriage as the most complete paradigm of earthly happiness; that what constitutes a good marriage consists of a very particular combination of adequate property (enough to engage and gratify the imagination), harmony between families, intellectual delight, sexual attraction, and moral respect; that errant opinion, more than any other actor, prevents the achievement of the moral and intellectual virtues necessary for good marriages and thus for happiness; and that the timely movement out of illusion into the truth constitutes the way to happiness and therefore the most permanently interesting action in human life. Austen tends to be a favorite of moral philosophers in the conservative tradition because, like Socrates, she finds the great enemy of happiness to be false opinion, and (unlike Mary Bennet) she understands how unique to each circumstance must be the discovery of right opinion. Orthodoxy in Austen does not mean stifling one's emotions and desires in conformity to an external standard but finding the fullest rational realization of them given the particular possibilities.

One can find a philosophic stance in Austen's work, then; discovering it leads to a certain stabilizing satisfaction. It becomes possible to regard the different novels as Austen's working through of the various kinds of wrong opinion arising from different types of characters in various economic and familial circumstances. Yet it also becomes possible to regard the plots themselves as ramifications of a pattern, almost a formula: the heroine is blinded to the truth of her affections by a, b, and c, but then when x happens, leading her to recognize y (and therefore to reinterpret a, b, and c), the happy result is z. To this extent, the plot of a Jane Austen novel resembles an article in the *Summa Theologica*, with its first "it seems that," its objections, its "on the contrary," its "I answer that," and its reply to the objections. Nevertheless, the pattern itself does not constitute the truth at which one arrives: Thomas's method would work as well to correct opinions about how to prepare garlic as to justify revelation. Austen's plots (like Flannery O'Connor's) give a predictable framework that allows one to concentrate on the fine points of perception and behavior that are the point. Any paraphrase of the novels willing to dismiss the interesting comic force of Elizabeth Bennet, Emma Woodhouse, or Anne Elliott getting herself married, or to articulate general principles of behavior without the local accent of one's pleasure in watching these heroines, would altogether miss the mode of knowledge peculiar to them as novels. For example, one does not come from reading *Pride and Prejudice* with useful extracts about the nature of virtue or the movement from prejudice to charitable recognition of others, but with a particular knowledge, for example, of the turn that enables Elizabeth Bennet to recognize the injustice of her judgments about Darcy.

Elizabeth has, the day before, sharply rebuked Darcy for proposing to her in a proud and condescending way, as though he were angry with himself for not being able to resist her, despite her embarrassing family. The proposal is itself a complete surprise, given his earlier disregard. When she receives Darcy's letter and reads his explanations, she realizes how little she has understood either of his own good intentions or of the skillful machinations of Wickham, whose attentions have flattered her:

> 'How humiliating is this discovery!—Yet, how just a humiliation!—Had I been in love, I could not have been more wretchedly blind. But vanity, not love, has been my folly.—Pleased with the preference of one, and offended by the neglect of the other, on the very beginning of our acquaintance, I have courted prepossession and ignorance, and driven reason away, where either were concerned. Till this moment, I never knew myself.' (Austen 236-37)

Her emotions hardly seem "grossly inarticulate," in Ransom's phrase: one cannot imagine her having the emotion without the inner articulation of its causes. A just humiliation does not *accompany* Elizabeth's complex realignments of understanding and reinterpretations of experience, it constitutes them, and her self-accusations bring out into the open the intimate, indeed inseparable, relation of feeling to intelligence. What she feels stems from what she understands, and what she understands is borne in upon her as what she feels.

In a strict sense, one cannot paraphrase Elizabeth's recognition and have it mean the same thing. Even the passage I have quoted is misleadingly rational unless one has a vivid sense of the moving continuum of the live text. Being inside, like being in a river or a tennis game, is a virtual body-knowledge of particular dips and swerves, dangers and releases, not of a distanced observation. To remove passages from this active flow, as textuality allows one to do, is useful in analysis, like a sequence of still photographs that breaks down, for posterity, Michael Jordan's drive to the basket, but it obviously cannot bring with it the living cross-tensions and momentums of the action. Elizabeth's self-accusations can come to light for the reader only because of the whole experienced movement that has led to this moment, and her emotion contains that essential *motion* in its new bearing, now internal both to Elizabeth and the reader. Her feelings are rich with the bodily particulars of intelligence—the flush and burning—not with the moral generalizations that one might associate with Mary Bennet. What teaches is what is borne in upon one by a combination of intense sympathetic shame, the glad sense of liberation from error, and a hope that the truth has not come too late for happiness. In this correction of bad opinion, feelings carry the change of perspective into a depth that conceptual recognition alone cannot reach, and the mode of knowing necessarily depends upon the whole experience of the fiction.

As Jacques Maritain writes in *Creative Intuition in Art and Poetry*, "poetic knowledge proceeds from the intellect in its most genuine and essential capacity as intellect, though through the indispensable instrumentality of feeling, feeling, feeling" (119). Maritain goes on to insist that although emotion itself does not *know*, but "the intellect knows, in this kind of knowledge as in any other," nevertheless the emotion of art must be distinguished from other kinds:

> It is not an emotion expressed or depicted by the poet, an emotion as *thing* which serves as a kind of matter or material in the making of the work, nor is it a thrill in the poet which the poem will "send down the spine" of the reader. It is an emotion as *form*, which, being one with the creative intuition, gives form to the poem, and which is *intentional*, as an idea is, or carries within itself infinitely more than itself. (119-20)[1]

This rich passage elucidates further what Eliot means by saying that poetry is "an expression of *significant* emotion, emotion which has its life in the poem and not in the history of the poet." Difficult as it is to articulate, this "emotion as *form*" through which poetic knowledge moves is crucial to any understanding of why literature matters. Maritain goes on to ask, "How can emotion be thus raised to the level of the intellect and, as it were, take the place of the concept in becoming for the intellect a determining means or instrumental vehicle through which reality is grasped?" (121).

Any discussion of meaning that does not move toward this essential apprehension of the work's nature—that its availability to the intellect lies not in a concept but in a form—will never get the point. Flannery O'Connor, in her wry and entirely unsentimental way, points out the fallacy of readers who want to cut directly to the "teaching," the paraphrase, the detachable meaning:

> People have a habit of saying, "What is the theme of your story?" and they expect you to give them a statement: "The theme of my story is the economic pressure of the machine on the middle class"—or some such absurdity. And when they've got a statement like that, they go off happy and feel it is no longer necessary to read the story.
>
> Some people have the notion that you read the story and then climb out of it into the meaning, but for the fiction writer himself the whole story is the meaning, because it is an experience, not an abstraction. (*Mystery* 73)

But from this kind of statement, other questions naturally arise. If the whole story is the meaning, how is it possible to hold that meaning in mind once the story itself is over, once one turns the page and other experiences begin to supplant it in one's consciousness? How is this experience held or kept in a way that makes it part of what one knows? O'Connor's "Greenleaf," for example, begins with Mrs. May waking to hear the escaped scrub bull of the Greenleaf boys chewing at the hedge outside her window and ends with the same bull goring her in the heart against her car, and all that passes between constitutes the experience, hence the meaning, of this great story. For a few hours after reading it, the whole action holds together—the image of Mrs. Greenleaf in the woods praying over her newspaper clippings, Wesley's ugly vindictiveness toward his mother, the gleaming modern dairy of the Greenleaf boys, Mrs. May's sense of a constantly martyred decency as she attempts to keep the "scrub" elements of Greenleaf-being, so to speak, from impregnating the "higher" May-being, with her whole barren defensive posture finally penetrated in the sexual and spiritual violence of the ending. Discussed fresh in a classroom or among friends, the story has a vivid unfolding complexity, and one can come to a clear recognition of what O'Connor means when she writes about the "anagogical vision" that "is able to see different levels of reality in one image or one situation" (*Mystery* 72). But what about a week later? A month or a year later? How does the story become a part of what one knows and is?

The answer—and I acknowledge the paradox—has a good deal to do with how well one has attempted to say what the experience teaches, what it means once it has been undergone. It is necessary to articulate what might otherwise remain, not exactly unconscious, but latent in consciousness. To do so strangely completes the story's act of being. This articulation is not a movement toward abstraction, but a movement into the reality that the story holds open. It is crucial not simply to feel but to say that Mrs. May embodies a way of hedging the self behind complacencies of status and property, and that she requires the Greenleafs, whom she constantly criticizes, to exhibit everything that she excludes from herself in fashioning her own identity. To the extent that the Greenleafs disappoint her expectations of general shiftlessness—for example, the success of the Greenleaf twins, both married to French wives and educated under the G.I. bill—she feels her carefully constructed identity being eroded by doubt and anxiety. The scrub bull eating her hedge, however, embodies more than the Greenleaf sensibility: he comes to her as a "patient suitor," the divine Bridegroom whose masculinity and fertility also terrify her and threaten her protected selfhood. Both the Dionysian stranger and the Christ, the Greenleaf bull, while remaining precisely a scrub bull, comes to disabuse Mrs. May of her barren self-sufficiency and to break open, with a violent grace, a world closed by its own fragile and desperate economy. Her horrific death becomes her most beautiful, most feminine moment, sensually and spiritually, one that recapitulates both a version of Pasiphae and St. Teresa's ecstasy when the angel pierced her heart—with perhaps a wry comment or two on Hemingway's "moment of truth."

This articulation, in turn, serves to deepen one's next reading of the story and to bring into perspective the mercy underlying O'Connor's vision of Mrs. May, whose name ought to suggest young fertility, the month of Mary when the green leaf emerges, a renewed permission to be, but whose feminine power can come about only through the event that she would most of all not choose. Thinking back into the action and articulating what happens also clarifies the emotional register of the whole: the conscious tone of Mrs. May's acidic feeling and brittle judgment of others gives way, once other levels come into conscious presence, to a deeper sexual longing with a full spiritual resonance. Needless to say, the *experience* of the story therefore does not mean only one's naïve first reading, important as the first impression is, but a deepening and increasingly articulated accuracy in entering the artistic emotion, through many repeated readings, with some losses and some gains each time. But what does one derive from it that has an influence on the way one lives, besides an admiration for the author or a sense that literature has a greater density than ordinary life? What does it add to one's intellectual bearing or moral disposition to have had the experience of Richard Wilbur's poem "On the New Railway Station in Rome" or Jane Austen's *Emma* or Dostoevsky's *The Brothers Karamazov* or Flannery O'Connor's "Everything That Rises Must Converge"? What does it matter that one has seen feelingly, as old Gloucester might put it, into the purgation of false opinion?

To the extent that one has *seen*, as O'Connor puts it, in an anagogical way, one takes away a promissory expectation that, reality having been so revealed, one will now occupy it differently. Certain kinds of delusion should no longer be as likely, given the liveliest interchange between insight into great literature and self-knowledge. "The type of mind that can understand good fiction," says O'Connor, "is not necessarily the educated mind, but it is at all times the kind of mind that is willing to have its sense of mystery deepened by contact with reality, and its sense of reality deepened by contact with mystery" (*Mystery* 79). One who attends the best literature with integrity will develop a disposition, a habit of seeing *what more might be present* in the "light of common day" that Wordsworth found almost intolerable. This kind of reading corresponds to what O'Connor, citing Jacques Maritain, calls the "habit of art":

> Art is the habit of the artist; and habits have to be rooted deep in the whole personality. They have to be cultivated like any other habit, over a long period of time, by experience; and teaching any kind of writing is largely a matter of helping the student develop the habit of art. I think this is more than just a discipline, although it is that; I think it is a way of

looking at the created world and of using the senses so as to make them find as much meaning as possible in things. (*Mystery* 101)

Reading literature well—that is, reading it anagogically—must also stem from and contribute to the cultivation of a habit, by experience. Necessarily, this habit requires that one be persuaded to give up the opposing habit of trying to extract, by the quickest means, the usable gist of people and experiences; it requires a recovery of the inner nature of time, a recognition of the deep givenness that requires every faculty of our active reception.

Poetic experience is a schooling of the emotions and feelings that give reason not only its warmth and pulse, but its general accuracy, so that the finest feeling is necessary for the most robust thought. The capacity of Nazi physicians to be enraptured by Schubert, on the one hand, and to experiment coldly on their Jewish victims, on the other, is not an argument to the contrary. Far from it: this dissociation of sensibility speaks precisely and obviously of the artificial anesthesis of the medium in which right reason informs and is informed by accurate feeling. It says nothing about the teaching capacities of art. To have the cultivated habit of finding, not one's own feelings, honored simply for being one's own, but rather the emotion of art in the work, corresponds to the habit of art as a virtue of the practical intellect. It requires a civil restraint, a self-discipline that releases higher possibilities of meaning, not by rejecting emotion and feeling, but by seeing them as distillates of intelligence like Emily Dickinson's "attar from the rose," essences wrung from the indispensable medium of meaning. Perhaps in the next age, greater attention to our natures—even to neurology—will begin to restore a kind of orthodoxy to literary criticism; Antonio Damasio's emphasis on emotion and feeling (his epigraphs to his latest book are from T. S. Eliot and Jorie Graham) might be an indication of this direction.

But the point is not to wait for confirmation from elsewhere. Poetry has its own authority, its own integrity. Great literature, as Keats knew well, proves itself on our pulses by the way that it reveals and forms both ourselves and the world. As this revelatory and formative agency, always working through the density of a particular experience that it constructs, poetry makes ranges of reality articulate that might otherwise evaporate from the surface of time. In Wilbur's sense, literature finds something to do, not only with the most important feelings, but with the quick of temporality in which they arise and from which an access to being might be permanently lost. It has to do, in its very nature, with the redemption of time.

6.

The Sacrifice of Achilles

O F all the poems in the history of the West, actual Scripture aside, but including the *Divine Comedy*, *Paradise Lost*, and all the devotional lyrics ever written, God loves the *Iliad* most. I should write this with the deflecting irony that such a statement needs: the poem is after all pagan and violent, full of wrath and terrible pride and mayhem and shameless deceptions by the gods. But no matter what arguments the lifted eyebrow might muster (Plato having anticipated them all), I know about the *Iliad* what the Scottish missionary in *Chariots of Fire* knew about the fact that he was a great runner. He tells his sister that the same God who made him a missionary also made him fast, "and when I run," he says, "I feel His pleasure." When I even think about the serious, unsparing world of honor and anguish and beauty that the *Iliad* brings before the imagination, I feel God's pleasure: not the tepid blessing of the sentimental Smiling Jesus that Flannery O'Connor's wonderful tattoo-covered prophet O. E. Parker finds in the recent section of the religious catalogue, but the stern approbation of the iconic Byzantine Christ, Son of Yahweh Sabaoth, the Lord of Hosts, the God who accepts Abel's blood sacrifice and the smoke of the flesh burning on the altar, because they signify the righteous and obedient heart. The *Iliad* presents the broken world as it is, fallen and savage, but capable of noble

formality and tender mercies; groaning ceaselessly for redemption but without undue self-pity; conscious of being kingly, masterful, and godlike, yet
also mortally aware of being subject to every loss and humiliation, including
the ultimate form, mortality itself.

In this book about why literature matters, the *Iliad* is the measure. Certainly, it was not always mine. In my early twenties, I read the poem twice,
dutifully, without particularly liking it, the first time in Samuel Butler's prose
translation, the second in Robert Fitzgerald's verse one. Both times it struck
me as unwieldy, full of unfamiliar names and long battles, and strangely
ignorant of what it was supposed to narrate: the theft of Helen, Achilles'
heel, the Trojan horse. I can remember the moment in the third reading (I
was twenty-five and in graduate school) when the poem emerged for me as
what it is, when it became—not to sound too Nietzschean about it—a
summons and a destiny. What would happen, I had asked myself, stirring
impatiently over Lattimore's thick, long-lined translation, if I did not skim
the details but gave my mind to them, if I truly lowered the plow through the
surface crust? Was it actually a well-imagined world, capable of engaging a
reader heretofore in love with the sorcery of Nabokov's prose? This passage
in Book I, describing Odysseus and his men returning from their trip to give
Chryseis back to her father, happened to be the next one in the poem:

> And Apollo who works from afar sent them a favouring stern wind.
> They set up the mast again and spread on it the white sails,
> and the wind blew into the middle of the sail, and at the cutwater
> a blue wave rose and sang strongly as the ship went onward.
> She ran swiftly cutting across the swell her pathway. (1. 479-83)

This passage might well have passed in the ancient world for boilerplate
formulaic description, but just there, for whatever reason, I entered the Homeric
world. The sea that Derek Walcott rediscovers in *Omeros* moved under me,
and I knew for the first time something of that characteristic Homeric *habitus*:
not failing to attend, in the middle of other concerns, the look of the wave at

the sea-plowing cutwater or the feel of a wind that blows solidly "into the middle of the sail"—the same attention to the look of things that gives the poem time later to compare the blood on the thighs of Menelaos to the special dyes Carian women use in staining ivory for the cheek pieces of horses.

It was not just the favoring wind that began to turn me: this was the *Iliad*, for that matter, not the more accessible, more amiable, more sea-fragrant *Odyssey*. Why the *Iliad*? Because it was about wrath and the devastation of that wrath, the burning *menis* of the great one unrecognized among the complacencies of piety and honor. Whoever has felt on any occasion what Milton ascribes to Satan—the "sense of injured merit"—has a way into the passion of Achilles, although the poem does not describe a satanic figure. Although many readers of the poem find Achilles an extremely harsh and unsympathetic man, oblivious of his role as the subordinate and at the farthest remove from Christian humility, Achilles did not strike me in that way at all, perhaps because I was thinking of his kind of excellence in a different context, against the background of the development of the Greek cosmic order. During that first real reading of the *Iliad*, I also happened to be studying Hesiod's *Theogony* in a class on Greek mythology. In the succession of divine regimes, Ouranos or Sky in his marriage to Gaia (Earth) begot the beautiful Titans, but then conceived monstrous children in her womb that he was unwilling to allow into the light. Gaia therefore arranged for the castration of Ouranos and his effective overthrow by Kronos, who still did not liberate the Hundred-Handed monsters from the depths, and who was in his turn overthrown by Zeus with the help of those very monsters. Zeus then consolidated his regime through crucial marriages and battles. His work of bringing about a more and more fully articulated and harmonious reality was threatened by the possibility of engendering a son greater than he was who would do to him what he had done to Kronos. According to prophecy, this son would be born of Metis (cunning intelligence). Zeus averted the threat by first impregnating, then swallowing her. Athena, born from his own forehead, is thus both the great daughter, supreme supporter of Zeus, and the averted Son. The whole *Theogony* is characterized by a sense of evolving complexity in which the reader is always made aware that something (possibly greater) might come into being to imperil the carefully begotten cosmos, with its Graces and Hours and Muses. While that new cosmos might be better still than the one brought about by Zeus, it would not come without a cataclysmic overthrow, and one's sympathies are therefore drawn to Zeus and his children, divine and human.

How did the *Iliad* fit into this pattern? Apparently not at all. Its action has very little to do with begetting, it would seem, or with being a son. Although the first line of the poem does say that the poem is about the wrath (*menis*) of *Peleus' son* Achilles, the mention seems more conventional than significant, at least at first glance. Although the first book does concern women either forbidden (as Chryseis is to Agamemnon) or taken away by force (as Briseis is from Achilles), the thrust of the action has to do with the masculine honor for which these women are a sign, rather than with the development of a new regime, divine or human, through marriage. But there was another tradition, explained by Pindar and later poets, in which the threat to Zeus was posed, not by his marriage with Metis, but by his liaison with the sea goddess Thetis, whose destiny was to have a son greater than his father. In the *Eighth Isthmian Ode*, Pindar writes:

> Zeus and bright Poseidon came to strife over Thetis,
> each desirous to be wed to her beauty
> and possess her; the passion was on them.
> But the will of the gods did not accomplish such union,
> for they had heard things foretold. Themis,
> lady of good counsel, rose up among them and spoke
> how it was destined for this sea-goddess to bring to birth a lord
> stronger than his father, to wield in his hand a shaft heavier than the thun-
>   derbolt
> or the weariless trident, if she lay with Zeus or his brothers. 'Let her go.
> She must come rather into a mortal bed.
> Let her look upon her son slain in battle,
> but a son like Ares for strength of hand, like the thundershaft for speed of
>   his feet.' (Lattimore 149)

Zeus prevented the possibility of his own overthrow by marrying Thetis to a mortal man—Peleus—instead of marrying her himself or allowing her any other divine husband. As Athena in Hesiod's account was the averted, threatening Son appearing as the obedient daughter, so in Homer's poem Achilles is the averted Son appearing as the mortal hero. Interpreted in this light, the *Iliad* not only concerns the succession of cosmic regimes, it is actually the central work about the place of man in the unfolding order. Why? Because the cosmos of Zeus comes to rest on the mortality of Achilles. In this context, Achilles has to be understood as a case apart, not as a general story about the great commander and the even greater subordinate. He is not a *type*: there can be only one Achilles, and the dimensions of his greatness do not translate any more readily into our egalitarian idiom than they did into the code of aristocratic honor. These dimensions, because they are *mythological*, lift the poem into a huge retracing of man's metaphysical anger and discontent. Achilles can rightly make claims upon Zeus himself, so much so that his decision to demand his honor can be regarded as the crucial test of the justice of Zeus.

Such a perspective is difficult to grant the poem if one expects something else from it, as I did initially, or if one believes that the existence of a tradition of Trojan War stories made its particular action a matter of happenstance rather than crucial significance. Mikhail Bakhtin misrepresents Achilles and the nature of the poem in distinguishing Iliadic epic from the form of the novel:

> The *Iliad* is a random excerpt from the Trojan cycle. Its ending (the burial of Hector) could not possibly be the ending from a novelistic point of view. But epic completedness suffers not the slightest as a result. The specific "impulse to end"—How does the war end? Who wins? What will happen to Achilles? and so forth—is absolutely excluded from the epic by both internal and external motifs (the plot-line of the tradition was already known to everyone). This specific "impulse to continue" (what will happen next?) and the "impulse to end" (how will it end?) are characteristic only for the novel and are possible only in a zone where there is proximity and contact; in a zone of distanced images they are impossible. (32)

I am not contesting the fact that the audience knew the whole story; no doubt they did, and no doubt they knew the Thetis myth as part of it. It is the "randomness" that is objectionable. Far from being a random excerpt, the *Iliad* concerns itself with the most important action that it could conceivably narrate in the world of its own tradition: the consent of Achilles to his death. In my essay on the *Iliad* for *The Epic Cosmos*, I compared reading the poem in ignorance of the central importance of the marriage of Peleus and Thetis to reading the *Inferno* (where references to holy things are scarce) in ignorance of the existence of Christ. The poem depends upon a cultural knowledge that it does not need to supply, and its form can therefore employ the kinds of omissions that give tacitness and truncation a grave poetic power. To that extent, Bakhtin is certainly right.

Laura Slatkin, in her book *The Power of Thetis* (1991), is the first critic to point out the significance of Achilles' mythological position. Slatkin's argument about the nature of Achilles' importance draws upon the same evidence in Pindar and elsewhere to reach the conclusion that the Olympians depend on his mortality. "If Themis had not intervened," Slatkin writes, "Thetis would have borne to Zeus or Poseidon the son greater than his father, and the entire chain of succession in heaven would have continued" (102). In other words, as Kronos deposed Ouranos, and as Zeus deposed Kronos, so the son of Thetis would have deposed Zeus. "Achilles would have been not the greatest of the heroes, but the ruler of the universe. The price of Zeus's hegemony is Achilles' death" (102). Her work explains why the gods made such importance of this "local row," and why the particular action of Achilles occasioned the poem preeminent in the ancient world and almost undiminished in power almost three millennia later. The reason is this: the *Iliad* addresses the problem of death, and it does so in such a way that *incarnation* itself—existence in the fleshly, even *edible*, decaying mortal body, given the simple fact that one can imagine being the supreme god— becomes the excruciating metaphysical preoccupation of the hero and the focus of the poem. More than any other work in the West, this one brings to a single incandescent point the question of what it means to be "the beauty of the world!" as Hamlet exclaims, and yet a thing that dogs and birds can feast on.

WHAT it might mean to be a godlike warrior tends to elude the contemporary, secularized imagination, largely because our images of heroic action are mediated by the superheroes of comic books or by films starring muscles and glands, whereas the spiritual warfare of the saint tends not to be photogenic. Almost lost to culture at large, even liturgically, is the sense of robust formality that accompanies real, conscious contact with divine powers. In our cultural understanding, it makes perfect sense to treat radioactive *matter* with extraordinary care or to exercise redundancies of caution in handling plague bacteria. We would look with pity and terror on people who, out of ignorance, simply because they could not *see* the invisible agency of the threat, handled uranium as though it were a mere metal or exercised no caution in hygiene around a typhoid victim. It might be similarly pitiable, since the divine things are immaterial and invisible, that we have lost the sense of ritual formality as the precondition for being able to temper the dangerous relation to divine power. In the same vein, Bakhtin is surely right about the effect of the novel on epic: it tends to incorporate elements that break the formal boundary of the epic world. Describing this phenomenon, he cites the way that the "high" genre begins to become "dialogized, permeated with laughter, irony, humor, elements of self-parody and finally—this is the most important thing—the novel inserts into [epic] an indeterminacy, a certain semantic openendedness, a living contact with unfinished, still-evolving contemporary reality" (7). The question is whether this "novelizing" of epic does not ignorantly destroy, like unprotected living contact with a disease, the formal wholeness that makes one able to undertake and achieve an encounter with what exceeds us.

Yet Bakhtin tends to treat the epic as though it had no contact at all with *us*, as though the formalities that separate it from ordinary experience simply make it irrelevant to the everyday:

By its very nature the epic world of the absolute past is inaccessible to personal experience and does not permit an individual, personal point of view or evaluation. One cannot glimpse it, grope for it, touch it; one cannot look at it from just any point of view; it is impossible to experience it, analyze it, take it apart, penetrate into its core. It is given solely as tradition, sacred and sacrosanct, evaluated in the same way by all and demanding a pious attitude toward itself. (16)

Bakhtin speaks of epic as "walled off" and bound to a national past; it forms "an absolute distanced image, beyond the sphere of possible contact with the developing, incomplete and therefore re-thinking and re-evaluating present" (17). Bakhtin associates the epic, *a fortiori*, with what Toni Morrison calls "official stories," whereas the novel comes from carnival and the "uncrowning" forms of laughter. By implication, the epic edges toward the officialdom of what Milan Kundera calls "Totalitarian Truth," as opposed to the novel's "concrete world of life." If the epic is "absolutely distanced," one can read it only at the cost of the imagination's vital complexity—like reading propaganda.

But in fact, this understanding of the nature of epic poetry is profoundly misleading. How is it, for example, that the political or cultural "nation" that gave rise to the *Iliad* (Mycenean Greece) no longer exists, no one has offered hecatombs to Zeus or Athene for some time, and yet a woman who read the poem for the first time last year told me that it exactly mirrored what went on in her corporate headquarters—the power moves of Agamemnon, the concern with how one appears before others? It is impossible to account for the powerful regenerative dynamism of the epic in Bakhtin's terms, either for ordinary readers or for other poets. How is it that Dante, exiled from his own city and witnessing an Italy without center or purpose (even the papacy had been removed to Avignon), could find in the *Aeneid* the intimate "mother and nurse" of his own poem? If the time of the epic genre is an "absolute past," how could Milton in his blindness and disfavor after the Restoration find in Homer and Virgil, as in the Bible, his powerful impetus and inspiration? Far from being the static and "complete" genre that Bakhtin portrays, the epic participates in a temporality both profound and accessible, though unlike the novel it requires a kind of ritual participation. Victor Turner's argument on the ritual process applies also to epic:

> For ritual...does not portray a dualistic, almost Manichean, struggle between order and void, cosmos and chaos, formed and indeterminate, with the former always triumphing in the end [as Bakhtin would have it]. Rather it is a transformative self-immolation of order as presently constituted, even sometimes a voluntary *sparagmos* or self-dismemberment of order, in the subjunctive depths of liminality. (83)

In epic, the cosmos in its imagined totality undergoes this "subjunctive" risk and renewal, nowhere more profoundly than in the *Iliad*.

Ritual transformation is not possible, of course, if one has to "grope for it, touch it" and "look at it from just any point of view," as the "novelized" modern wants to do. With the *Iliad*, this question of novelization arises particularly in translation. The poem itself, of course, remains what is has always been. The test comes whenever someone attempts to bring it across into contact with our own idioms, in our own time. A contemporary translation—one that *feels* contemporary—either has to reproduce the formal redundancies and displacements of the poem in an age resistant to formality or to novelize the work in order to break down the "distancing" epic boundary. Richmond Lattimore's translation of the *Iliad*, the Chapman of my experience, attempts the first approach. It allows one to stand outside the powerful Shakespearean and Miltonic associations of blank verse and hear Homer as a different kind of voice. Lattimore realized that to translate him into iambic pentameter would not make the Greek poem seem natural in English, so much as it would take away a certain necessary Homeric spaciousness of line. Critics of Lattimore find his translation prosy (Garry Wills dismisses him as an "unoffending *prosateur*"), lacking in the verbal bite that gives poetry its particular life, and it is true that one would rarely be moved to quote Lattimore's translation for its excellence as English poetry. On the other hand, it does not obscure the look of the original. To my mind, it allows one to experience the actual pace of the Homeric poem better than any other English translation. The rhythm at least accommodates the very different naturalness of Greek hexameters, if it lacks their massive rumble, their capacity to expand or contract, their firm spondaic endings, their centrifugally taut enjambments. Line by line, Lattimore succeeds in recreating a measure in which the large imagistic and symbolic patterns have room to move across to the other strand of the great helix. The poem moves with alternating speed and delay in a slightly defamiliarized diction, neither archaic nor novelized, with a formal boundary but in a language not deliberately archaic.

Lattimore's translation makes it possible to assess the difference between Homer's way of handling Achilles' mythological importance—of which I believe Lattimore himself (judging by his introduction to the translation) has no suspicion—and the way in which a contemporary "novelizing" translator would bring it to the fore. What is the difference, in other words, between an accurate translation of Homer by a man who does not suspect who Achilles is and a novelized translation by a contemporary poet who sees the place of Achilles and the Olympians very clearly, but does not respect the formal indirections of the ancient poem? In *War Music*, the latter, Christopher Logue, gives what he calls an "account" of certain sections of the *Iliad*. Two major interpretations color his vivid and engaging version. First is that Achilles has already made his choice to die in coming to Troy at all. Logue seems impatient with all the Homeric tiptoeing around the foregone conclusion that Achilles will choose glory. As Achilles' first words in the *Iliad*, Logue has him speak to Thetis out of a very conscious awareness of his place in the Olympian plan and therefore of the character of his own life.

> "Source, hear my voice.
> God is your friend. *You had me to serve Him.*
> In turn, He swore: If I, your only child,
> Chose to die young, by violence, far from home,
> My standing would be first; be best;
> The best of bests; here; and in perpetuity.
> *And so I chose....*" (5, my emphasis)

The promise of undying glory becomes explicitly dependent in Logue on the second interpretation, which has, in part, a faultless logical accuracy. The

Olympian decision to marry Thetis to Peleus and so "mortalize" her threatening son meant that Zeus had to guarantee the son of Thetis the "best of bests" in honor. Not so clear, at least in the *Iliad* itself, is whether Achilles would ever say explicitly, as Logue's hero says, "You had me to serve Him," and whether he would overtly connect the option of a short glorious life to the marriage of his mother to Peleus. Homer's Achilles gives every evidence of understanding the logic of his birth, but he exercises a mannerly tact, as I hope to show, that transforms the character of his knowledge.

Logue's other point—that Achilles has already knowingly *chosen* to die young—seems to me premature on the first page of the poem, since it undercuts the force of Achilles' withdrawal from battle and his decision to re-enter it to avenge Patroklos. The logic of the *Iliad* supports Logue only to a degree. In Lattimore's translation, Achilles says—350 lines into the poem—much the same thing as Logue has him say, but with some crucial differences:

> 'Since, my mother, you bore me to be a man with a short life,
> therefore Zeus of the loud thunder on Olympos should grant me
> honour at least. But now he has given me not even a little.' (1.352-54)

Several crucial things are left unsaid. Why should the fact that Thetis bore Achilles to be "a man with a short life" lead to the conclusion that Zeus should *therefore* grant him honor? One must *infer* the causal connection between Achilles' birth and the agency of Zeus, as well as the gift-character of Achilles' short life, his very mortality. The fact that many generations of readers have not felt compelled to understand why Achilles feels that Zeus has a pressing *obligation* to honor him testifies to the tact with which Achilles speaks. His mother knows exactly what he means, as do we once we recognize the reference to the threat posed by the son of Thetis, but enough room is left in Achilles' speech to prevent the relation from being treated as though it were basely contractual.

In Logue's account, directness of statement and explicitness of motive directly counter the mode of indirection and courtesy that mortals use in

dealing with each other and with gods, even when those gods are their moth-
ers. Logue begins by having the naked Achilles "Fast walk, face wet with
tears" out from the Greek camp, then run down the beach and kneel and
"beggar his arms" to beseech his mother for her help. Logue makes this
opening dramatic, cinematic in conception, urgent in its feel, in order to
foreground this plea unforgettably at the outset and thus to govern one's
whole experience of the action, like a vivid opening scene in a film. No
conventional invocation, no proem—just the theme itself, conveyed by the
unmediated image of Achilles' naked beauty and the explicit statement of
his grievance. In seeking this kind of immediacy, though, Logue ignores the
branching, coral-like displacements that both obscure and amplify the central story. Why "displacements"? Because, given the elements, there could be
the more direct and compact narrative that Logue imagines. In fact, one
could take this stripping even further. In Derek Walcott's *Omeros*, for example, the characters named Achille and Hector contend for the St. Lucian
island beauty Helen, the former housemaid of an aging British couple. Walcott
prunes away accretions and complications to render what he sees as the thing
itself: the quarrel over who possesses the beautiful woman. In effect, Walcott
suggests that in the essential core story of the *Iliad* Hector would steal Helen
from Achilles, and Achilles would kill Hector to get her back. Once the three
principals are imagined in this basic triangular relation, the actual displacements (or "instead-of's") in the *Iliad* begin to be evident. Instead of Hector,
Paris steals Helen, who is married to *Menelaos* instead of Achilles. Achilles
does in fact have his girl stolen from him, but it is *Briseis* instead of Helen,
and instead of Hector, *Agamemnon*, brother of Menelaos, takes her.

The intricacies multiply, because the original deed of Agamemnon against
Achilles ultimately leads Achilles to kill Hector instead of Agamemnon, not
for stealing Briseis but for killing *Patroklos* and taking Achilles' armor. Because
each of these characters has his or her own story, these displacements include
more and more people and meanings—ultimately, the whole army of the
Greeks and the population of Troy—in the ramifying action and complicate
the "original" motives with many others, though all are governed by the same

fundamental passion for justice. At the beginning of the poem, the reprisals
of the Greeks on the Trojans for the theft of Menelaos' wife give way to the
more encompassing and devastating reprisals on the Greeks that Achilles will
exact for stealing his honor and bringing about the occasion of his mortality.

Logue pares away what must seem to him needless subtleties. But what
does he lose by this approach? To ask this question is to ask why Homer
composed the poem as he did. I would suggest that by making Achilles'
metaphysical grounds of complaint explicit, Logue immediately sacrifices
most of the moral complexity of Achilles. In the cinematic opening scene,
the poem's camera closes in on the fleet of the Greeks arrayed along the
beach; then Logue tells the reader to picture

> A ten-foot-high reed wall faced with black clay
> And split by a double-doored gate;
> Then through the gate a naked man
> Whose beauty's silent power stops your heart
> Fast walk, face wet with tears, out past its guard,
> And having vanished from their sight
> Run with what seems to break the speed of light
> Across the dry, then damp, then sand invisible
> Beneath inch-high waves that slide
> Over each other's luminescent panes.... (5)

The advantage of this description is that it is so visually idiomatic for us. We
are accustomed to recognize the introduction of characters by seeing them
first cross through a threshold, and in this disclosure the guards and the beach
and Achilles' nakedness give the scene a strong liminal feel. The difficulty here
comes with a peculiar effect that Logue has worked into the lines. When
Achilles comes naked through the gate, Logue ascribes *to us* a first powerful
reaction to Achilles' beauty, so that before anything else, the hero is a *look* of
naked male beauty on the beach, like a figure in a homoerotically lavish Calvin
Klein ad.

Just after the poem makes the reader register Achilles' looks, it makes
one see him "fast walk" past the guard before breaking into a run down the
beach. This line in particular summarizes, for me, almost the entirety of

what offends me in Logue's presentation of Achilles: we are to see a beautiful naked man "Fast walk, face wet with tears, out past the guard." The alliterative spondees at the beginning—"Fast walk, face wet"—with their slightly greater emphasis on the first syllable of each spondee, adeptly suggest Achilles' almost lunging pace, his just-held-back urgency, but his face wet with tears and particularly his concern for keeping himself from running until he passes the guard strike me as deliberately feminized. One is forced to picture Achilles just barely containing his hot, bursting emotion, as though he were a publicly shamed girl trying to get through a room of onlookers before running to her room to bawl, but in this case, one has to imagine the guards as a lounging group of tough, cynical soldiers from whom the sensitive boy-Achilles has to hide his feelings as he runs to call his mother. This Achilles is too young, too girlishly anxious, to be the terrifying sacker of twenty-three cities in the generous Troad. Logue's account seems to assume that in the Homeric world, men like Achilles were looked at as women often are in ours, first in terms of their looks; that if women are "shes," little better than useful animals, and Chryseis (Cryzia in Logue) is described as "a gently broken adolescent she," this kind of emphasis on the higher *male* beauty actually elevates Achilles' worth; and that constant awareness of one's looks being assessed would give the hero of the *Iliad* the same sense of himself at any given social moment as, say, Anna Karenina or Mme. de Vionnet. In the aesthetic overtones of that one crucially offending line, Logue invites the poem's audience into a sophisticated connoisseurship, somehow knowingly gay and ironic and novelized, though not Wildean so much as Foucauldian.

In the *Iliad* itself, the first question is not how Achilles looks but how the devastating quarrel between Agamemnon and Achilles breaks out when an old priest attempts to ransom back his captive daughter. The first figure to appear in the poem is not a beautiful naked man but old Chryses with the treasures he has brought to offer for his daughter, "holding / in his hands wound on a staff of gold the ribbons of Apollo / who strikes from afar" (1.13-15). An old man comes along the beach as a supplicant to the powerful king: he has no beauty but the dignity that makes him risk this approach on behalf of Chryseis, whom he loves more than all his wealth. When Agamemnon publicly dismisses the old man and mocks the god's ribbons, contradicting his public responsibility for his private pleasure in the girl, Chryses goes away calling upon Apollo, who then sends down a plague that devastates the Achaian army. Logue includes these scenes in a flashback from Achilles' opening dialogue with Thetis, but in Homer, the crucial difference is that Achilles first appears when he calls an assembly after nine days of corpse fires. He makes his entrance as a man acting responsibly on behalf of the army to ascertain from a prophet or dream-interpreter why Apollo is so angry, not as a Mapplethorpe study. Homer does not mention his good looks, nor, unlike Logue, does he have Ajax first suggest the assembly. What is lost in Logue's cinematic opening is an Achilles who is already a serious man, by no means the "boy Achilleus" that Logue's Agamemnon calls him.

Picture the poet, in a negotiation before the poem begins, bargaining with several goddesses, who offer him different possibilities. Promised a potent opening image with a sexual frisson, Logue trades away the old man for the beautiful naked one and puts the old priest later in the section as a flashback. In exchange, he gives up certain effects far away in the poem. As he progresses, he also rewrites every character who would act out of self-conscious self-restraint as well as every god urging the long view. Here is the scene in Lattimore's translation when Athene intervenes to stop Achilles from killing Agamemnon:

> The goddess standing behind Peleus' son caught him by the fair hair,
> appearing to him only, for no man of the others saw her.
> Achilleus in amazement turned about, and straightway
> knew Pallas Athene and the terrible eyes shining. (1.197-200)

After Athene tells him that Hera loves Agamemnon and Achilles equally and cares for both, the goddess goes on to make this promise:

> 'Come then, do not take your sword in your hand, keep clear of fighting,
> though indeed with words you may abuse him, and it will be that way.
> And this thing also will I tell you and it will be a thing accomplished.

> Some day three times over such shining gifts shall be given to you
> by reason of this outrage. Hold your hand then, and obey us.' (1.210-14)

Athene's persuasion has less to do with greed than with self-restraint and the trust that the plans of the gods will eventually bring about something better than what he is losing in the moment. In effect, Athene tells Achilles to invest his lost prize and his present humiliation with her for a greater future return.

Logue's version, more immediately engaging on the level of imagery, entirely omits this kind of persuasion on her part. With his startling use of contemporary similes for events in the world of the *Iliad*, he gives Athene a memorable entrance:

> And then,
> Much like a match-flame struck in full sunlight,
> We lose him in the prussic glare
> Teenage Athena, called the Daughter Prince—who burst
> Howling and huge out of God's head—sheds
> From her hard, wide-apart eyes, as she enters
> And stops time.
>
> But those still dying see:
> Achilles leap the 15 yards between
> Himself and Agamemnon;
> Achilles land, and straighten up, in one;
> Achilles' fingertips—such elegance!—
> Push push-push push, push Agamemnon's chest;
> The King lean back; Achilles grab
> And twist the mace out of this royal hand
> And lift it.... Oh...flash! flash!
> The heralds running up...
>
> But we stay calm,
> For we have seen Athena's radiant hand
> Collar Achilles' plait,
> Then as a child its favourite doll
> Draw his head back towards her lips
> To say:

"You know my voice?
You know my power?

"Be still.

"God's wife has sent me:
'Stop him. I like them both,' she said.
    I share her view.
If you can stick to speech, harass him now.
But try to kill him, and I kill you." (19-20)

Notice that Logue has this terse, intimidating, comic-book Athene simply omit the promise that Achilles (the "elegance" of whose fingertips gets an appreciative comment) will be amply rewarded later for his self-restraint. She merely threatens him. Over and over, in any circumstance when this central formal principle of the Homeric world—delay—could emerge as a possibility, Logue chooses instead the immediate effect. At any point when he can bring out an interpretation rooted in sex or power or both, he does so, brushing aside any language that disguises the great principles that connect the Homeric world, as he sees it, with our own.

When Thetis presents her petition on behalf of Achilles to Zeus, to take another example, the goddess in Logue's account does not hesitate to mention every obligation that Zeus has incurred in asking him for the temporary victory of Hector. She

reminds him of her conscientiousness;
Then (seating Him) of her enforced, demeaning coitus;
Then (as she keeps His hands) repeats
The promise He had given to her son.... (37)

Logue's champion-breeder Zeus, for his part, does not hesitate to tell Thetis that the request will make trouble, because

Next to her detestation of the Trojans,
My wife likes baiting Me:
'So you have helped the Dribbler *again*,'

That is how Hera styles My favourite king,
Priam of windy Troy,
A stallion man—once taken for Myself—
Who serviced 50 strapping wives from 50 towns,
Without complaint—to unify My Ilium,
Though all she says is,
   'From where I sit Your city on the hill
Stinks like a brickfield wind.' (38)

Entirely gone from Logue, it goes without saying, is any principle of decorum; in the *Nicomachean Ethics* Aristotle mentions the scene in Homer as an example of the way that one approaches the magnanimous man who does not like to be reminded of his specific obligations:

> [The great-souled man] is fond of conferring benefits, but ashamed to receive them, because the former is a mark of superiority and the latter of inferiority. He returns a service done to him with interest, since this will put the original benefactor into his debt in turn, and make him the party benefitted. The great-souled are thought to have a good memory for any benefit they have conferred, but a bad memory for those which they have received (since the recipient of a benefit is the inferior of his benefactor, whereas they desire to be superior); and to enjoy being reminded of the former but to dislike being reminded of the latter: *this is why the poet makes Thetis not specify her services to Zeus...* (1124b [Loeb 221,223]; my emphasis)

The reluctance of the great-souled god to remember the benefit done for his reign by Thetis must therefore be extreme, because it was the greatest possible benefit, and in Lattimore's translation, Thetis simply says, "'Father Zeus, if ever before in word or action / I did you favour among the immortals, now grant what I ask for'" (1.503-4).[1]

Logue's account relies upon Homer as the display of nakedness relies upon clothing. If Logue's poem sometimes seems revelatory, it is because he has made explicit what the *Iliad* holds in reserve. For this reason, what Garry Wills says about Logue's work seems to me precisely wrong, especially when he says that "Logue is striving to reach the essence of Homer, including those things hardest to bring over into our culture, the things most easily jettisoned

THE SACRIFICE OF ACHILLES

if one is inventing a contemporary entertainment," and Wills includes in his list "theophanies, animal sacrifice, catalogues, epithets, or repeated speeches" (Logue xi). The hardest things in Homer to bring over are rather the enormous patient restraint, the elaborate displacements, and the almost tectonic scale of the indirection that allows the poem to delay Achilles' re-emergence for nearly two-thirds of its length in order to accumulate a sufficient massiveness of value in his return. What contemporary poet after the *Star Wars*, *Alien*, and *Mad Max* films could fail to find something appealing about theophanies, animal sacrifices, and catalogues, if not epithets and repeated speeches? But the patience *not* to sacrifice everything for the stunning graphics of Aphrodite and Ares is much more difficult to come by.

T HE choices that Logue makes are paradigmatic of our age's choices, but the great advantage of literature is that we are not limited to our own age. Let me begin again by thinking about the old man at the beginning of the *Iliad* and why Homer puts him there. One reason is that, twenty-four books later, one can recognize that it exactly balances the embassy of Priam coming to ask for the return of the body of Hector and thus comprises part of the poem's much-analyzed geometric form. But then one has to ask this question: why should the action of the epic poem about the choice to die young—the choice made by the one man on whose death the Olympian order of Zeus might be said to rest—be framed or bracketed by the appearances of these old men? Chryses literally appears as part of the answer to the question that the poet asks about the quarrel between Achilles and Agamemnon: "What god was it then that set them together in bitter collision?" (1.8). Emerging from the explanation of the plague that occasioned their quarrel, the old man is suddenly "beside the fast ships of the Achaians" carrying his "gifts beyond count" to offer as ransom for his daughter Chryseis, the war-prize or *geras* of Agamemnon after the sacking of the city of Chryse. When Samuel Johnson was writing about *King Lear*, he was at some pains to convince his readers that the old king would act in such a primitive way with his daughters, but he satisfied himself that there might still be chieftains like

Lear in such places as Madagascar. The actions of Chryses have to be exam-
ined in a similar, if less condescending, light, because it is difficult, at first
glance, to register the emotional tone of this scene accurately.

In modern circumstances of ransom, the kidnapper or terrorist being
appeased already carries the stigma of the worst kind of criminal, and everyone knows, not only that the ransom itself is the last desperate measure, but
that if possible the criminal will be caught and punished. But in the world of
the *Iliad*, ransom is an understood and respected concomitant of war. It is
treated as a version of gift exchange, since it is both a way of gaining wealth
from the rich families of well-connected captives and a form of clemency:
the victor spares the life and restores the freedom of the one ransomed. In
this practice of wary, formal gift-exchange between enemies, the beautiful
Chryseis has a mercurially delicate position, since she has been captured as a
war-prize and publicly awarded to the great king, whose public honor she
embodies. When the men defending her city were killed, she and the other
women were rounded up as the booty of war, like other chattel, in a scene
that must have been like the one described in a famous simile of the *Odyssey*,
when Odysseus weeps like a woman who has just seen her husband killed
and who is being prodded with spear butts as she is led off into slavery.
Logue perhaps overstates the case by having captive women referred to as
"shes," but not by much. They are slaves whose remaining dignity depends
solely upon the kind of treatment that personal beauty, rank, and elegance
of demeanor can earn them from the lords on whom they are bestowed.

Golden Chryseis (father, daughter, and city all bear the root *chryse*, gold,
in their names) has obsessed Agamemnon to such an extent that he later says
in the public assembly that he likes her better than Klytaimestra, his own wife
(1.113-14). He is so taken with her that he ignores what might be called the
currency of public honor, in which possession of a woman as a war-prize
might be treated as the equivalent of other forms of wealth that also signify
one's status. When old Chryses approaches him, hoping that this kind of
equivalence will be accepted—not because *he* thinks of his daughter as property, but because he does not—Agamemnon, who has accepted her as a thing

and no doubt taken her sexually, is not expected to treat her as personally as Chryses does. The old man has to hope that Agamemnon will consent to exchange her for his "gifts beyond count," and in making the plea, he renounces any political loyalty of his own and emphasizes his own private affection. But he also complicates the exchange by saying that accepting the ransom will honor Apollo, the god whose priest he is:

> 'Sons of Atreus and you other strong-greaved Achaians,
> to you may the gods grant who have their homes on Olympos
> Priam's city to be plundered and a fair homecoming thereafter,
> but may you give me back my own daughter and take the ransom,
> giving honour to Zeus' son who strikes from afar, Apollo.' (1.17-21)

On the first level, Chryses has to be respected because his very presence among enemies requires the kind of courage that has already put aside his own shame. In circumstances when it might be natural to consider the girl as damaged by her enslavement and lost to him, he makes a gesture that restores her worth in the eyes of all, not least Agamemnon, who sees unmistakably how much her father values her—that is, far above his property. The old man's dignity lies in his unconcern about himself, his love for his daughter, and his service to the god. Agamemnon, deafened by his feeling for the girl, lacks ears to hear it, but this is less a conventional request for exchange than an oracle sent by the god himself in the person of a priest "holding / in his hands wound of a staff of gold the ribbons of Apollo." If one regards what Chryses says as both a literal plea and an indirectly delivered divine message, it becomes more pointed. The situation itself becomes part of a test. If Agamemnon recognizes the sacredness of the old man and accepts the ransom, then he will also have what he desires in the long run: the capture of Troy and a safe homecoming. If he does not, then he has given up the moral authority of his cause. Why? Because Apollo has so structured (or revealed) golden Chryseis' importance that she becomes a displaced Helen, with whom Agamemnon is another Paris. He possesses a woman who pleases him very much. When he refuses Chryses and drives him away with threats, he acts as shortsightedly toward his own people as Paris has acted in Troy.

In fact, Agamemnon's refusal embeds the cause of the war—the refusal to return a woman whose alliances make her taboo—in the very core of the Achaian army. Humiliated and frightened by Agamemnon, Chryses goes away along the beach praying to the god whose ribbons the Achaian king has just mocked, and the incensed god, whom the priest has indirectly and thus deceptively represented all along, sends a plague among the Greeks—one that rages for nine days, exactly reiterating on a smaller fractal scale the greater nine-year plague that the crime of Paris brought on Troy. Who is the first to act, not only on behalf of the army, but also on behalf of the old priest, his daughter, and the insulted god?

> Nine days up and down the host ranged the god's arrows,
> but on the tenth Achilleus called the people to assembly;
> a thing put into his mind by the goddess of the white arms, Hera,
> who had pity upon the Danaans when she saw them dying. (1.53-56)

One would have to have in mind at the beginning the *completed action*—that is, the experience of the whole poem, including Hera's rage at the temporary defeat of the Achaians, through Priam's visit to ransom Hector in Book 24—to be able to take a prophetic perspective and see what this embedded sign *will have meant* by the end. It already anticipates Achilles' eventual return to battle after the death of Patroklos, when he walks along the beach "crying his terrible cry" to call all the Achaians once more into assembly. It foresees his pity toward old Priam, who makes the same brave and profoundly humble gesture to Achilles that Chryses makes to Agamemnon, this time for the corpse of his son.

But something even more remarkable is already going on in this opening intervention of Achilles: a first revelation of the sacrificial meaning of his life. In order to see this meaning, one must think in the subjunctive mood: if Zeus had not given up his desire for Thetis because of the destiny she bore, he would have brought the same kind of ruin on Olympos that Paris is bringing on Troy and Agamemnon on the Achaians. Since Achilles embodies—*is*—the divine *avoidance of ruin* through the forbidden woman, his destiny necessarily begins to be disclosed, first through the war over a forbidden woman, and now through the still more acute focus of this dispute. When the Achaians are threatened by Agamemnon's refusal to give up Chryseis, Achilles steps in to insure that Apollo's intentions become manifest. He protects Kalchas from the threats of Agamemnon, but in doing so Achilles also enacts a sacrificial role on behalf of the army: he has to suffer the humiliating loss of his own prize of honor, Briseis; later, to lose Patroklos; and eventually to accept his own death as the condition for honoring his friend. Given the logic of consequences, it is possible—in fact, necessary—to understand Achilles' eventual self-sacrifice (paradoxically, killing Hector) as the price of this very first intervention on behalf of the army. It is also possible to see that his self-sacrifice ultimately fulfills the gesture of the forbidden Thetis in giving Zeus and the other Olympian gods her mortal son.

But back to the literal level: why the sacred *old man* as the poem's first image, the figure who precipitates the action that will lead Achilles to accept his sacrificial destiny? Again, one must think in a great loop. If Chryses anticipates and balances Priam at the end of the poem, then one should also recall that in Book 24, Priam's appeal to Achilles explicitly evokes a figure absent from the literal action of the poem but everywhere present by implication: Peleus. "'Achilleus like the gods, remember your father, one who / is of years like mine, and on the door-sill of sorrowful old age'" (24.486-87), Priam says when he first comes to Achilles in supplication, and he closes his plea by urging the killer of his son, "'take pity upon me / remembering your father'" (24.503-4). Priam, then, makes explicit an allusion already present (but disguised) in Chryses at the beginning: the old father of Achilles, the man ultimately responsible for the fact that Achilles will have to die. The first line of the poem, some ten lines before the appearance of Chryses, refers to Achilles as Peleus' son, and it does so in a particularly telling way. Milton imitates the effect in the first line of *Paradise Lost*, "Of man's first disobedience and the fruit." The pressure of the iambic pentameter forces the blending of distinct sounds known in Greek metrics as synezesis, pronouncing two syllables as one. The fact that the "disobedience" of the meter comes in the word *disobedience* has a symbolic import for *Paradise Lost* as a whole, since it signifies man's original sinful attempt to exceed the measure—a "first dis-obedience" already in the first line. Milton very pointedly imitates Homer in this beginning. In the first line of the *Iliad*, there is an extra syllable in the genitive ending of *Peleiadeo*, translated by Lattimore as "Peleus' son." When the meter forces the extra syllables to be consciously forced together, it signi-fies the difficulty with which the divinity of Achilles will be forced into the mortal measure that comes from being the son of Peleus.

Old Chryses comes along the beach a few lines later. In this context, he is a visible reminder of Peleus who also embodies the alternative destiny—homecoming and the sight of his aged father and his own eventual old age—that Achilles will give up by reentering the battle. But an old Achil-les hobbling down the beach, supplicating younger, more powerful men, is unthinkable. His life, sacrificial since his conception, needs the focus and intensity befitting the unique sacrifice of the Olympian gods. If he cannot be a god, he must die young, for reasons perhaps best described by Priam pleading with Hector from the walls:

> 'For a young man all is decorous
> when he is cut down in battle and torn with the sharp bronze, and lies there
> dead, and though dead still all that shows about him is beautiful;
> but when an old man is dead and down, and the dogs mutilate
> the grey head and the grey beard and the parts that are secret,
> this, for all sad mortality, is the sight most pitiful.' (22.71-76)

Achilles' sacrificial death—itself never described in the poem but displaced onto Hector, as we shall see—needs the frame of pitiable old age, the rejected future in which even Achilles would falter and lose his particular excellence, in order to stand out tragically in its superlative beauty.

Much of this formal significance Christopher Logue loses by rearrang-ing the first book. Homer constructs an effect whose import will be delayed for almost 15,000 lines; Logue cuts to the immediately revealing image and makes Achilles talk openly about the reason he was born mortal. In Homer, a fact kept from overt expression becomes manifest through the indirection

of form—so manifest that the poem exceeds all others in beauty and grandeur, so indirect that until recently no one seemed to remember why it might
be important for the Olympians of the *Iliad* that Thetis married Peleus. This
significant indirection, I am arguing, governs the entire formal construction
of this massive poem. But at no point does it feel self-consciously artistic,
like Flaubert or James, largely because its indirections and restraints seem to
be coming from open negotiations with the order of reality itself, an order
governed by the gods and most jealously guarded, it seems, by what Apollo
will allow. Among the many themes that Chryses introduces—old age, gift-
giving for ransom, supplication to the powerful, prayer for retribution, and
so on—he also announces the fatal power of Apollo, the god who will stun
Patroklos with a blow that knocks the armor from him in the midst of battle
(16.78-805) and whom Achilles will call "most malignant of all gods" (22.15).
The poet himself answers the opening question about Achilles and
Agamemnon, "What god was it then set them together in bitter collision?"
with the reply, "Zeus' son and Leto's, Apollo" (1.8-9).

Never truly foregrounded (as Zeus, Hera, or Athene are) either in the
Iliad or in the *Odyssey*, Apollo somehow attracts mortal scorn, yet this "most
malignant," most inimical god, apparently envious of human greatness, violently enforces the limits of powers and natures. At the point when
Agamemnon, for example, seizes too much privilege and becomes forgetful,
Apollo becomes the Mouse-god, Smintheus, who sends his plague among
the Achaians, first to "the mules and the circling hounds" (1.50), then to the
men thus denigrated by their comparability in disease and death to their own
animals. This quarrel, in turn, leads to the still more devastating "plague" of
Achilles' absence. Where formal boundaries—of gift exchange, honor, piety,
achievement in battle—are violated, Apollo sends a virulent ugliness or exerts a particularly violent counter-force to strengthen the demarcation between what is whole and what is unclean. If Blake is right in his "Proverbs of
Hell" that "The road of excess leads to the palace of wisdom," it must be
because, in Homeric terms, Apollo hates excess and "malignantly" reveals
the exact line of violation. Wisdom comes, if one survives, from the repeated

experience of formal delineation through the testing of limits. The *Iliad* would lack its fire and greatness of soul—like the otherwise admirable opus of Henry James—if it were not always claiming as much splendor of revelation as it could get, and getting it by a violence, less blind than that of Patroklos attacking Troy, that forces Apollo to show himself. Whenever too much explicitness or overt power would dissipate the poetic effect instead of increasing it, Apollo rages, but one does not know what is enough, as Blake has it, until Apollo says "too much." Apollo jealously drives the imagination back inside the measure to bring about a paradoxical intensity of beauty. His presence at the beginning of the *Iliad* already foreshadows the splendor that springs into being when the tantalizing dream of a godlike adored self, removed from contingency and subject to no will other than its own, is suddenly and forcibly cut off, in the full consciousness of its condition.

S ACRIFICE pacifies Apollo in Book I of the *Iliad*, and poetic form, closely associated with Apollo in the Western imagination, has exact analogies to this profound and universal ritual. At the heart of form, if I think into the nature of the *Iliad*, lies the deliberate destruction of whatever is most prized, so that it might be revealed and preserved. Form in this sense is the whole intuition of lost being, etched into the immortal, sustaining medium of absence. But even the simplest lyric has this basic character. The poet consecrates existence to the revelatory matrix of loss, and the consecration consists in submission to the form. I have already cited in the previous chapter John Crowe Ransom's view that "Given an object, and a poet burning to utter himself upon it, he must take into account a third item, the form into which he must cast his utterance. (If we like, we may call it the *body* which he must give to his passion.) It delays and hinders him. In the process of 'composition' the burning passion is submitted to cool and scarcely relevant considerations" ("Forms" 40). In being cooled and made deliberate, the consciousness invested in what is being deliberately lost raises it to a level altogether different from the consciousness present in the heat of passion: compare, for example, killing in a hunt to the deliberate, formal killing of an

animal in sacrifice. Because ritual requires heightened awareness, it takes
its participants more deeply into the experience being "imitated" than the
experience itself can do. Similarly, emotions and feelings are made more
articulate and intelligent in poetic form. But this formal character does not
solve them in advance or free the reader from the dangers that attended the
"original" of the ritual. To repeat the passage from Victor Turner, ritual "is a
transformative self-immolation of order as presently constituted, even sometimes a voluntary *sparagmos* or self-dismemberment of order, in the subjunctive depths of liminality" (83). Form always emerges from these subjunctive
depths—the *if* or *might* or *would be*—that fear and desire postulate through
the imagination, and in the process of becoming actual, it ascends into the
light of common day. Being revealed at all—like being born mortal—means
risking belittlement and misunderstanding because of the reliance of revelation on an action in time and, perhaps even more, on the docility of those to
whom the truth should come.

Nowhere is this belittlement and misunderstanding more evident than
when Agamemnon in effect punishes Achilles for saving the army by replac-
ing his own lost prize with Achilles' war-prize Briseis, scorning his greatest
warrior. Enraged, experiencing the *achos* (anguish or sharp sorrow) that
underlies his name, Achilles very nearly slaughters Agamemnon on the spot,
as we have seen in Logue's version, but when Athene halts him with the
promise of later recompense, he takes up the scepter instead and formally
curses Agamemnon and his army:

> 'And this shall be a great oath before you:
> some day longing for Achilleus will come to the sons of the Achaians,
> all of them. Then stricken at heart though you be, you will be able
> to do nothing, when in their numbers before man-slaughtering Hektor
> they drop and die. And then you will eat out the heart within you
> in sorrow, that you did no honour to the best of the Achaians.'
>   Thus spoke Peleus' son and dashed to the ground the sceptre
> studded with golden nails, and sat down again. (1.239-46)

Agamemnon's insult triggers a deeper sense of "injured merit" than Agamemnon
or anyone else in the army realizes. Given this insult and the removal of his

prize, Achilles' request for honor invokes the much larger debt that Zeus owes to him. His words to Thetis bitterly underscore the irony of his situation:

> 'Since, my mother, you bore me to be a man with a short life
> [*minunthadios*, "minute-lived"]
> therefore Zeus of the loud thunder on Olympos should grant me
> honour [*time*] at least. But now he has given me not even a little.
> Now the son of Atreus, powerful Agamemnon,
> has dishonoured me, since he has taken away my prize and keeps it.'
> (1.352-56)

"Honour at least": that is, in the narrow circumstances of his mortal life, honor will have to serve as his compensation. Agamemnon identifies himself with "Zeus of the counsels" (175), and in the logic of Achilles' request, Agamemnon's insult appears to be the deed of Zeus: "he [Zeus] has given me not even a little [honor]." Treating Agamemnon as a mask, Achilles indirectly challenges the personal adequacy of Zeus as the distributor of prizes, the one who either does or does not acknowledge his indebtedness to those who sustain him in power. He refuses the conventional mechanisms of honor and insists that Zeus either do better or admit his own similarity to Agamemnon.

But in his insistence, he unwittingly asks to fulfill his role as the sacrifice of the Olympians. When Thetis forwards this request to Zeus himself, the background of Thetis' wedding unmistakably underlies both her demeanor and her words,[3] even the mildly ironic *Pater* with which she begins her plea, although she does not "specify her services to Zeus," as Aristotle notes:[4]

> 'Father Zeus, if ever before in word or action
> I did you favour among the immortals, now grant what I ask for.
> Now give honour to my son short-lived beyond all other
> mortals. Since even now the lord of men Agamemnon
> dishonours him, who has taken away his prize and keeps it.
> Zeus of the counsels, lord of Olympus, now do him honour.
> So long put strength into the Trojans, until the Achaians
> give my son his rights, and his honour is increased among them.'
> She spoke thus. But Zeus who gathers the clouds made no answer
> but sat in silence a long time. (1.503-12)

For Zeus, brought into the foreground by Achilles' dishonor, the request
entails a strange kind of service, not unlike the servitude of Poseidon and
Apollo when they built the walls of Troy (7.446-53). If he nods his head, Zeus
will be laboring on behalf of a mortal to build something even more lasting
than Troy itself. If he begins to afflict the Achaian army, it will not be because
Agamemnon has dishonored *him* in a representative figure, a king or priest,
such as Chryses was for Apollo. Achilles does not stand for Zeus; on the
contrary, he stands for an averted threat to Olympos, an enemy who would
have put Zeus into the position of Priam and Hektor—and Agamemnon—
if Zeus had insisted on marrying the forbidden goddess, who now kneels in
front of him and whose very presence will get him in trouble with Hera. The
honor done to Achilles by the destruction of the Achaians will not go to
Achilles as the representative of Zeus; it will come from Zeus as the
representative of Achilles. Yet the paradox is that this reversal will not in any
way alter the pitiable contingency of Achilles as a flawed man subject to death,
while it will subject countless others to suffering and death, including a son
of Zeus, and bring to the surface the deepest divisions among the gods. On
the other hand, if he does not honor Achilles, he will fail to repay the debt on
which his rule rests. Although his reasons for hesitation are more than
understandable, the arguments of Thetis have the greater power:

> And Thetis, as she had taken
> his knees, clung fast to them and urged once more her question:
> 'Bend your head and promise me to accomplish this thing,
> or else refuse it, you have nothing to fear, that I may know
> by how much I am the most dishonoured of all gods.' (1.512-16)

Diplomatically, Zeus blames Hera for his hesitation, but he grants Achilles'
request:

> 'I will look to these things that they be accomplished.
> See then, I will bend my head that you may believe me.
> For this among the immortal gods is the mightiest witness
> I can give, and nothing I do shall be vain nor revocable
> nor a thing unfulfilled when I bend my head in assent to it.'

> He spoke, the son of Kronos, and nodded his head with the dark brows,
> and the immortally anointed hair of the great god
> swept from his divine head, and all Olympos was shaken. (523-30)

Another reason for Zeus's long pause is that the purpose of the plan to which he nods in this absolute fashion is not simply the temporary victory of the Trojans; Zeus fashions—in fact, has been fashioning since the wedding day of Thetis—a fitting circumstance in which the devastating metaphysical wrath of Achilles can become the form of the hero's *kleos aphthiton* or undying fame, embodied in the poem itself, a beautifully crafted and unperishing fame, the only fitting compensation for the mortality of the son of Thetis. His problem in crafting it is the epic poet's problem: how he can make the mythical significance of one man appear in its permanent singularity when many others have claims to honor and when time has such erosive effects.

When I first began to read the *Iliad* seriously, I had no idea of its importance in the formation of the Western imagination. It seems to me now that, huge as it is, it establishes once and for all the fundamental principle of limitation—what Fr. William Lynch calls "the finite"—through which the amplitude of meaning must come. Because the life of Achilles has an absolute limit that cannot be violated, both Zeus and Homer have to find a way to bring all the possible meaning of the potential "ruler of the universe," all the subjunctivity of his averted destiny, into a single action that compensates him for his short life and reveals his greatness. The actual life of Achilles, in other words, becomes the "literal level," in which all the other meanings have to be contained—and only a small portion of that short life. This does not mean that the texture of the poem is "realistic" in a modern sense. If one looked at it in that light, what could it mean to speak of "the limitations of the real" and the "literal level" when goddesses congeal out of sea mist, or high gods take the form of vultures to sit in a tree and watch mortals? What about the fire that springs from the head of Achilles, or the immortal horse that turns and speaks to him? Rather, the literal level means the indicative plane of action on which things must come to light, the field of appearance, the light of a common day in which gods are present as forces and contrasts, but their own plenitude of being is always denied in advance to mortals. The gods are like wealthy, beautiful, free people constantly appearing among prisoners or slaves, sometimes fooling them with hopes, sometimes intervening to suit their own preferences, sometimes bestowing particular favors. In a world constantly penetrated by these divine presences, the greatest mortal—the one who *subjunctively* rules them all—nevertheless remains bound absolutely to a measure from which not only rule, but the crucial element of immortality has been removed.

Poetically, this one restraint means everything, because what the later exegetical tradition called the anagogical level therefore becomes possible: another action, in a "mythological" dimension having to do with the order of the cosmos, both does and does not take place through the literal events narrated in the *Iliad*. Imagine a slave narrative about a black man of extraordinary genius limited in his capacity to express it by the circumstances of his enslavement: everything that he actually accomplished would have to stand for what he *might have* done. In the same way, the withdrawal of Achilles from the Achaian army and his voluntary return after the death of Patroklos have to stand for what he might have done on the cosmic level, but in this case the significance lies in the fact that this action also literally *is* the cosmic level.

The mortal measure in which Zeus has to work paradoxically gives this cosmic significance its most powerful effect. Every action of Achilles bears within it the seismic tremor that accompanies the conversion of a great cosmic subjunctive into a lesser actuality. Yet the actuality brings mortal action onto the stage of universal significance for the first time. What does that mean? It means, on one level, that the beautiful, well-heeled people have to acknowledge, through the extraordinary honor that they bestow, the fact that their whole world of deathless privilege depends upon the suffering and death of the one who would have been greatest among them but who instead was born as a slave. On another level, it means that the deathless realities—what Melville calls the "joyous, heartless, ever-juvenile eternities"—come to have their focus and being in the limited frame of mortal life.

The great genius of the *Iliad* lies in a principle of metaphysical reticence that can be summarized in this way: whatever absolutely must be revealed will be delayed, and the more crucial it is, the longer it will be put off through substitutions; every momentous reality that emerges will therefore do so through multiple displacements and premonitions of itself; and when it does finally come to light its manifestation will leave the greater part concealed. The absolute necessity in the poem as a whole is the revelation of Achilles—given the nod by Zeus at the end of Book I—who has been mortally insulted a few lines after the poem begins. In order to bring about the manifestation of what this hero is in his "ontological splendor," to borrow a phrase from Maritain, the whole action of the poem is necessary, in this sense: Achilles' destiny includes every other mortal in the poem, each of whom shares his condemnation to death, so that every striving for distinction or drawing back, every victory or death, reflects upon his own, and in the course of fashioning a single great word by the end, the poem shatters at first into many images and possible substitutes, before contracting gradually into a more powerfully focused substitution, in Patroklos and Hektor. The principle of the *Iliad's* form comes closest to showing itself when one reflects that the poem about the hero uniquely conceived to die does not end with his death, but with the death and burial of his greatest enemy, Hektor.

H EKTOR, Hektor, Hektor. The greatest son of Priam often convinces readers that he is the real hero of the poem, because of his deep bonds to his wife, his son, his parents, and his city—or I should say, his abandonment of what seem to have been those bonds. Unlike Achilles, he seems, on occasion, to be moved by pity and kindness, at least in the past. Seth Schein writes in his discussion of the hero's relation to Troy that

> Hektor, as Redfield has said, is "above all else a hero of *aidos*," which means
> a hero of social obligations and responsibilities.... For *aidos*, in addition to
> denoting the impulse toward warrior-bravery owed to comrades and com-
> munity and associated with the honor and glory to be won in battle, signi-
> fies the generosity and pity owed to the weak and helpless who are directly
> dependent on one's kindness and mercy for their survival and welfare. (179)

But this interpretation of Hektor as "preeminently a familial and social hero" (Schein 181), true as it is, neglects his ambition. His obligations and responsibilities gradually dissolve in the experience of glory that Achilles provides him by being absent. His own is to accept, then to become, a gift of glory. His sudden ascendancy over all the other Greeks and Trojans in the war takes place for one reason: so that Achilles' request for honor can be fulfilled. In a way terrible to contemplate, Hektor is the sacrifice that Zeus makes to Achilles. Given the opportunity provided by Achilles' quarrel with Agamemnon, no other warrior, not even Diomedes in the first day of battle without Achilles, not even Patroklos in his *aristeia*, so consciously and with such outright relish tries to replace Achilles in glory. Because he tacitly accepts the terms of Achilles' own oath to Agamemnon in Book I ("'Then stricken at heart though you be, you will be able / to do nothing, when in their numbers before man-slaughtering Hektor / they drop and die'"), Hektor will act not only *in* but *as* the absence of Achilles, named by Achilles himself to embody his metaphysical wrath.

   Let us pick him up at the center of the poem, on the day after the Achaian embassy to Achilles, when Hektor is moving toward his greatest glory. While Achilles watches the action from the deck of his own ship, Hektor's attack centers on breaking through the Achaian wall built since Achilles' departure from the fighting. At first, the Achaians rally and push the Trojans back, but by afternoon, when the major Achaian warriors— including Agamemnon, Diomedes, Odysseus, and the healer Machaon— begin to succumb to wounds, Hektor drives the Greeks streaming back once again to the ships. But as soon as he begins to pursue them, assured by a message from Iris that Zeus will guarantee his success, ambiguous divine messages and warnings from his friends begin to impose a hateful limit on Hektor's sense of expanding power. Only the night before, after the previous day's victories, he had said to his men as they camped on the plain for the first time since the beginning of the war, "'Oh, if I only / could be as this in all my days immortal and ageless / and be held in honour as Athene and Apollo are honoured" (8.538-40). But now, just as Hektor is about to break through into the interior of the Achaian camp, a bird sign comes—flying ominously to the left of the Trojans, an eagle flies up holding a snake, but the snake rears back and bites it, and the bird drops it among the Trojans (12.200ff.). Poulydamas, though not an official soothsayer like Kalchas, interprets the sign to mean that temporary victory over the Achaians will result in their striking back, and "the Achaians / will cut down [many] with the bronze as they fight for themselves by their vessels" (12.226-27). Hektor will not accept this interpretation because it would mean giving up the assault; moreover, his friend is telling him "to forget the counsels of thunderous / Zeus, in which he himself nodded his head to me and assented" (12.235-36). Within his own interpretive frame, Hektor would be impious to listen to Poulydamas, because it would mean mistrusting Zeus, who has allowed him to taste the intoxicating kind of glory always reserved, before this time, for Achilles. Tempted out of himself into the trap that Zeus is laying for him, Hektor seems to become two people, as Achilles will when he sends Patroklos out a little later. Abandoning the restraints of his *aidos*, Hektor leaves behind his wiser self: Poulydamas "was companion to Hektor, and *born on the same night with him,* / but he was better in words, the other with the spear far better" (18.251-52; my emphasis).

Shortly after Poulydamas' warning, Hektor heaves a great stone through the gate built in the Achaian wall and breaks into the interior of the camp:

> Then glorious Hektor burst in
> with dark face like sudden night, but he shone with the ghastly
> glitter of bronze that girded his skin, and carried two spears
> in his hands. No one could have stood up against him, and stopped him,
> except the gods, when he burst in the gates and his eyes flashed fire.
> (12.462-66)

The broken gate momentarily and dramatically frames him as the great hero who breaks through boundaries. Unfortunately for Hektor, the real boundary for him is a moral one, because he cannot yet see that when he feels like Athene or Apollo, he is in fact only the instrument that Zeus uses. As the victorious enemy of Agamemnon and the Achaians, he embodies Achilles' wrath and acts on behalf of a form whose absolute limits he cannot yet sense. Ironically, by breaking into the Greek camp, he first exposes the intact body of his own city to his contaminating passions for glory. Through this rupture stream the events leading to the return of Achilles, his own death outside the Trojan Wall, and the eventual fall of Troy.

Zeus immediately looks away (13.1-9)—and perhaps not out of disinterest alone. The irony of Hektor's delusion is not pleasant to watch. Shortly afterward, the poem reiterates the point that Zeus must deceive Hektor in order to work out his plan:

> Zeus willed the victory for the Trojans and Hektor,
> glorifying swift-footed Achilleus, yet not utterly
> did he wish the Achaian people to be destroyed before Ilion,
> but only was giving glory to Thetis and her strong-spirited
> son.... (13.347-51)

And as Hektor presses ever closer at the end of Book 15, the point is stressed once again:

> Zeus' desire was to give glory to the son of Priam,
> Hektor, that he might throw on the curved ships the inhuman
> weariless strength of fire, and so make completely accomplished
> the prayer of Thetis. (15.596-99)

Because of the scene earlier in the poem with Andromache, the irony of Hektor's success is almost unbearable. Despite his own mother's useless prayers and his wife's pleas not to expose her to the violation sure to come, this son and husband has become the agent of a great wrath that will sacrifice every "unbought grace of life," in Edmund Burke's luminous phrase, to the lust for destruction. The more the divine power infuses him with its intensity, the shorter Hektor's life becomes:

> A slaver came out around his mouth, and under the lowering
> brows his eyes were glittering, the helm on his temples
> was shaken and thundered horribly to the fighting of Hektor.
> Out of the bright sky Zeus himself was working to help him

and among men so numerous he honoured this one man
and glorified him, since Hektor was to have *only a short life*
and already the day of his death was being driven upon him
by Pallas Athene through the strength of Achilleus.
(15.607-14; my emphasis)

At first glance, the logic of honor for Hektor seems to be the same that Achilles used in Book I, when he said, "'Since, my mother, you bore me to be a man with a short life, / therefore Zeus of the loud thunder on Olympos should grant me / honour at least.'" But Hektor would not be a man with a short life were it not for the framing priority of the short life of Achilles. Hektor is beside himself, displaced from his own proper meaning by this experience of glory and brought more and more to be an unwitting simulacrum of Achilles. Unlike the thief in Akira Kurosawa's *Kagemusha*, a double who must suppress everything personal in himself in order to imitate the warlord Shingen, Hektor has no suspicion that he is being glorified in order to die and that his life is being dramatically foreshortened as a divine gift to Achilles.

ONE major difference between the world of the *Iliad* and our own lies in the understanding of glory. Peter Berger has very helpfully distinguished between societies of honor, such as those of the Greeks and Trojans, and societies of "dignity," like our own, and his ruminations "On the Obsolescence of the Concept of Honor" are well worth bringing to bear on the poem. But there is also a deeper difference between our culture and that of Homer. To give and receive glory, to bestow honor and be its recipient— these things that seem so crucial in the ancient world—have a different valence in our culture because sacrifice is no longer recognized as the major metaphor of the human condition. The very necessity of sacrifice means that man does not occupy the place in the cosmos that would allow him most to appear, to shine, to manifest an "I Am." Any glory is contingent on what the gods allow, based on what one can sacrifice. The order of reality that operates in the Homeric world is one in which beauty is not a matter of "aesthetics" and the achievement of form lies at the very heart of the metaphysical penetration open to human beings. This world takes it for granted that there is a powerful drive toward the *manifestation* of things, a "will to appearance" neither entirely identical with nor separate from what Nietzsche calls the "will to power." Glory involves utmost *appearance*, which is tantamount, in many ways, to saying "utmost being." In his *Introduction to Metaphysics*, Heidegger argues that for the early Greeks (based on his analysis of *physis* in Pindar), appearing was the same thing as Being:

> Being is the fundamental attribute of the noble individual and of nobility (i.e. of what has a high origin and rests in it). In regard to this Pindar coins the saying *genoi' hoios essi mathon* (Pythian Ode II, 72). "Mayest thou by learning come forth as what thou art." But for the Greeks standing-in-itself was nothing other than standing-there, standing-in-the-light. Being means appearing. Appearing is not something subsequent that sometimes happens to being. Appearing is the very essence of being....

According to Heidegger's reading, Greek truth (*aletheia*) means that "The power that manifests itself stands in unconcealment," and nonbeing means "to withdraw from appearing, from presence" (101-02). When Antonio Damasio uses the striking figure of an actor stepping from the shadows into the full light of the stage to describe the phenomenon of consciousness, he comes close to this Greek sense of appearance that underlies glory. To achieve the greatest fame is to step most fully into the greatest consciousness in a sense almost synonymous with *recognition*.

But crossing from the shadows into appearance in this way requires enormous sacrifice. The theologian Hans Urs von Balthasar, who has taken glory more seriously in its theological sense than anyone else in our time, writes that for the Greeks, "The world is to be understood as the *epiphaneia* of the divine to man and as man's being broken open so that he may grasp this appearing" (21). Breaking open requires violence, especially sacrificial violence, without which man cannot grasp the shining that lies in things, because, paradoxically, nature also loves to hide. With the same great truth— the significance of Achilles—to be both hidden and revealed, the *Iliad* shines with violence. As the poem about giving due honor to the figure on whom the Olympian hegemony rests—that is to say, the sacrificial victim whose breaking open sustains the epiphany of the divine things to men—the *Iliad* uniquely makes the divine construction of glory for a mortal its central action, and this construction, necessarily beautiful, also becomes the unique paradigm of dynamically unfolding poetic form.

The plot of the *Iliad is* the making of poetic form. If the aim is glory, then the well-being of individuals must be sacrificed to the effect of the whole flow of events as they form a single cumulative effect. To honor Achilles does not mean to make him happy, but it does mean that he must have some "objective correlative," as Eliot puts it, of the thing being fashioned of his life. Zeus deceives Achilles even more than he does Hektor in order to give him the glory that he wants, but at the same time, he uses the events to give a premonition of the appearance of Achilles' eventual *kleos aphthiton*. For Eliot, the emotion of a poem depends upon effectively establishing "a set of objects, a situation, a chain of events which shall be the formula of that particular emotion; such that when the external facts, which must terminate in sensory experience, are given, the emotion is immediately evoked" ("Hamlet and His Problems" 789). The language of "formula" here grates a little, but certainly a complex pattern of emotion comes to center on *appearing* as Achilles, in keeping with the suggestion that Nestor first makes to Patroklos in Book XI, when he first proposes the idea: "let him give you his splendid armor to wear to the fighting, / if perhaps the Trojans might think you are he" (11.797-98). To wear Achilles' armor is to enter his epiphany. This substitutional role gives Patroklos the chance to experience the terrifying effect that Achilles has when he enters battle as though it were a reaction to himself, but to choose the epiphany also requires the acceptance of the short life. Around this armor, darker meanings begin to proliferate. At first glance, it would seem that Patroklos, dressed in the armor of Achilles, simply *represents* his friend in this action, but it becomes difficult to say whether Patroklos fights as Achilles, for Achilles, or against Achilles. Like Hektor, who has also been lured almost entirely into the Achillean role, he is a deeply ambiguous figure who goes out in a rage against the devastation that Achilles' deliberate absence has caused, but no sooner does he experience success in driving back the Trojans than he, like Hektor, is overcome by the intoxication of being in Achilles' glory.

The momentum of the poem in its great tidal surges into and out of appearance carries Patroklos into the scene in which he kills Sarpedon, the son whom an agonized Zeus sacrifices to this unfolding form. Patroklos then attacks Troy itself, almost as a phantom of the Achilles who, in actuality, will never have this victory to constitute his immortal action. Apollo turns him back, and when the god strikes the helmet, shield, and corselet from Patroklos' body in the midst of battle, this stripping is like breaking the shell from a turtle: it brings to light an almost obscenely naked vulnerability, in the greatest possible contrast to the illusion of appearance. Once the brilliant metal falls away, he is revealed as *only Patroklos*, not Achilles. But at the same instant, Achilles himself becomes palpably mortal for the first time. His helmet rolls under the feet of the horses:

> Before this time it had not been permitted
> to defile in the dust this great helmet crested in horse-hair;
> rather it guarded the head and the gracious brow of a godlike
> man, Achilleus; but now Zeus gave it over to Hektor
> to wear on his head, Hektor whose own death was close to him.
> (16.796-800)

The poem puts such an ominous emphasis upon this transfer that it almost seems that the helmet bears the meaning of Patroklos' death, as though he merely brought a gift from Achilles to Hektor, or he himself were the gift, in some Stygian undercurrent of intentionality. Hektor sees him shrinking back among his companions to avoid death, already wounded in the back by Euphorbos, and cuts through the battle to stab him "in the depth of the belly" with his spear. Since Hektor has acted *as* Achilles through much of the poem, there is an uncanny appropriateness to the exchange: the dead Patroklos, noted for gentleness, moved by *aidos*, overcome by the fury of battle and the lust for glory, is offered to Hektor. What Hektor is to Achilles, Patroklos is to Hektor: a displaced self, both intimate and inimical—that is, a sacrifice— who prophesies as he dies Hektor's destiny to die at the hands of Achilles.

But the lost armor of Achilles has an even greater momentum. In Book XVII, Hektor withdraws from the fighting and gives his own armor to the Trojans to carry back into Troy—the gesture a warrior usually makes when he has killed an enemy and taken his armor. Then, having symbolically killed his former self, he puts on

> that armor immortal
> of Peleid Achilleus, which the Uranian gods had given
> to his loved father; and he in turn grown old had given it
> to his son; but a son who never grew old in his father's armor. (17.194-97)

Zeus watches the change of armor with remorse at what he himself is bringing about:

> When Zeus who gathers the clouds saw him, apart from the others
> arming himself in the battle gear of godlike Peleides,
> he stirred his head and spoke to his own spirit: 'Ah, poor wretch!
> There is no thought of death in your mind now, and yet death stands
> close beside you as you put on the immortal armor
> of a surpassing man. There are others who tremble before him.
> Now you have killed this man's dear friend, who was strong and gentle,
> and taken the armor, as you should not have done, from his shoulders
> and head. Still for the present I will invest you with great strength
> to make up for it that you will not come home out of the fighting,
> nor Andromache take from your hands the glorious arms of Achilleus.'
> He spoke, the son of Kronos, and nodded his head with the dark brows.
> (17.194-209)

On the one hand, Zeus gives Hektor the helmet to wear (16.799-800); on the other, he says that Hektor should have refused a gift that will cost him his return to Andromache. This reminder of Andromache, so close to Zeus's reiterated nod and his compensatory gift of honor for a short life, brings Andromache increasingly into an analogous relation to Thetis and points forward to another passage about marriage in Book XVIII. Mourning the loss of Patroklos, Achilles says to his mother,

> I have lost him, and Hektor, who killed him,

has stripped away that gigantic armor, a wonder to look on
and splendid, which the gods gave to Peleus, a glorious present,
on that day *they drove you to the marriage bed of a mortal.*
I wish you had gone on living then with the other goddesses
of the sea, and that Peleus had married some mortal woman. (18.82-87; my
emphasis)

It is a wedding gift that Hektor puts on, but not a gift that he will ever take
home. On the other hand, unlike his own marriage, the celebrated union that
the armor recalls and symbolizes was an act of force, for the gods "drove"
Thetis to Peleus' bed. As Thetis mourns when she goes to Hephaistos to ask
for new armor, "Of all the other sisters of the sea [Zeus] gave me to a mortal,
/ to Peleus, Aiakos' son, and *I had to endure mortal marriage* [in Greek, *the bed*] /
though much against my will" (18.432-34; my emphasis). From the perspective
of Peleus, marriage to Thetis is unimaginable glory, and his armor is its sign.
But there is also a sense in which Peleus resembles Paris, who identifies glory
with the most beautiful and desired woman and who says to Hektor, "Never
to be cast away are the gifts of the gods, magnificent." In some stories, the
apple "To the fairest" that led to the judgment of Paris—thus to the choice
of Helen and the Trojan War—was cast down by Eris on the day that the gods
drove Thetis to the marriage bed of a mortal. The armor brings that day back
in all its meaning, and Hektor puts it on like a bridegroom.

Hektor is increasingly short-lived the more he occupies the exact bodily
space of Achilles and his father Peleus. In the destructive downhill momentum of the gift of the armor, the gods gave it to Peleus, who gave it to his
son, who, in a gesture reflecting the motives of the gods (averting his own
destruction) and of his father (honoring his son) gives it to Patroklos—
from whom Hektor seizes it. His reward for being the proxy of Achilles is to
enter the meaning of Achilles, glorious and short-lived. This glorious shining compensates Achilles—and through him, any other mortal who enters
his meaning, indeed, mortality per se—for averting the threat to Olympos,
but it cannot come fully into appearance without its other side, its condition:
the bitter *achos* or anguish of ultimate loss.

Book XVIII of the *Iliad* has a greatness unique even in this poem. One comes to it immediately after a book of desperate fighting defined by the exact space of Patroklos' body. Hektor has rather ambiguously promised half the spoils (17.231) and an honor as great as his own to anyone who succeeds in dragging Patroklos' body back among the Trojans. The Greeks have an equal motivation: they must save it because the Trojans would mutilate it and dishonor them before Achilles. For them to yield would be intolerable, unforgivable—as Menelaos feels more than anyone else—but their best men are already injured, and the burden of defense again falls on great Aias, who has already fought nobly but unsuccessfully to stave off the Trojans from the ships. Out of their moiling labor runs Antilochos, now stripped of his armor (like Patroklos and Achilles) to be able to run quickly with the news of Patroklos' death. What follows upon his appearance to Achilles breaks the *Iliad* open into dimensions of emotional grandeur that are scarcely approachable elsewhere in literature. When Antilochos tells Achilles that Patroklos is dead and that the armor has been taken, this moment condenses into it the ultimate helplessness of Achilles before death and intensifies his rage beyond the mortal scale. Because of Patroklos' death, Achilles directs his supernatural *menis* so much against himself that Antilochos has to hold his hands to keep him from cutting his own throat (18.32-34). Like Othello murdering Desdemona, he has pushed his friend ahead of him into his fate, and the gleaming sign of Achilles' sacrificial origin in Peleus' glory and Thetis' *achos* covers the body of Hektor. In the wedding armor, Hektor now embodies Achilles' birth as a mortal, Achilles himself—the self that Achilles hates, the one who gave Patroklos over to death, the one who killed his friend. Hektor becomes the shining target of Achilles' self-hatred and fathomless despair.

The most famous part of Book XVIII is the set piece about the new armor that Hephaistos fashions for Achilles; the famous shield has garnered the most commentary and I will not add to it. I find the more compelling passages of this book at the beginning, in passages like this one:

> He cried out
> terribly, aloud, and the lady his mother heard him
> as she sat in the depths of the sea at the side of her aged father,
> and she cried shrill in turn, and the goddess gathered about her,
> all who along the depth of the sea were the daughters of Nereus.
> (18.34-38)

Then follows the beautiful naming, the litany of the sea-daughters ("For Glauke was there, Kymodoke and Thaleia, / Nesaie and Speio and Thoe, and ox-eyed Halia" and so on—thirty-three names in all) who take up her cry. When Achilles' anguish finds its immediate response, magnified in a threnody that comes up from the maternal depths, the uncanny effect is far more moving than Zeus's tears of blood over Sarpedon. Thetis comes this second time, not alone, but leading the sea daughters among the ships and shelters of the Achaians, and with bitter irony, she asks why Achilles is not happy with how things have gone since his request for honor. He makes the formal reply that we have seen, telling her (with a bitterness of his own) that Patroklos is dead, that the armor is taken, and that she should never have consented to the request of the gods to marry a mortal—or to marry at all. Since, as Thetis tells him, "it is decreed your death must come soon after Hektor's" (18.96), he must accept his own death as the cost of avenging his friend. He does so with a kind of resigned graciousness in what strikes me as his first fully conscious consent to his sacrificial destiny: "I will accept my own death, at whatever / time Zeus wishes to bring it about, and the other immortals" (18.115-16). In order to die, paradoxically, he will need new armor, and he will have to kill the man who wears Peleus' gift.

Hephaistos' gift will mark the moment at which Achilles fulfills the prophecy to be greater than his father. Perfectly fitted to his mortal body but separable from it, it will provide an objective earnest of the glory to come and a way of understanding how a living man might inhabit the immortal form being made from his life. But before the famous passage in which Hephaistos fashions the great shield comes the scene that to my mind best exemplifies the beginning of the revelation of Achilles. As he was in the first book after Agamemnon's insult, Achilles is at his most vulnerable when he encounters his divine mother. She comes to him once again in his *achos*. Despite the immediate provocation of Patroklos' death, he cannot fight, because when Apollo struck the armor from Patroklos, he reduced and exposed Achilles in the same instant. The difference is that Achilles in this interim of nakedness is also being moved toward an epiphany of his momentous hidden nature, one brought about by the intervention of Hera, who sends Iris to Achilles. Midway through Book XVIII, the greater and lesser Aias are still trying to pull the body of Patroklos from the fighting, but Hektor keeps charging in upon them and seizing Patroklos' feet to capture the corpse. At the point when he would have succeeded, Iris comes to Achilles with the message that he must intervene quickly, because "glorious Hektor / rages to haul [the corpse] away, since the anger within him is urgent / to cut the head from the soft neck and set it on sharp stakes" (18.175-77). When Achilles asks how he can fight without armor, she tells him simply to go to the ditch: "show yourself as you are to the Trojans" (198).

In Christopher Logue's version of the scene, Achilles makes an agonized cry that seems to sum up the misery of loss:

> Look north.
> Achilles on the rampart by the ditch:
> He lifts his face to 90; draws his breath;
> And from the bottom of his heart emits
> So long and loud and terrible a scream,
> The icy scabs at either end of earth
> Winced in their sleep; and in the heads that fought
> It seemed as if, and through his voice alone,
> The whole world's woe could be abandoned to the sky.
> And in that instant all the fighting glassed. (196)

All the emphasis here falls on Achilles' mortal anguish (and its effect on the polar icecaps), but in Homer, Achilles begins to appear as uniquely favored by the gods just at this moment. Others in the *Iliad* have been helped by gods (Paris snatched from Menelaos in Book III, for example, or Aineias hurled from danger by Poseidon); others, such as Diomedes in Book V, not to

mention Hektor, have had their own powers divinely enhanced. But there is
nothing like this:

> Achilleus, *the beloved of Zeus*, rose up, and Athene
> swept about his powerful shoulders the fluttering aegis;
> and she, the divine among goddesses, about his head circled
> a golden cloud, and kindled from it a flame far-shining. (18.203-6; my
> emphasis)

Has Achilles before his consent to die been called "the beloved of Zeus"?
Clothed with the terrifying aegis, Achilles becomes a form of fire, burning yet
still intact and unconsumed. In the *Aeneid*, the image of unconsuming fire that
plays upon the head of Ascanius signifies his protected destiny, and the
Christian imagery of the Pentecostal descent of the Holy Spirit is emblematic
of divinization. Rather than focus on the specific meaning of this manifestation of Achilles' ironic divinity, however, Homer directs one's attention to an
entirely different scene:

> As when a flare goes up into the high air from a city
> from an island far away, with enemies fighting about it
> who all day long are in the hateful division of Ares
> fighting from their own city, but as the sun goes down signal
> fires blaze out one after another, so that the glare goes
> pulsing high for men of the neighboring islands to see it,
> in case they might come over in ships to beat off the enemy;
> so from the head of Achilles the blaze shot in the bright air. (18.207-14)

This simile poses what Steven Pinker, the cognitive scientist, calls a problem
in reverse-engineering: one has to start with the made thing and then decide
what it was designed to do. From an obvious point of similarity—the flame—
one is taken into a world of island kingdoms whose only communication,
ambiguous at best, is by means of signal fires after dark, across all the thwart
currents and uncertain winds and saltwater distances between them. What
purposes do the excess and apparent irrelevance in the simile serve?

Someone sees the signal fires go up from a distant island. Who?
Ultimately, it must be someone who can decide whether to muster the ships

and help, or rather to let the battle go as it will, since it is someone else's trouble. If he decides to help, he puts himself and his own men at risk, but he makes an ally, forges a reciprocal bond, and seizes upon the chance of winning glory. There is really no hint, however, about who this watcher might be—whether, for example, his married daughter lives in the city under attack, whether his estranged brother is its king. Like the simile itself, the fires signal without specification, without a particular address. Why are the signal fires compared to the fire coming from the head of Achilles? One's first impulse would be to identify him, not as the besieged city, but as the one seeing the distant signal fire. The Achaians fighting for Patroklos' body seem comparable to those defending the island city under attack. By appearing beside the ditch, Achilles acts as the rescuer; he has already committed himself to help, even at the cost of his own life. But like so many other similes in Homer, this one keeps turning its reflective surface, and Achilles becomes—in this same act of appearing— the one who needs rescuing, but for whom there can be no help. Vulnerability, friendship, and desperate beseeching seem implied by the signal fire in the simile, whereas in his person he has never appeared more terrifying and immortal. Patroklos' dead body is his own; he is himself the isolated city, whose very signaling means that it will soon be burning. This flame prophesies both his divinization in fame and the coming funeral pyre that will consume his flesh. At the same time, as the simile keeps turning, the blaze announces the end of the only besieged city literally present: Troy, whose destruction is certain from this moment of his return. This simile therefore anticipates the one that will describe the reaction of Troy to seeing the naked body of Hektor, newly stripped of the Peleian armor, tied to the back of Achilles' chariot and dragged around the city: "It was most like what would have happened, if all lowering / Troy had been burning top to bottom in fire" (22. 410-11).

Aflame, savior and victim, heralding both his own destruction and Troy's, Achilles stands beside the ditch focused and burning as though all the daylight were condensed into one incandescent human form and all sound of battle into his body as its instrument. Logue omits both the help of Athene, who augments his shout, and the simile that immediately follows:

> As loud as comes the voice that is screamed out by a trumpet
> by murderous attackers who beleaguer a city,
> so then high and clear went up the voice of Aiakides.
> But the Trojans, when they heard the brazen voice of Aiakides,
> the heart was shaken in all, and the very floating-maned horses
> turned their chariots about, since their hearts saw the coming afflictions.
> The charioteers were dumbfounded as they saw the unwearied dangerous
> fire that played above the head of great-hearted Peleion
> blazing, and kindled by the goddess grey-eyed Athene. (18.219-27)

Besieged city, rescuer, and now attacker as well, Achilles increasingly attracts all the roles and likenesses, like a god. Twelve Trojans, Homer says, died "upon their own chariots and spears" (18.231) in the panic caused by his appearance, and Patroklos' body is easily rescued by the Achaians, as the Trojans tremble for the destruction to come.

In the plan of Zeus, this moment of unveiling seems necessary to counterbalance the glorification of Hektor that has already taken place. In other words, if Hektor can now appear on the battlefield shining in the Peleian armor, then Achilles himself, naked of armor, must somehow be shown to be even greater. Like a Moses, he stands for an instant disclosed by the miracle. Or perhaps even more, he resembles Christ in the Transfiguration, since this moment for all its practical effect seems meant primarily to reveal who he is and what he will do rather than what he has done before. It does little good to ask what Achilles has accomplished to merit this revelation. Morally, he has no ground to stand on. In his pride, he has brought the bloodlust of Hektor down on his own army, he has haughtily refused the offer of reconciliation that would have spared more lives, including that of Patroklos, and in doing so he has even allowed his friend to die in his place. Regardless of what his acts might have been before Agamemnon's insult, he has *done* nothing in this poem but to allow the gods to enhance his own honor until it occupies a new, incomparable place, no longer dependent on men like Agamemnon. But the very character of divine honor under these conditions—first the loss of Briseis, then the estrangement of his friends, and finally the death of Patroklos—has been emptied of desirability: it is anguish and stark isolation, not divine plenitude. The satisfactions that lie before him are those of Hell. Having sought a godhead of honor, he has found instead the *achos* of endless absence, because his true nature is not divine but human. If he could kill himself with sufficient satisfaction, he would do so, but his own suicide could not begin to propitiate the self-loathing that has now opened within him. He will shortly turn his own Hell toward Hektor and the Trojans, even there despairing of adequate recompense, since his injury is bottomless and metaphysical. Yet at the same time, the causes of Achilles' anguish—his illusions, his losses, his ties to his father—also keep him within the range of humanity, and even now in the nobility of his nature, he is consenting to give up his single great life in magnanimous recompense for another, lesser man.

Christ is true God and true man, but what is Achilles? By no means a god incarnate; in fact, it makes little sense to think of him as "half-divine," since his mortality is not partial, but total. Neither is he a dying god, like Dionysus, nor a hero whose death will divinize him, like Herakles. Achilles is a man like Hektor—yet his distance from Hektor is as great as the distance between a man and a god. His only real privilege stems from being poised in his ontological splendor against what has been taken from him by his being born at all: his "what-if" existence as the Son of Zeus, the ruler of the universe. His very life as a mortal—in anyone else the condition of being able to appear and *be* at all—is the supreme deprivation, and he is made to feel *that* loss as part of his greatness. But how is his state of mind even recognizable, as it certainly is, if every mortal does not somehow intuit the same prior deprivation? In fact, in one way of thinking, the worst, least gifted man has the greatest claim against cosmic justice, since he was deprived, not only of supreme immortality, but even of the character and talents and looks that might have made him a respected human being. In the bitter egalitarian language of rights—the kind of thinking that characterizes a Thersites—this "ugliest man" has a *right* to be Zeus, if there is going to be a Zeus. Achilles does not skew the nature of gifts this radically, but on the other hand he clearly thinks of his mother's marriage to a mortal from the perspective of a metaphysical plaintiff, and he is a long way from being able to say of Zeus, as Dante's Piccarda says of God, "In His will is our peace."

It would be easy, in the Romantic tradition that praises Milton for being of the devil's party without knowing it, to claim that Achilles exceeds Christ in the high, unsparing pathos of his character—that Christ pities too readily, that Achilles' anticipated *pieta* in Book XVIII is made even more anguished by the fact that his mother is immortal, and so on. The crucial comparisons, however, lie in the questions of conscious mortality and of obedience to the frame of the given destiny. Achilles clearly faces what Heidegger calls "death as death," but can Christ do so, if He is conscious of the power to overcome it? In *Paradise Lost*, for example, before the fall of Adam when the Son first accepts the necessity of His sacrificial incarnation, he says to the Father:

> Though now to Death I yield, and am his due,
> All that of me can die, yet, that debt paid,
> Thou wilt not leave me in the loathsome grave
> His prey, nor suffer my unspotted soul
> For ever with corruption there to dwell;
> But I shall rise victorious, and subdue
> My vanquisher, spoiled of his vaunted spoil. (3.246-52)

In the Gospels, He weeps when Lazarus lies dead in the tomb, but He also has the power to restore the life of his friend by calling on His father. Achilles, like Othello, looks on the dead body of Patroklos, unable to muster "that Promethean heat / That will [his] former light relume." Yet like Christ, Achilles can call on his divine parent to effect a miracle, in this case the incorruptibility of Patroklos' body. On the morning that Thetis brings him his new armor from Hephaistos, Achilles expresses his fear "that flies might get into the wounds beaten by bronze in his body / and breed worms in them, and these make foul the body, / seeing that the life is killed in him, and that all his flesh may be rotted" (19.25-27). She promises him that even if he lies there a year, Patroklos' body will be firmer than ever, and to guarantee it, "through the nostrils of Patroklos she distilled / ambrosia and red nectar, so that his flesh might not spoil" (19.39-40). Still, Thetis does not restore the life itself, as the Father does for Jesus. Does death that can be miraculously overcome remain "death as death," or does one rather have to feel, as Lear does with the corpse of Cordelia, "Thou'lt come no more, / Never, never, never, never, never!" to experience its true character?

The relation between Achilles and Christ seems to me the crucial one because, first in the Greek world with its succession of divine hegemonies, then in the Jewish one prepared by Scripture, the centrally destined figure does not become a sacrifice as a result of his circumstances, but is in fact *conceived* to be sacrificed, so that the whole of his mortal life bears the particular consecrated radiance and intimacy of the victim about to be consumed. As true man, Christ lives His life toward this destiny; every healing and exorcism has as its inner meaning a restoration of the divine image, brought about by the man whose deep intimacy with the body and the psyche of those He heals comes from His own sacrificial consecration of His mortal being, in its emergent change, as a free gift of obedience to the Father. Being true man requires that He not consider equality with God something to be grasped at, that he deliberately refuse occasions of being made manifest in terms of glory. Otherwise, he would not experience the sacrificial nature of limitation, nor would he undergo the truly obliterating metaphysical evil of death as death. If death is the result of sin, its inmost character lies in the turn away from the divine plenitude of being, into the ungrounded self whose illusions are ultimately revealed as an abyss. Christ's sacrificial merit lies in undergoing this abyss of divine absence as true man, yet without turning away from the Father. He enters the inmost character of sin without sin. This act means emptying Himself of all divine plenitude and accepting this predestined deprivation of being, even to the point when He cries out, "My God, my God, why have you abandoned me?" Only the absolute refusal of pride, given more profound temptations and darker ironies than those that wrack Achilles, can make possible the glorification of God in His transformation of mortality.

Achilles, on the other hand, has never *chosen* to take on the excruciating limitation of time and death; rather, mortality has been forced onto him through a divine mother who never said, with the graciousness of Mary, "Be it done to me according to thy word." Instead, she was forced into bed with a mortal. The skies have never opened above her son with the assurance, "This is my beloved Son." Everything about his being lies athwart; everything has a profound unfairness that comes most fully into focus when one watches the desperation of his attempt to seize upon the recompense of glory. When Milton conceived the figure of Satan, he drew largely upon Achilles, especially the "sense of injured merit." But it bears repeating that Achilles is not a satanic figure. In Milton's account, Satan rebels from God precisely at the moment when the Son is "begotten" in Heaven and elevated above Lucifer. Satan's pride immediately converts into envy of the privileged Son—more like Iago than Achilles. Achilles has no rival in glory, either in the generations of heroes before him (not even Herakles), or in the ages after him. According to Plutarch, Julius Caesar wept because he had not accomplished as much as Alexander at the same age, but Alexander the Great envied Achilles. When Odysseus speaks to Achilles in the underworld, he wonders at his incomparable blessedness, receiving, of course, the famous reply that Achilles would rather be thrall to another man and still alive than king of all the dead; at the end of the *Odyssey*, Agamemnon also emphasizes how blessed Achilles remains. After describing how "immortal crying arose and spread over / the great sea" (24.48-49) when Thetis came out of the ocean depths with her "sea girls," how "all the nine Muses in sweet antiphonal singing / mourned you" (24.60-61), he tells Achilles how "even now you have died, you have not lost your name, but always / in the sight of all mankind your fame shall be great, Achilles" (24.93-94). In terms of honor, then, Achilles has no reason to envy anyone. His problem is rather that all glory, even as he begins the destruction that will guarantee it, has been revealed to him as bitter vanity, and he has not yet found his way to that inner authority from which he can act with gracious benignity. He has not met the man of sorrows.

MOMENTS after Achilles stands by the ditch and shouts, Poulydamas once again cautions Hektor not to trust in glory. Alone among them, this man "born on the same night" as Hektor (18.251) sees that if Achilles catches them still on the plain in the morning, "there will be many Trojans the vultures / and dogs will feed on" (18.271-72). Instead, he wants to go back inside the city he evokes with an almost childlike longing:

> If all of us do as I say, though it hurts us to do it,
> this night we will hold our strength in the market place, and the great walls
> and the gateways, and the long, smooth-planed, close-joined gate timbers
> that close to fit them shall defend our city. Then, early
> in the morning, under dawn, we shall arm ourselves in our war gear
> and take stations along the walls. (18.273-76)

Homer himself calls this advice "good sense," but Poulydamas' fate seems to be like Cassandra's, because neither Hektor nor the other Trojans will listen to him. If they could hear him, they would recognize the way in which Achilles' presence has already revealed the city to them once again, with its "long, smooth-planed, close-joined gate timbers." Instead they follow Hektor's "counsel of evil" to stay on the plain and win glory the next day. So doing, they commit themselves to Hektor's fate.

As his own course of action inevitably overtakes him and Hektor stands outside the walls of the city "in front of the gateway" (22.35), his parents plead with him, both making one request: that Hektor come inside. Old Priam looks out at Achilles coming across the flat land, remembers the loss of his other sons to this man, and has no expectation that Achilles will give up Hektor for ransom:

> 'Come then inside the wall, my child, so that you can rescue
> the Trojans and the women of Troy, neither win the high glory
> for Peleus' son, and yourself be robbed of your very life.' (22.56-58)

Even when Priam pictures himself cut down in front of his own doorway, with his own dogs licking his blood, he cannot move his son. His longing, the whole longing of Troy, is to have the walls of Troy *contain* Hektor. No one has the slightest doubt that Achilles will win this contest. Hektor's own mother reveals her breasts and tells him to reverence them—to have *aidos* for what once comforted him—and to defend Troy from inside the wall, because

'if he kills you I can no longer
mourn you on the death-bed, sweet branch, of child of my bearing,
nor can your generous wife mourn you, but a big way from us
beside the ships of the Argives the running dogs will feed on you.' (22.86-89)

Unfortunately, all these supplications simply add to Hektor's shame. How can he appear before Andromache now, having caused the destruction of his people—including his own brothers—by refusing Poulydamas' advice (22.99-103)? How can he hear someone say, "'Hektor believed in his own strength and ruined his people'" (22.107)? If he frightened Astyanax before (in his visit home in Book VI), how much more would he if he came inside wearing Achilles' four-horned and hollow-eyed helmet, the very one worn by the man who killed Andromache's father and brothers and who now comes toward him like the star that brings on fever and death?

Aidos should have kept him inside the walls and could draw him there still—but the ironies of the pleading are almost too intense. Held in place by the armor of Achilles and his past deeds *as* Achilles, he stands outside *looking like* his city's enemy, which he has indeed become through the refusal of Poulydamas' advice. He would not be Troy's enemy if he were able to come inside without being shamed, but the very excess that makes him look like Achilles makes him unable to come inside. From all appearances, then, Priam and Hekabe call out to Achilles; they plead with Achilles to come inside the wall. In one sense, they unknowingly plead for their own destruction. But in another sense, as Hektor stands in this terrible, intimate estrangement from his parents and his wife, kept out rather than in by *aidos*, his appearance uncannily begins to make Achilles himself a displaced son being beckoned back into the human bonds. Once Hektor appears as Achilles, what happens to him also happens to his great enemy.

It is in this sense that one should see Hektor's actual death as a sacrifice: not simply Hektor *for* or *as* Achilles, but Achilles as Hektor. After Hektor flees three times around the city and Athene finally brings him to a stand, then betrays him, Hektor realizes that no one can help him; at this point, when he becomes most completely himself, not so much disillusioned as undeluded, Hektor is no longer the snake (22.93) or the fawn (22.190), but someone

> like a high-flown eagle
> who launches himself out of the murk of the clouds on the flat land
> to catch away a tender lamb or a shivering hare; so
> Hektor made his swoop....(22.308-12)

Seth Schein misses this simile when he writes that "Hektor is never compared to a predator, but instead several times to a predator's potential victim" (180). The simile presents Achilles, not Hektor, as the victim: Hektor swoops at him, as though *Achilles* were a "tender lamb or a shivering hare." Almost as though he were the image in a mirror, Achilles responds:

> and Achilleus
> charged, the heart within him loaded with savage fury.
> In front of his chest the beautiful elaborate great shield
> covered him, and with the glittering helm with four horns
> he nodded; the lovely golden fringes were shaken about it
> which Hephaistos had driven close along the horn of the helmet.
> (22.311-16)

The whole poem has insured that the outcome of this battle will not be a question: Hektor will die. Moreover, Achilles *nods*, the necessary gesture of the victim; the helmet's four horns are taken, no doubt, from sacrificed beasts, while its fringes recall the head of Zeus in the nod to Thetis, when the hair swept down from his divine head and shook Olympos (1.528-30). Achilles accepts his death—and the whole plan of Zeus that includes his begetting— by accepting the gift of Hektor, who occupies the same intimate space (this armor that is the womb of glory for those who are short-lived) given to Peleus at the same time that Achilles was engendered. In the reversibility of the gesture, Hektor concedes to his death by dedicating his whole meaning to *kleos*: he does not want to die "inglorious [*akleios*]," but to "do some big thing first, that men to come shall know of it" (22.304-5). Everything will be destroyed in being given, and everything that rises to its Achillean destruction will be preserved forever in song.

The destruction that preserves, the sacrifice that speaks, finds its image in the way that Hektor dies. As the two charge each other, Achilles looks for the weak spot in his own armor:

> He was eyeing Hektor's splendid body, to see where it might best
> give way, but all the rest of the skin was held in the armor,
> brazen and splendid, he stripped when he cut down the strength of Patroklos;
> yet showed where the collar-bones hold the neck from the shoulders,
> the throat, where death of the soul comes most swiftly; in this place
> brilliant Achilleus drove the spear as he came on in fury,
> and clean through the soft part of the neck the spearpoint was driven.
> Yet the ash spear heavy with bronze did not sever the windpipe,
> so that Hektor could still make exchange of words spoken. (22.321-29)

Certainly others in the poem have died speaking, most notably Sarpedon (16.492-501) and Patroklos (16.844-54), but no one else dies in a way that combines the imagery of sacrificial death with the capacity for speech specifically necessary for *kleos*. Hektor's last words, like Patroklos', are a prophecy of his killer's death, in this case Achilles' destruction by Paris and Apollo *in the Skaian gates* (22.360). Hektor's last words in life recapitulate his whole movement in the poem, because, as Achilles says in Book 9,

> 'when I was in the fighting among the Achaians
> Hektor would not drive his attack beyond the wall's shelter
> but would come forth *only so far as the Skaian gates* and the oak tree.
> There once he endured me alone, and barely escaped my onslaught.' (353-56; my emphasis)

As Hektor dies because he left the gates and so broke into his own city, so Achilles will die meeting Apollo, and the fateful man who took the glorious forbidden woman, in the Skaian gates.

F ROM a distance, Hektor's career in the *Iliad* has a clearly discernible trajectory. It begins in Book 2 with a call from Iris to organize the Trojan troops. His first day of battle is undistinguished, but Book 8 marks the beginning of his glorification, when Zeus directly inspires (that is, deludes) him and continues to bend the battle for him until Hektor sets fire to the ships in direct fulfillment of Achilles' request. From the time that he kills Patroklos in Book 16 and then puts on his armor, until his death in Book 22, Hektor hubristically and fatally enters the exact, intimate space of Achilles' own body, so that, in Zeus's plan, he can be sacrificed to Achilles, *as* Achilles, and Achilles can himself be fittingly glorified in being sacrificed for the gods. From the end of Book 22 until his return to his kinsmen for burial at the end of the poem, he is a corpse in Achilles' possession, an emblem of hated mortality, completely subject to the will of his conqueror, except that the gods themselves protect his now-exalted body from decay and mutilation.

After the death of Patroklos, Achilles can hardly eat, because he appears to feel a particular new horror—a prohibitive nausea—at the dead body and its edible flesh. How can he eat when his beloved friend, in death, might attract birds or hungry dogs, as we have seen, and "'flies might get into the wounds beaten by bronze in his body / and breed worms in them, and these make foul the body, seeing / that the life is killed in him, and that all his flesh may be rotted'" (19.25-27)? The condition of mortality has nothing worse in it than this capacity of the living form to become noxious flesh—except perhaps the eagerness of other life to feed on it. Precisely because he loathes the flesh, Achilles wants for Hektor the opposite of everything sacrificial. Sacrifice, with its purifying fire, not only invites men into communion with the dazzling bodies of gods untainted by the decay that inheres in *flesh*, but also alleviates the horror of flesh by the sacred process of cooking. In the funeral pyre, by analogy, one loses the recognizable bodily image of the beloved, but on the other hand, one saves this likeness from rotting or being eaten.

As the inimical self, soaked in Achillean identity, Hektor's body comes into Achilles' possession to be loathed and molested. In the plan of Zeus, Hektor's body in its pure, dumb passivity can fully satisfy Achilles' dark lust to treat the flesh that is his own condition as an abject object. Achilles wants to deny Hektor's body participation in any kind of formal communion that mitigates the horror of being mere flesh; he *wills* Hektor to be torn apart by speechless beasts without the capacity for *kleos*, to be eaten, to rot; he longs to keep Hektor away from the rite of fire that holds men and gods both apart and together in the beautiful and melancholy forms of sacrifice. It is in this light, I think, that one should read Achilles' "cannibalism," when he says to the dying Hektor,

> 'I wish only that my spirit and fury would drive me
> to hack your meat away and eat it raw for the things that
> you have done to me. So there is no one who can hold the dogs off
> from your head....' (22.346-49)

Achilles means to say that he wants no ritual formalities for the man who reduced Patroklos to dead flesh; therefore, he represents Hektor's body as itself nothing but flesh to be eaten. Ironically, however, Achilles' savage wish to be bestial enough to consume his enemy and live off his flesh is subtly converted into the larger design, provided for in the plan of Zeus, to take in his enemy and make him over into himself, to be in communion with Troy and have "Hektor"—that is, a profoundly relational *aidos*—within him. The transformation of the darkest human passions into noble generosity is the ultimate aim of the plan of Zeus. Through this transformation of Hektor's loathed body into the sacred gift that Achilles himself gives, he will insure the justice and efficacy of the sacrifice to which the son of Thetis has already nodded his great gold-fringed and four-horned head.

From the time that he kills Hektor until the end of the poem, Achilles exists in the liminal space of intimacy and anguish that characterizes the sacrificial victim chosen but not yet killed. The gods especially are aware that he is *about to die*: his treatment of Hektor's corpse seems to hold them on Olympos, gathered in a kind of suspense, but for a long time unable to intervene. Apollo, with his instinct for the formal limit, complains vehemently about the abuse:

> 'So Achilleus has destroyed pity, and there is not in him
> any shame [*aidos*], which does much harm to men but profits them also.
> For a man must some day lose one who was even closer
> than this; a brother from the same womb or a son.' (24.44-47)

Equally bitter in her rebuke of Apollo, Hera distinguishes Achilles from Hektor by reminding all the gods of the occasion that underlies the whole poem and the whole war:

> 'Hektor was mortal, and suckled at the breast of a woman,
> while Achilleus is the child of a goddess, one whom I myself
> nourished and brought up and gave her as bride to her husband
> Peleus, one dear to the hearts of the immortals, for you all
> went, you gods, to the wedding; and you too feasted among them
> and held your lyre, o friend of the evil, faithless forever.' (24.58-63)

The verb used of the gods' participation in the wedding (*antiao*) is used elsewhere in the poem (1.67) to signify their acceptance of a sacrifice. They all *accepted* the sacrificial wedding of Thetis, and now there must be no question about the honor due to Achilles, begotten to die for their sakes and celebrated at his conception by Apollo himself.

    Zeus fulfills his initial promise to Thetis and places the whole of the last book in the framework of sacrifice by the way he sets about to retrieve the body of Hektor:

> 'Hera, be not utterly angry with the gods, for there shall not
> be the same pride of place given both. Yet Hektor also
> was loved by the gods, best of all the mortals in Ilion.
> I loved him too. He never failed of gifts to my liking.
> Never yet has my altar gone without fair sacrifice,
> the smoke and the savour of it, since that is our portion of honor.
> The stealing of him we will dismiss, for it is not possible
> to take bold Hektor secretly from Achilleus, since always
> his mother is near him night and day; but it would be better
> if one of the gods would summon Thetis here to my presence
> so that I can say a close word to her, and see that Achilleus
> is given gifts by Priam and gives back the body of Hektor. (24.65-76)

In Book I, Achilles sent Thetis to Zeus with a request for an honor owed him; now Zeus sends Thetis to Achilles with a request for him to let go, to relent and have mercy, to accept gifts and to give the gift of Hektor in return. This will not be an occasion in which the gods intervene directly by taking advantage of their specifically divine strengths. Earlier, with other men, Aphrodite felt no scruples, for example, about snatching Paris from the duel with Menelaos in Book 3 or saving Aineias in Book 5. Apollo similarly intervened with the body of Sarpedon in Book 16, and Poseidon hurled the differently fated Aineias from the battle in Book 20. Zeus seems concerned, however, that Achilles be approached even more carefully than he approaches the other Olympian gods; he issues no direct threat, as he did with Athene and Hera (8.399-406) and with Poseidon (15.162-67), but says only that he is angered. Instead of letting "clear-sighted Argeiphontes" steal the body (24.109), he alerts Achilles to the fact that Priam will be coming and lets the actual request for the body be played out movingly and beautifully on the mortal level.

After Hermes has lifted the "huge door-bar" of the gate of Achilles' camp for him (24.455), the old man comes unexpectedly into Achilles' shelter as a suppliant. Tall Priam rushes in, grasps Achilles' knees as Thetis had grasped the knees of Zeus, kisses the manslaughtering hands, and says: "'Achilleus like the gods, remember your father, one who / is of years like mine, and on the door-sill of sorrowful old age'" (24.486-87). What is it, then, being played out here? Why is this scene, which ends with Priam taking away the body of his son, the necessary completion of the whole action that began with an old man offering ransom for his daughter?

In the immediate context, Priam's astounding consciousness of his position moves Achilles far more than the deed alone would have: "I have gone through what no other mortal on earth has gone through: / I put my lips to the hands of the man who has killed my children" (24.505-6). Hearing the knowledge of abjection spoken and consciously accepted, Achilles recognizes it as ennobling: this is the man of sorrows. Only Priam's suffering (or Niobe's) can approximate the intensity of Achilles' own; with the death of most of his fifty sons, nineteen of them "from the womb of a single mother," and the greatest of them Hektor, he has known the loss of the future at Achilles' hands in a way that is like Achilles' experience of Patroklos' death and mortality itself as infinite loss. Strangely, he saves Achilles from despair.

All through the poem, he has been witnessing in Hektor a version of himself, first as the one who acted as the displaced embodiment of his *menis* in his absence from battle, then as the object—dressed as himself—of his direct hatred. Now in this long-prepared, complex instant of recognition, Achilles experiences Troy from the inside, as though his own stark pride had been its walls. Priam's grief for Hektor, so far beyond fear and ordinary shame, finally lets him inside the gates of the isolated and despairing self. His signal fires had called to Priam, and now Achilles has been broken into, not by rage, but by sorrow and the speech of supplication. He discovers a new communion with the great enemy sacrificed to him as part of the gift-obligation of the gods. Hektor's return for the terrible Achillean gift of *kleos* is this miraculous presence: a father, a city within.

Achilles warns Priam not to be too hasty about taking back Hektor or to make too much of his body, because he knows that his rage can flare out again. But already his disposition toward the body he has tried for so long to mutilate and punish has changed. The gods have not let the corpse suffer corruption. As Hermes describes him to Priam,

> 'now here is the twelfth dawn
> he has lain there, nor does his flesh decay, nor do worms feed
> on him, they who devour men who have fallen in battle.
> It is true, Achilleus drags him at random around his beloved
> companion's tomb, as dawn on dawn appears, yet he cannot
> mutilate him; you yourself can see when you go there
> how fresh with dew he lies, and the blood is all washed from him,
> nor is there any corruption, and all the wounds have been closed up
> where he was struck, since many drove the bronze in his body.' (24.413-21)

The incorrupt body, understood as a sign of holiness in all religions, is a gift not only to Priam but to Achilles as well. When he has his serving women wash and anoint the corpse, he has to recognize in the miracle of Hektor's freshness and healing the futility of his own rage against the flesh. His enemy's body becomes the object of his care, largely because Achilles can now imagine Peleus,

'who outshone all men beside for his riches
and pride of possession, and was lord over the Myrmidons. Thereto
the gods bestowed an immortal wife on him, who was mortal.
But even on him the god piled evil also. There was not
any generation of strong sons born to him in his great house
but a single all-untimely child he had, and I give him
no care as he grows old, since far from the land of my fathers
I sit here in Troy'.... (24.535-42)

The mortal body that Achilles has from Peleus—symbolized here by the body from which Achilles actually stripped his father's armor—is not his enemy. Not flesh, but what Milton's Satan will call "that fixed mind, / And high disdain from sense of injured merit"—he who could have been the mightiest of gods —has been Achilles' enemy, and this proud despair has tempted even good Hektor into the space of its isolated grandeur.

The miraculous body becomes a sign from the gods of the greater immortal nature of *kleos*; onto this displaced corpse of Achilles comes the great condensation of the poem's significance. When Achilles puts Hektor's body on the litter himself and lifts it into the mule wagon, then goes in to eat with Priam, the son of Thetis does the greatest honor to the son of Peleus. The central sacrifice on which the gods depend, in being accepted by its victim, the one man whose objection to mortality has the greatest justice, makes possible for other mortals a participation in this beautiful depth of kindness. Achilles in the end will not have been born as a sacrifice *to* the gods, but by the gods for the immortal poem. By sustaining the immortals and binding them forever to the speech of men, Achilles' death sustains the infinite dignity of mortality. But he gives up his metaphysical quarrel in a gesture that widens the gift and makes it eternally dynamic: he gives Hektor to Priam for the rite of burning. He lets Hektor's burial stand for his own.

T HE *kleos aphthiton* or everlasting glory promised to Achilles *is* poetic form, understood as the completion of a unique sacrifice. Given our own modern (or postmodern) context, the acceptance of this sacrificial dimension might seem belittling, like consenting to the enslavement of others because their pitiable lot allows one to meditate with exquisite poignancy on thwarted opportunity. It might seem more noble to defy the rhetorical structures of limitation as though they were "mind-forged manacles" that suborned one's freedom in advance; it might feel more righteous to reject the principle of sacrificial form on ideological grounds.

Percy Bysshe Shelley, for example, intuited how crucially the *Iliad* enforces a deep, tragic acceptance of mortality and limitation under the divine regime of Zeus. In the spirit of the early French Revolution, he scorned the idea of reconciling "the Champion [Prometheus] with the Oppressor [Zeus] of mankind." In Aeschylus' lost play *Prometheus Unbound*, the one who reveals the threatening destiny of Thetis is not Themis (as in Pindar) but Prometheus, and his disclosure of the secret becomes the condition of his liberation and reconciliation. In high mythological dudgeon, exercising his prerogative to be the unacknowledged legislator of mankind, Shelley has Prometheus withhold the secret and thus prevent Thetis from saving the order of Jupiter by marrying a mortal. In his own *Prometheus Unbound*, Jupiter, unwarned, consummates the marriage with Thetis and conceives the "son," symbolized not in any one figure but in a new age of equality. The mortal son is never conceived at all, the *Iliad* vanishes (a deft solution to the "anxiety of influence"), and by implication, the sacrificial life of Achilles no longer supports an order of tyranny very much like, one supposes, either the *ancien regime* or the reign of the "old, mad, blind, despised and dying king" in England. When Spirit of the Earth praises the new regime after the overthrow of Jupiter, she stresses the absence of "Sceptres, tiaras, swords, and chains, and tomes," all the regalia that

> imaged to the pride of kings and priests
> A dark yet mighty faith, a power as wide
> As is the world it wasted, and are now
> But an astonishment; even so the tools
> And emblems of its last captivity,
> Amid the dwellings of the peopled earth,
> Stand, not o'erthrown, but unregarded now. (3.173-79)

Without the mortality of Achilles, in other words, Jupiter would long ago have been overthrown by his successor, and man would now be "Sceptreless, free, uncircumscribed," not to mention "Equal, unclassed, tribeless, and nationless, / Exempt from awe, worship, degree, the king / Over himself; just, gentle, wise" (3.194-97).

Shelley finds in tragic limitation mere waste and slavery and captivity and humiliation and self-contempt, not the intensification of form. But next to the *Iliad*, Shelley's poem, to quote one of its own climactic lines, is "Pinnacled dim in the intense inane." Thinking that he has been liberating poetry from its eons of oppression under a kind of Nobodaddy, he gives away the crucial principle of form that Homer discovered in the implications of a sacrificial mortality; he tries to literalize the anagogical level—the poetic equivalent of what Eric Voegelin calls "immanentizing the eschaton." There can never be, in the poetry of Shelley, any scene to match in its sublimity the night on the beach at Troy when, after all the elaborate preparations, the funeral pyre of Patroklos will not light:

> Then swift-footed
> brilliant Achilleus thought of one more thing that he must do.
> He stood apart from the pyre and made his prayer to the two winds
> Boreas and Zephyros, north wind and west, and promised them splendid
> offerings, and much outpouring from a golden goblet entreated them
> to come, so that the bodies might with best speed burn in the fire
> and the timber burst into flame. (23.192-98)

With the habitual delay of the poem, one then leaves the immediate scene: the goddess Iris hears Achilles' prayer and goes to the house of Zephyros, where all the winds are having a feast. Despite their polite invitations to have her join them, she refuses to take a seat because of her urgency but entreats them to do the bidding of Achilles and set ablaze the funeral pyre of Patroklos. These graceful and courteous Weathers, personified at their ease, now resume their full elemental natures in a scene that raises the hair on the back of one's neck:

> She spoke so, and went away, and they with immortal
> clamour rose up, and swept the clouds in confusion before them.

They came with a sudden blast upon the sea, and the waves rose
under the whistling wind. They came to the generous Troad
and hit the pyre, and a huge inhuman blaze rose, roaring.
Nightlong they piled the flames on the funeral pyre together
and blew with a screaming blast, and nightlong swift-footed Achilleus
from a golden mixing-bowl, with a two-handled goblet in his hand,
drew the wine and poured it on the ground and drenched the ground with it,
and called upon the soul of unhappy Patroklos. (23.212-21)

This kind of scene, with its balances of exquisite courtesy and barbaric splendor, is impossible either for Logue or Shelley. Its power depends upon the sacrificial *habitus* of formal intensification and transformation of violence through indirection and delay. The ritual of destruction derives its superb melancholy from one's recognition that Achilles has not only lost Patroklos and killed Hector, but also that he acts in full consciousness of what is coming. Achilles knows that his own death will come soon, very soon, and this great pyre on the beach at night is the signal fire that his mortality sends into the dark. Its beauty is what beckons God.

Not Conclusion

Perhaps you smile at me. I could not stop for that. My business is circumference. An ignorance, not of customs, but if caught with the dawn, or the sunset see me, myself the only kangaroo among the beauty, sir, if you please, it afflicts me, and I thought that instruction would take it away.

— Emily Dickinson to Thomas Wentworth Higginson, July 1862

W HY does literature matter? Mistrusting theory, not so much in itself as in its recent displacement of literature, I have been drawn, in trying to frame an answer, to contemporary novelists and poets who have garnered certain kinds of honor and to the greatest poets of the past, whose freshness has never left them. Several dimensions of literature that seem to me insufficiently addressed in the current discussion have kept emerging: the experience of form as the poetic mode of knowledge, the essential pleasure in world becoming word, the intelligence of feeling, and the revelation literature affords that reality is polysemous, including historical and moral levels, but ultimately disclosing an anagogical meaning.

The greatest works achieve form in ways inseparable from their meaning, none more so than the *Iliad*; they give the highest pleasure to the imagination, for reasons that can be analyzed but not entirely explained; they both elicit and inform emotions in ways that require the whole intelligence of the work, as when Priam says, "I have kissed the hands of the man who has killed my children"; and they have a vertical openness, analogous to what Mircea Eliade describes architecturally as a hole left in the roof, even if it comes to be there through a Keatsian capability *not* to close off possibilities, rather than through a positive knowledge of divine things. As I write this, just before the turn of the millennium, astronauts venturing out from the space shuttle, with lifelines back to the ship, have just replaced the gyroscopes and computers on the Hubble telescope. It seems somehow an appropriate image of what literature at its heights also tries to do: by elaborate craft, to render a Dante momentarily weightless above the great sphere of the earth; to allow him to labor at restoring a vision directed outward past our own atmospheres and weathers; and to return him to his fitting habitation, where the air is general and the gravity substantial.

One of the mistakes of the New Critics, with whom my own strongest sympathies obviously lie, was to put too much emphasis on lyric poetry, probably because the form of a single poem could be apprehended whole in a single essay. At the risk of repeating the error, I want to conclude with a single poem, apparently insignificant next to the *Iliad*, a small lyric by a woman who rarely *appeared*, either in person or in print, and who therefore seems at the farthest remove from an Achilles. One might be tempted to say that her correspondent and sometime editor Thomas Wentworth Higginson was the Agamemnon who dishonored her. After citing some of the poems she sent him in her first letters, he admits in an essay for the October 1891 *Atlantic Monthly* that he could not fit her into the categories of criticism:

> The impression of a wholly new and original poetic genius was as distinct on my mind at the first reading of these four poems as it is now, after thirty years of further knowledge; and with it came the problem never yet solved, what place ought to be assigned in literature to what is so remarkable, yet so elusive of criticism. The bee himself did not evade the

schoolboy more than she evaded me; and even at this day I still stand somewhat bewildered, like the boy.

Was Higginson to blame for not championing her more forcefully? I suspect that he felt an ambivalence that came from being personally implicated in her genius, but unable to overcome the strangeness of it, like Heaney's St. Kevin, who is holding his hands outside the window of his cell in prayer when a blackbird lands and lays an egg in one of his upturned palms.

Dickinson's poetry, once encountered in its true strangeness, keeps turning up surprises. When I look through the Johnson edition, the range of the poems I never remember reading before is a little staggering. This, for example, seems perfectly characteristic in its oddity:

1062

He scanned it — staggered —
Dropped the Loop
To Past or Period —
Caught helpless at a sense as if
His Mind were going blind —

Groped up, to see if God was there —
Groped backward at Himself
Caressed a Trigger absently
And wandered out of Life.

Apparently, a man reads something so calamitous that it makes the world suddenly void of meaning. Desperation leads him to kill himself—but almost inattentively, in a mood not unlike the "regardless" one of "After Great Pain." But suppose the poem is a mordant little satire. What *is* it that "He scanned"? A poem of Emily Dickinson's perhaps? Such as *this* one, a poem that neither scans nor rhymes in the usual ways? The critic (alas, poor Higginson) who cannot hang it by its "Loop" on the poetry of the "Past" or assign it a tidy literary-historical "Period" staggers back, grasping helplessly at a "sense"— doubts God—doubts himself—and caresses the Trigger from sheer bewilderment.

Even the smallest poems, left without explanation or commentary, contain the whole character of Dickinson's imagination. Should one necessarily take this one, for example, as serious evidence that Dickinson suffered from profound depression, or simply as evidence that she knows that the analogy will lead one to speculate about her?

1095

To Whom the Mornings stand for Nights,
    What must the Midnights — be!

Another, never anthologized to my knowledge, contains the whole character of Dickinson's ironic diction:

1069

Paradise is of the option.
Whosoever will
Own in Eden notwithstanding
Adam and Repeal.

Particularly noteworthy: the fishy real-estate irony of "owning" property in Eden, played off against the other sense of "owning" that accompanies covenant theology, as in Melville's Ishmael telling the reader to "own the whale." Is she speaking of the boldness of Christian love ("The kingdom of Heaven suffers violence, and the violent bear it away"), or of a kind of option (in its dictionary sense, "a contract conveying a right to buy or sell designated securities, commodities, or property interest at a specified price during a stipulated period") on a Paradise—with its sexual suggestion of nakedness—that remains available notwithstanding the "Repeal" or curse in Genesis, one that also entails husband Adam lording it over owned wife Eve? A teasing ambiguity—a perversity, in some moods of reading—plays around the poem. And Dickinson can also turn with considerable acuity to the kinds of large political commentaries one would more readily associate with Burke or Tocqueville:

1082

Revolution is the Pod
Systems rattle from
When the Winds of Will are stirred
Excellent is Bloom.

But except its Russet Base
Every Summer be

The Entomber of itself,
So of Liberty —

Left inactive on the Stalk
All its Purple fled
Revolution shakes it for
Test if it be dead.

Whatever moves her to write this poem—observation of milkweed?—the mistrust of "systems" and "Will" evident from it indicates that she would not have been surprised by the revolutions and tyrannies of the twentieth century.

The "public" of Civil War America, one suspects, could not readily accommodate the kind of mind that would think to say, as she did when she sent Higginson a second group of poems to read, "While my thought is undressed, I can make the distinction; but when I put them in the gown, they look alike and numb." What kind of comment is *that*? It burns on the imagination like the lash of a nettle. It is no wonder that Higginson would remark, gentleman that he seems, that she evaded his questions about her circumstances with "a naive skill such as the most experienced and worldly coquette might envy"—except that the quality of naïvete seems rather obviously misnamed. What looks naïve is instead a very forthright awareness of metaphor in its effects, a language almost maddening in its capacity to infuse the unmediated perceptual nakedness of a child with a knowing verbal dalliance: "You ask of my companions. Hills, sir, and the sundown, and a dog large as myself, that my father bought me. They are better than beings because they know, but do not tell; and the noise in the pool at noon excels my piano." How can Higginson go on being what he is after receiving such a letter? What should he reply when he reads, "I had a terror since September, I could tell to none; and so I sing, as the boy does of the burying ground, because I am afraid"?

Dickinson's fear, when it comes to occasions, most resembles that of Achilles: mortality weighs upon her. One could search her biography to try to find the provocations for particular poems, but the fact of death, sometimes personified as a lover because of the intimacy with it that she cannot ultimately avoid, as she might a husband, focuses her attention with shifting bursts and pauses, preternaturally acute, on the things that *are*, each of which (against the backdrop of discriminating annihilation) can awaken more feelings than, say, the third day at Gettysburg might in someone else.

This is a woman who does not need momentous circumstances to feel the depth of any emotion. Her bent is evident from what she says in reply to Higginson, who, working from his conventionally gown-numbed mind, asks about her life in ways that she finds almost unanswerable: "You ask great questions accidentally. To answer them would be events." One can speculate about what might have occasioned the poem that seems to me a fitting epilogue to the *Iliad*, "After great pain, a formal feeling comes," but it need not have been much, at least outwardly. "Great pain," even as a phrase, has a ranging ambiguity that could apply to the fall of Troy or to receiving a letter containing an irrevocable rejection:

> After great pain, a formal feeling comes—
> The Nerves sit ceremonious, like Toombs—
> The stiff Heart questions was it He, that bore,
> And Yesterday, or Centuries before?
>
> The Feet, mechanical, go round—
> Of Ground, or Air, or Ought—
> A Wooden way
> Regardless grown,
> A Quartz contentment, like a stone—

This is the Hour of Lead—
Remembered, if outlived,
As Freezing persons recollect the Snow—
First—Chill—then Stupor—then the letting go—

The poem is, in effect, an extended simile in which the unspecified pain is compared to and might be *mistaken for* the loss of someone through death, after the original passion of grieving dies down; the poem could almost describe Achilles in the time after the pyre of Patroklos has burned out and the ashes are gathered up and the sheer waiting sets in. But the central numbness of this poem speaks of a different kind of loss, an emotional shock closely allied to the most burning shame and involving the bright original of every negative in the poem. In other words, it is necessary to imagine a feeling the opposite of formal, one with no sense of imposed restraint; the "Nerves" not ceremonious—in fact, not summoned out of the anatomized self to be Capitalized and Personified, but alive in their unanalyzed anonymity; the heart not "stiff" and male, boring, dully bearing things, but far otherwise—feminine, pliant, racing. The poem does with numbness something like what St. Augustine does with forgetfulness, when he wonders that he can remember it at all, since the very nature of forgetfulness is loss of memory. Describing the absolute absence of feeling, these lines evoke not only the feeling of this absence, but also its original opposite and the extraordinary pain of emotional immolation that must have come between *that* happy condition and *this* dead one. Something or someone once intensely experienced will "come no more," as Lear says, "Never, never, never, never, never."

What arrests me in this poem is the intensity with which it focuses on the doubleness of the "formal feeling" that must underlie it. On the one hand, it speaks of the deadliest, coldest experience of mere form, form emptied of every living motion, like a body "formally" operated by a soul no longer of it. If the "Nerves sit ceremonious," they do so at first glance like blank mourners at a funeral or very public figures crucified to the demands of self-abnegation on high occasions—or like statues of such people, or statues on tombs—or, stripped of all human likeness, like the purely ceremonial tombs themselves. No longer nerves, they mark a permanent absence with their heatless formality. Yet at the same time that the poem evokes the chill of this "formal feeling," another "formal feeling," very lively and different, is actively finding the pleasure of the simile, stiffening the ceremonial lines with spondees, and making the verb "bore" ambiguously intransitive. There is an excitement of making, in which Dickinson as poet necessarily stands aside from the actual emotion of the words in order to observe them and weigh the effect of her comparisons.

Writing of the way that art stands "outside the human sphere," Jacques Maritain comments that art "has an end, rules, values, which are not those of man, but those of the work to be produced. This work is everything for Art; there is for Art but one law—the exigencies and the good of the work" (*Art and Scholasticism* 9). Dickinson's second formal feeling, in other words, is this excitement of intelligence that can, in effect, penetrate the very numbness of the state being described in order to describe it less and less numbly. "Hence," says Maritain, "the tyrannical and absorbing power of Art, and also its astonishing power of soothing; it delivers one from the human; it establishes the *artifex*—artist or artisan—in a world apart, closed, limited, absolute, in which he puts the energy and intelligence of his manhood at the service of a thing which he makes" (9). For Maritain, the specifically human dimension of the end that art pursues comes through the particular spirit that prepares and shapes it: "Its *formal* element, what constitutes it in its species and makes it what it is, is its being ruled by the intellect. If this formal element diminishes ever so little, to the same extent the reality of art vanishes" (9, his emphasis). Somehow Dickinson arrives at the paradox of poetry when her making intellect masters formal feeling in order to evoke the loss of all affect after great pain.

Nowhere is this achievement more evident than in the apparent loss of form in the second stanza. John Crowe Ransom, writing about the ambiguous ending of a poem by Edna St. Vincent Millay, faults it for using an ambiguous word because "the finish of the metre gives the illusory sense of an equal finish in the sense, and if there comes any doubt about the sense it may be argued to be even better because the range of its possibilities is wider" ("The Poet as Woman" 109). Ransom knows "too well" this temptation to fudge, no doubt from his own work with meter. "Let us remember Procrustes, who will symbolize for us the mechanical determinism of metrical necessity, a tyrant against whom only pure-hearted and well-equipped champions will consistently prevail" ("Poet" 110). I do not know of Ransom having written about the second stanza of "After Great Pain"; I doubt that, much as Ransom cares for meter, he would find the same difficulties with it that he finds with Millay's work, because of the peculiar brilliance of Dickinson's violations:

> The Feet, mechanical, go round—
> Of Ground, or Air, or Ought—
> A Wooden way
> Regardless grown,
> A Quartz contentment, like a stone—

This stanza is "elusive of criticism" in Higginson's sense only if one cannot imagine how a poem that apparently breaks down, as this one does, could at the same time have a high formal excellence. The same play on Ransom's "mechanical determinism" is in Dickinson, and the word "Feet," ostensibly describing the steps one takes in the state of numb formal feeling, also calls attention to the metrical line and to its mechanical pattern of iambic stresses—though one trips a little on the spondee "go round." The first quatrain was composed in iambic pentameter, but in the second, the poem seems forgetfully to lapse into the standard meter of hymns, with their alternating lines of eight and six syllables (like "Amazing Grace"). If one understands the word "comes" as a half-rhyme with "toombs," then the first stanza is composed of two couplets, and the second line of the second stanza should not only match the first in length, but rhyme with it. Instead the feet, literally and metrically, become ungrounded after six syllables, and where a rhyme might be, the word "Ought" comes instead. Ironically, "ought" means "duty," here where the rhyme *ought* to be. It also means "nothing." One's mechanical feet go round on "ought," following a pattern of duty completely emptied of meaning, a form that has become nullified in the very act of one's attempting to fulfill it. We speak of people "going through the motions," but in this kind of emotional nullity, the customary things that have their objective correlative in the stanza forms prove untrustworthy. Which ones? The poem seems to wander off distractedly. The way one goes has become "wooden"—that is, stiff and unfeeling. The word "regardless," straying from its more conventional meaning, now takes on the literal sense of unseeing.

But again, behind the violations of the stanza lie remnants of ecstasy— walking on air, treading down duty to enter an Edenic "wooden way" as untended and "regardless grown" as the garden in *Paradise Lost*, where the pathways needed clearing of "wanton growth" (4.629) and where Eve "as a veil, down to the slender waist / Her unadorned golden tresses wore / Di- shevelled, but in wanton ringlets waved / As the vine curls her tendrils" (4.304-7). The "quartz contentment" might also—in brighter circum- stances—call to mind the New Jerusalem of Revelation 22, "coming down out of heaven from God, prepared as a bride beautifully dressed for her husband" (22.2): "It shone with the glory of God, and its brilliance was like that of a very precious jewel, like a jasper, clear as crystal" (22.10-11). The reference might very well have been on her mind. In her second letter to Higginson, Dickinson writes, "You inquire my books. For poets, I have Keats, and Mr. and Mrs. Browning. For prose, Mr. Ruskin, Sir Thomas Browne, and the Revelations." In Keats' "The Eve of St. Agnes," Madeline was so rapt in her reverie, anticipating the prophetic dreams of that night, that "She danc'd along with vague, *regardless* eyes, / Anxious her lips, her breathing quick and short" (VIII, my emphasis). In other words, if the "great pain" of the poem describes, not the grief of death per se, but loss of love after the complete surrender of the self, then the transgressions of Dickinson's stanza might reflect both the nature of an original antinomian joy and the loss that makes this deadening grief so extreme, that dims even a lucid "quartz" to stony opacity. In exploring woodenness, Dickinson also recapitulates the inspired improvisations, the forgetfulness of ordinary things, and the transgressions that characterize the first transports of love. Here are the movements again, all the more deadening for their irony. Everything uniquely intimate and light yields to impersonal gravity, to stone.

What seems a breakdown in the second stanza is Dickinson's boldest formal art. The very improvisations seem to lead, in the third stanza, to the recognition that everything was formally predestined and foreknown, as inevitable as death itself—as if part of the first joy of love had been the unlikelihood of any such bliss, and one had always known that it was ground-less, one had felt very well all along that great pain would be the price of any private happiness. This inevitability makes the short opening lines of the stanza seem impersonally predestined as well:

> This is the Hour of Lead—
> Remembered, if outlived,
> As Freezing persons recollect the Snow—
> First—Chill—then Stupor—then the letting go—

Like Augustine, Dickinson explores the paradox that the "Hour of Lead" can be written about at all, since its inmost quality is lack of affect and forgetfulness. But under the influence of the felicitous simile that her art suggests, the original form of the poem begins to reassert itself, and the last two lines regain the iambic pentameter couplet as though returning from a trance or coma. Ironically, under the Procrustean tyranny of meter, "persons who have been revived after undergoing the experience of losing conscious-ness while freezing to death" must be condensed into the ambiguous phrase "Freezing persons." The experience that can only be described after a miraculous recovery, in other words, becomes the very one that the poem enters, as though these persons were only now undergoing the experience of freezing: "First—Chill—then Stupor—then the letting go—". To recount the experience—to "recollect" in tranquility both icy rigidity and release—recapitulates it, makes it present, transforms it.

The sheer artistic delight of this ending astonishes me. How can it be that in describing death by frozen numbness the poet can awaken the most intense imaginative pleasure? The fact that deadly impassivity can be described at all is not in itself the source of this ending's particular greatness.

In part, it owes to the sudden broadening of the poem's scope into a large outer landscape. To think of "Freezing persons" who "recollect the snow," one first has to summon up a blizzard sufficiently sudden and overwhelming to defeat those accustomed to the climate. People freeze, in such circumstances, because they are caught traveling, the snow covers and obscures all forms, the way becomes impassable, and they feel themselves yielding as the cold overcomes them: "First—Chill—then Stupor—then the letting go—". Dickinson's punctuation, edited out of the first editions of her poems, perfectly modulates the rhythms of this last line: the distinct word "—Chill—" set out nakedly between the dashes, yielding to "—then Stupor—" in the slightly longer phase beyond the sensation of chill, and giving way entirely (without the typographical closure of a period) to the emotionally tense but metrically placid ending "—then the letting go—".

Exactly coinciding with the poem's formal conclusion and the strong fulfillment of the last rhyme is the trope of surrendering consciousness and life. But to imagine the blizzard, the "Freezing persons," and the *recollection* that provides this last line, there has to be another moment, before actual death but after the "letting go," when someone else finds and saves the victim. Just beyond the range of the loss of consciousness, already drawing near, must be this rescuer who makes possible the reviving and recollection of the self—if the "Hour of Lead" is outlived. It takes an effort of intellect to remember that the tenor of the metaphor is not *dying* but letting go of the original joy whose absence has caused, first extreme pain, then numbness, then the necessity of releasing it. To release the cause is like the soul letting go of the freezing body, the condition of its earthly life. It is letting go of the beloved. It is also like the poet letting go of the poem. I am reminded of Heaney's remark that "The achievement of a poem, after all, is an experience of release. In that liberated moment, when the lyric discovers its buoyant completion and the timeless formal pleasure comes to fullness and exhaustion, something occurs which is equidistant from self-justification and self-obliteration" (*Government* xxii). In Dickinson's poem the "liberated moment" of completion comes with the formal feeling of release that ends the poem:

despair perfectly balanced by the hope of its expression, numb loss awakened by the discovery of its true likeness.

Like the *Iliad*, Dickinson's poem—wrung a bit for its essential oils—might yield an anagogical understanding: that immortal form becomes manifest, from a perspective outside the human sphere, only in renunciation. In this regard, poetry for her, as for Heaney, might be a promissory intimation of what lies beyond "this world." These intimations waver, and their substance might come down to the differences between Dickinson's word choice and the one substituted by Thomas Wentworth Higginson and Mabel Loomis Todd, her first editors. In the 1896 edition, "This World is Not Conclusion" begins in this way:

> This world is not conclusion;
> A sequel stands beyond,
> Invisible, as music,
> But positive, as sound.

In Thomas Johnson's edition, based on the actual Dickinson manuscripts, the opening differs in punctuation and in one crucial word:

> This World is not Conclusion.
> A Species stands beyond —
> Invisible, as Music —
> But positive, as Sound —

"Sequel" has a certain appeal, suggesting that the world is an engaging text that calls for a continuation. But the substitution introduces Higginson's and Todd's wholesale rewriting of this edgy and troubling poem, including the omission of the last eight lines.[1] Dickinson's "Species" must have struck them as oddly off-key, unpleasantly abstract. Why literature matters might come down to a single word like this one. A species can be a class of individuals designated by a common name, in which case the "Species" here might be the heavenly choir, the saints in glory "Invisible, as Music." The word *species* also means a biological classification, a sense of course made extremely prominent by Charles Darwin in *The Origin of Species* (1859) a few years before this poem was written; the Species that stands beyond might be the future race that follows man—if Dickinson can be suspected of intimations of the *Ubermensch*. Species can also mean an object of thought correlative with a natural object, in which case "this world" is always undergoing a transformation into thought that makes its physical being inconclusive. Species also denotes the consecrated elements in the Roman Catholic Eucharist, the bread and wine under whose appearance dwells the Real Presence of Christ, and in this metaphorical application, the appearances of earthly things might be understood in the sense that Dickinson meant when she wrote in a letter to Higginson, "Abroad is close to-night and I have but to lift my hands to touch the 'Heights of Abraham.'"

Each of these meanings gives its own particular cast to the word "Conclusion" in the first line. Taken together, however, they immediately begin to modify the meaning that Higginson and Todd took from the word, when they willed Dickinson to be saying, as Longfellow puts it, "Life is real! Life is earnest! / And the grave is not its goal"—an instance of what Allen Tate calls "the feeble poetry of moral ideas that flourished in New England." But as the poem develops, "Conclusion" more and more seems to mean the necessary consequence drawn from premises, as in a syllogism. In other words, to be in this world means to be prey to uncertainties: "Narcotics cannot still the Tooth / That nibbles at the Soul—" she writes at the end of the poem. But the greatness of poetry lies precisely, as Keats says, in the negative capability of remaining in "uncertainties, mysteries, doubts, without any irritable reaching after fact and reason."

T HIS capacity to remain with and endure uncertainty is not skepticism but a faith in the formal feeling of art, an image, it may be, of waiting for completion from elsewhere. In Dostoevsky's *The Brothers Karamazov*, the novice Alyosha undergoes a crisis of faith when his mentor Fr. Zosima not only fails to maintain his bodily freshness after his death but develops an odor with scandalous rapidity. Even Patroklos and Hektor in the *Iliad*— pagans long before Christianity—keep ambrosially fresh after death because of their favor with the gods, and as a widely respected holy man, Fr. Zosima was expected to exhibit the same miraculous defiance of corruption. Far from it. That night, after hearing the triumphant remarks of Fr. Zosima's envious accusers and skirting a spiritual disaster, Alyosha has a vision that combines two scriptural images into one: the first miracle of Christ at the wedding feast of Cana, and the final descent of the Bride of the Lamb in Revelation 22. Fr. Zosima appears to him in the vision to invite him to the wedding feast of the Lamb, this mystical union between the Son of God and His Bride the Church. Embedded as it is in the movements and emotional textures specific to this novel, the scene has a current of meaning that moves from Zosima's bodily corruption through Alyosha's experience with the temptress Grushenka to a redemptive vision, but it serves to put the focus on one particular feature of the account in the Book of Revelation: the fact that the Bride of the Lamb, the Holy City, *descends* from heaven. One has the sense that Fr. Zosima has deliberately sacrificed his own honor for Alyosha in order to show him in this vision that the beauty of form, like the resurrected body, cannot be made by human will and expectation. Something else— some super-added grace—must descend with the transformed matter. The earthly church, like the individual soul that espouses the divine Bridegroom, must be taken up and given divine form.

The point is not a denigration of art or *techne*, but an emphasis on a kind of gift exchange. At its heights, art, like religion, must be a kind of pure receptivity. Homer suggests the same thing. When Achilles moves toward his glory, his armor cannot be fashioned by mortal hands, but brought down from Olympos by his divine mother, already complete. Similarly, the *kleos aphthiton* of immortal song must be divinely given, and the poet—for all the labor of the poem—therefore asks at the very beginning that the goddess give him what he sings. The matter hungers for the form, yet the form is never something distinct from the matter, never something that pre-exists it, like an idea. Literature is not *about* ideas. In its own proper nature, it does not illustrate philosophies or popularize doctrines, political or religious. Doctrines and ideas as such can be better expressed in more direct ways than literature affords. It does not exclude them, either. In fact, it works in and with the greatest ideas precisely because they most affect human action and lead to the greatest consequences; they most inform and are informed by the intelligence of feeling. Abstractions and systems literature puts in their place, as Dickinson means to when she writes,

> Philosophy — don't know — And through a Riddle at the last — Sagacity, must go —

In effect, art is that riddle, with its own luminous intelligence. In art, to repeat what Maritain says, the intellect rules the work in its "*formal* element, what constitutes it in its species and makes it what it is." Umberto Eco argues that St. Thomas Aquinas, Maritain's guide in these matters, did not exclude from consideration the view of form

> as a sort of ontological *quid* in the broadest sense.... When form is conceived of in this way, it is synonymous with the organization and completeness of an experienceable object or a lived experience. It does not mean the rational structure within a thing. It refers, not to the relations within it, but rather to the thing itself as something organized and made what it is by those relations. It does not mean a pure structure or pattern, which can be abstracted by the mind from a complete object and imposed upon a shapeless stuff, but rather a structure or pattern which is materially at one with the object—something in virtue of which an object lives and is what it is, but which itself possesses reality and character only in virtue of being materialized in the object. (68)

Literature matters because nothing can better approach the form, in this sense, of life in its felt reality, as it is most deeply experienced, with an intelligence that increases in power the more it explores the most unbearable dimensions of joy and suffering. Without being specifically religious in itself, it can give an experience of "a common glory" that intimates something otherwise unsayable about the nature of the Word through whom all things were made. It can turn even the loss of life and meaning not only into the rediscovery of meaning but into an occasion of promissory joy.

Works Cited

Adams, Hazard, ed. *Critical Theory Since Plato.* Revised edition. New York: Harcourt Brace Jovanovich, 1992.

Allison, Jonathan. "Seamus Heaney and the Romantic Image." *Sewanee Review.* Spring 1998. Vol. 106 , Issue 2 . 184-202. *MasterFILE Premier on-line.* EBSCO Publishing. January 7, 2000 <http://ehostvgw15.epnet.com/ehost1.asp>.

Allums, Larry, ed. *The Epic Cosmos.* Introduction by Louise Cowan. Dallas, Tex.: The Dallas Institute Publications, 1992.

Anaya, Rudolfo A. *Bless Me, Ultima.* Reprint Edition. New York: Warner Books, 1995.

Aristotle. *The Nicomachean Ethics.* Trans. H. Rackham. The Loeb Classical Library. Cambridge: Harvard University Press, 1934.

Austen, Jane. *Pride and Prejudice.* New York: Penguin Books, 1985.

Bakhtin, M. M. *The Dialogic Imagination: Four Essays.* Ed. Michael Holquist. Trans. Caryl Emerson and Michael Holquist. Austin: University of Texas Press, 1981.

Balthasar, Hans Urs von. *The Glory of the Lord: A Theological Aesthetics.* Volume I. *Seeing the Form.* Trans. Erasmo Leiva-Merikakis. Eds. Joseph Fessio and John Riches. San Francisco: Ignatius Press, 1983.

Berger, Peter. "On the Obsolescence of the Concept of Honor." *Revisions: Changing Perspectives in Moral Philosophy.* Eds. Alasdair Macintyre and Stanley Hauerwas. Notre Dame: University of Notre Dame Press, 1983.

Bloom, Allan. *Shakespeare's Politics*. With Harry Jaffa. Reprint Edition. Chicago: University of Chicago Press, 1996.

Bloom, Harold. *Shakespeare: The Invention of the Human*. New York: Riverhead Books, 1998.

Brooks, Cleanth. "The Heresy of Paraphrase." *Critical Theory Since Plato*. Ed. Hazard Adams. New York: Harcourt Brace Jovanovich, Publishers, 1992. 961-968.

Cameron, Sharon. *Choosing Not Choosing: Dickinson's Fascicles*. Chicago: University of Chicago Press, 1993.

Cinthio, Giraldi. *Hecatommithi*. In *The Tragedy of Othello the Moor of Venice* by William Shakespeare. Revised Edition. New York: Signet, 1998. 134-146.

Coleridge, Samuel Taylor. "The Charm of Chemistry." Essays from *The Friend*. Volume III, Section the Second, Essay vi. <http://etext.lib.virginia.edu/ stc/Coleridge/phil_theo/Friend.html#charm>.

_____ . "Biographia Literaria." *Critical Theory Since Plato*. Ed. Hazard Adams. New York: Harcourt Brace Jovanovich, Publishers, 1971.

Cowan, Louise. "Introduction." *The Epic Cosmos*. Ed. Larry Allums.

_____ . *The Southern Critics: An Introduction to the Criticism of John Crowe Ransom, Allen Tate, Donald Davidson, Robert Penn Warren, and Cleanth Brooks*. Reprint Edition. Dallas: Dallas Institute Publications, 1997.

Curtis, Tony, ed. *The Art of Seamus Heaney*. Chester Springs: Dufour Books, 1994.

Damasio, Antonio R. *Descartes' Error: Emotion, Reason, and the Human Brain*. New York: Grosset/Putnam, 1994.

_____ . *The Feeling of What Happens: Body and Emotion in the Making of Consciousness*. New York: Harcourt Brace & Company, 1999.

Dante. *Paradiso*. Trans. Allen Mandelbaum. New York: Bantam Classic, 1986.

Davison, Peter. "A Certain Logic: An Interview with Richard Wilbur." September 9, 1999 <http://www.theatlantic.com/unbound/poetry/wilbur.htm>.

De Man, Paul. *Blindness and Insight: Essays in the Rhetoric of Contemporary Criticism*. Second Edition. Minneapolis-St. Paul: University of Minnesota Press, 1985.

Dostoevsky, Fyodor. *The Brothers Karamazov*. Trans. Richard Pevear and Larissa Volokhonsky. New York: Vintage, 1991.

Douglas, Mary. *Purity and Danger: An Analysis of the Concepts of Pollution and Taboo.* London: Ark Paperbacks, 1989.

Eco, Umberto. *The Aesthetics of Thomas Aquinas.* Trans. Hugh Bredin. Cambridge: Harvard University Press, 1988.

Eliot, T. S. "Hamlet and His Problems." *Critical Theory Since Plato.* Ed. Hazard Adams. New York: Harcourt Brace Jovanovich, Publishers, 1992. 764-766.

_____ . "The Perfect Critic." *The Sacred Wood: Essays on Poetry and Criticism.* London: Methuen & Co., 1920.

_____ . "Tradition and the Individual Talent." *Critical Theory Since Plato.* Ed. Hazard Adams. New York: Harcourt Brace Jovanovich, Publishers, 1992. 761-764.

Ellis, John M. *Literature Lost: Social Agendas and the Corruption of the Humanities.* New Haven: Yale University Press, 1997.

Evdokimov, Paul. *The Art of the Icon: A Theology of Beauty.* Trans. Stephen Bigham. Festal Creations, 1989.

Franklin, R. W., ed. *The Poems of Emily Dickinson: Variorum Edition.* Cambridge: The Belknap Press, 1998.

Garber, Marjorie. *Symptoms of Culture.* New York: Routledge, 1998.

Giegerich, Wolfgang. "The Opposition of 'Individual' and 'Collective'—Psychology's Basic Fault: Reflections on Today's Magnum Opus of the Soul." *Harvest,* 1996, V. 42, No.2. 7-27. <http://www.cgjung.com/articles/giegerich1.html>.

Ghazoul, Ferial. "The Arabization of Othello." *Comparative Literature.* Winter 1998. Volume 50, No. 1; pages 1-31.

Gioia, Dana. "Can Poetry Matter?" *The Atlantic Monthly.* May 1991. Volume 267, No. 5; pages 94-106. <http://www.theatlantic.com/unbound/poetry/gioia/gioia.htm>.

Graham, Jorie. *The End of Beauty.* Hopewell, N.J.: Ecco Press, 1987.

Greenblatt, Stephen. *Renaissance Self-Fashioning: From More to Shakespeare.* Chicago: University of Chicago Press, 1980.

Griffin, Jasper. *Homer on Life and Death.* New York: Oxford University Press, 1980.

Hall, Donald. *Life Work*. Boston: Beacon Press, 1993.

Hanson, Victor Davis, and John Heath. *Who Killed Homer? The Demise of Classical Education and the Recovery of Greek Wisdom*. New York: Free Press, 1998.

Heaney, Seamus. *The Government of the Tongue: Selected Prose 1978-1987*. New York: The Noonday Press, 1990.

_____. *The Haw Lantern*. New York: Farrar Straus & Giroux, 1987.

_____. *Opened Ground: Selected Poems 1966-1996*. New York: Farrar Straus & Giroux, 1998.

_____. *Preoccupations: Selected Prose 1968-1978*. New York: The Noonday Press, 1981.

_____. *The Redress of Poetry*. New York: The Noonday Press, 1995.

_____. *Selected Poems 1966-1987*. New York: Farrar Straus & Giroux, 1990.

_____. *The Spirit Level*. New York: Farrar Sraus & Giroux, 1996.

_____. *Station Island*. New York: The Noonday Press, 1986.

Heidegger, Martin. *An Introduction to Metaphysics*. Trans. Ralph Manheim. New Haven: Yale University Press, 1986.

_____. *Poetry, Language, Thought*. Trans. Albert Hofstadter. New York: HarperCollins, 1985.

Higginson, Thomas Wentworth. "Emily Dickinson's Letters." *The Atlantic Monthly*, October 1891 <http://www.theatlantic.com//unbound/poetry/emilyd/edletter.htm>.

Hillman, James. *Healing Fiction*. Reprint Edition. Dallas: Spring Publications, 1994.

Homer. *The Iliad*. Trans. Richmond Lattimore. Chicago: University of Chicago Press, 1987.

Johnson, Thomas H., ed. *The Complete Poems of Emily Dickinson*. Boston: Back Bay Books, 1960.

Keats, John. "Ode to a Nightingale." *English Romantic Poetry and Prose*. Ed. Russell Noyes. New York: Oxford University Press, 1956.

Kernan, Alvin. ed. *The Tragedy of Othello the Moor of Venice* by William Shakespeare. Revised Edition. New York: Signet, 1998.

Klinghoffer, David. "Black Madonna." *National Review*. 02/09/98, Vol. 50 Issue 2, p30, 3p. *MasterFILE Premier on-line*. EBSCO Publishing. January 10, 2000 <http://ehostvgw6.epnet.com/ehost1.asp>.

Kundera, Milan. *The Art of the Novel*. Trans. Linda Asher. New York: Grove Press, 1988.

Lattimore, Richmond. Trans. *The Odyssey of Homer*. New York: Perennial Classics, 1967.

_____ . Trans. *The Odes of Pindar*. Chicago: University of Chicago Press, 1947.

Lloyd, David. "'Pap for the Dispossessed': Heaney and the Post-Colonial Moment." *The Art of Seamus Heaney*. Ed. Tony Curtis.

Logue, Christopher. *War Music : An Account of Books 1-4 and 16-19 of Homer's Iliad*. Introduction by Garry Wills. New York: Noonday Press, 1997.

Longley, Edna. "North: 'Inner Emigre' or 'Artful Voyeur'?" *The Art of Seamus Heaney*. Ed. Tony Curtis. Chester Springs: Dufour Books, 1994.

Lynch, William F. *Christ and Apollo: The Dimensions of the Literary Imagination*. Revised Edition. Notre Dame: University of Notre Dame Press, 1975.

Maritain, Jacques. *Art and Scholasticism* and *The Frontiers of Poetry*. Trans. Joseph W. Evans. New York: Charles Scribner's Sons, 1962.

_____ . *Creative Intuition in Art and Poetry*. The A. W. Mellon Lectures in the Fine Arts, 1952. Bollingen Series XXXV.1. Princeton: Princeton University Press, 1977.

Melville, Herman. *Moby Dick; or The Whale*. Ed. Tony Tanner. Oxford: Oxford World's Classics, 1988.

Milton, John. *Paradise Lost* and *Paradise Regained*. Ed. Christopher Ricks. New York: Signet Classics, 1982.

Morrison, Toni. *Beloved*. New York: New American Library, 1988.

_____ . *Paradise*. New York: Alfred A. Knopf, 1998.

_____ , ed. *Birth of a Nation'Hood: Gaze, Script, and Spectacle in the O. J. Simpson Case*. With Claudia Brodsky Lacour, ed. New York: Pantheon Books, 1997.

_____ . *Playing in the Dark: Whiteness and the Literary Imagination*. Cambridge: Harvard University Press, 1992.

_____ , ed. *Race-ing Justice, En-Gendering Power : Essays on Anita Hill, Clarence Thomas, and the Construction of Social Reality.* New York: Pantheon Books, 1992.

_____ . "The Future of Time: Literature and Diminished Expectations." The Jefferson Lecture in the Humanities. March 25, 1996.

Noyes, Russell, ed. *English Romantic Poetry and Prose.* New York: Oxford University Press, 1956.

O'Connor, Flannery. *The Complete Stories.* New York: The Noonday Press, 1999.

_____ . *Mystery and Manners.* New York: The Noonday Press, 1969.

Paglia, Camille. *Sexual Personae: Art and Decadence from Nefertiti to Emily Dickinson.* New Haven: Yale University Press, 1990.

Pinsky, Robert. *The Sounds of Poetry.* New York: Farrar Straus & Giroux, 1998.

_____ . *Poetry and the World.* Hopewell, N.J.: Ecco Press, 1992.

Pollak, Vivian. "Attempting the Impossible." *Women's Review of Books.* January 1999, Vol. 16 Issue 4. 13-14. *MasterFILE Premier on-line.* EBSCO Publishing. January 10, 2000 <http://ehostvgw14.epnet.com/ehost1.asp>.

Ransom, John Crowe. "Criticism as Pure Speculation." *Critical Theory Since Plato.* Ed. Hazard Adams. New York: Harcourt Brace Jovanovich, Publishers, 1971. 881-890.

_____ . "Forms and Citizens." *The World's Body.* Baton Rouge: LSU Press, 1968. 29-54.

_____ . "The Poet as Woman." *The World's Body.* Baton Rouge: LSU Press, 1968. 76-110.

"St. Catherine of Siena." *The Catholic Encyclopedia.* Robert Appleton Company, 1907-1914 <http://www.newadvent.org/cathen/03447a.htm>.

St. John of the Cross. *The Collected Works of St. John of the Cross.* Trans. Kieran Kavanaugh and Otilio Rodriquez. Washington: ICS Publications, 1973.

Schein, Seth L. *The Mortal Hero: An Introduction to Homer's Iliad.* University of California Press, 1985.

Shelley, Percy Bysshe. *Prometheus Unbound* in *English Romantic Poetry and Prose.* Ed. Russell Noyes. New York: Oxford University Press, 1956. 981-1015.

Showalter, Elaine. "From He-Man to Holy Man." <http://www.salon.com/books/feature/1998/11/cov_12feature.html>.

Slatkin, Laura M. *The Power of Thetis: Allusion and Interpretation in the Iliad*. Berkeley, CA: University of California Press, 1992.

Strauss, Leo. "On the Interpretation of Genesis." *Jerusalem and Athens: Reason and Revelation in the Works of Leo Strauss*. Ed. Susan Orr. Lanham, Md.: Rowman & Littlefield, 1995. 202-225.

Taplin, Oliver. *Homeric Soundings : The Shaping of the Iliad*. Oxford U P, 1995.

Tate, Allen. *Essays of Four Decades*. Wilmington, Del.: ISI Books, 1999.

Todd, Mabel Loomis, ed. *Poems, Third Series*. Boston: Little, Brown, & Co., 1896. www.bartleby.com. January 10, 2000 <http://www.bartleby.com/113/ed101.html>.

Turner, Victor. *From Ritual to Theatre: The Human Seriousness of Play*. New York: PAJ Publications, 1982.

Vendler, Helen Hennessey. *Seamus Heaney*. Cambridge: Harvard University Press, 1998.

Walcott, Derek. *Omeros*. New York: The Noonday Press, 1992.

Wolfe, Tom. *A Man in Full*. New York: Farrar Straus & Giroux, 1998.

Wood, James. "The Flying Trapezius." *The New Republic*. Dec. 14, 1998. Vol. 219, Issue 24, p37, 6p.

Wordsworth, William. "London, 1802." *English Romantic Poetry and Prose*. Ed. Russell Noyes. New York: Oxford University Press, 1956.

_____ . "The World Is Too Much With Us." *English Romantic Poetry and Prose*. Ed. Russell Noyes. New York: Oxford University Press, 1956.

_____ . "Preface to the *Lyrical Ballads*." *English Romantic Poetry and Prose*. Ed. Russell Noyes. New York: Oxford University Press, 1956.

Young, R. V. *At War with the Word: Literary Theory and Liberal Education*. Wilmington, Del.: ISI Books, 1999.

Notes

INTRODUCTION: THE MONEY OR THE MINE

1. Allen Tate had already said in his 1928 essay that Dickinson's poetry is "a magnificent personal confession, blasphemous and, in its self-revelation, its honesty, almost obscene. It comes out of an intellectual life towards which it feels no moral responsibility. Cotton Mather would have burnt her for a witch" (298).

2. Major schools of contemporary thought—the movement of historical writing away from large political events toward what anthropologist Clifford Geertz calls "local knowledge," the academic emphasis on the texture of private life, the belief in the "social construction" of identity, sexual and otherwise—inform the contemporary biographical curiosity about such things as the feminism of Dickinson's texts, her opposition to publication, and her supposed erotic interest in Susan Dickinson.

3. Cited from the unpaginated online version. One wonders how cyberprint, with its disciplinary inclusiveness, will be "gendered."

4. If one says, "the poems," then how does one decide what the texts are and how they should be reproduced? If Dickinson left different versions of the same poem, did she do so in order to deconstruct the idea of a final text, or because she was still trying to write the poem that satisfied her? One has to decide, one way or the other, and "choosing not choosing"—as Sharon Cameron does—seems to me clever and disingenuous. Still, it is difficult to dismiss the problem to which Cameron and others point. When there are two good poems that share lines but that differ from each other, is one of them simply to be *decreed* the "real" one? Pollak obviously thinks not when she claims that "it is no longer possible to believe in New Critical ideals of

definitive editing." But did the "ideal" to establish a text not considerably precede the New Critics? Classical scholars such as Richard Bentley come to mind. Dickinson's poems pose no more of a problem than, say, the differences between the folio and quarto versions of Shakespeare's plays. Both Alexander Pope and Samuel Johnson considered it worthwhile to try to establish a best version. Both considered this attempt the highest act of practical criticism. With Dickinson, it is difficult to be sure about her preferences; she obviously loves a teasing relation to her reader.

2. SEAMUS HEANEY AND THE "GRAND ELEMENTARY PRINCIPLE OF PLEASURE"

1. Coleridge continues, "from all other species (having *this* object in common with it) it is discriminated by proposing to itself such delight from the whole, as is compatible with a distinct gratification from each component part" (471). According to Coleridge, the poet can accomplish his end when he "brings the whole soul of man into activity, with the subordination of its faculties to each other according to their relative worth and dignity." The result will be "a tone and spirit of unity, that blends, and (as it were) *fuses* each into each, by that synthetic and magical power, to which we have exclusively appropriated the name of imagination" (471).

2. For example, in his commentary on Stefan George's poem "Words," Heidegger writes that:

   > The poet must relinquish the claim to the assurance that he will on demand be supplied with the name for that which he has posited as what truly is. This positing and that claim he must now deny himself. The poet must renounce having words under his control as the portraying names for what is posited. As self-denial, renunciation is a Saying which says to itself: "Where word breaks off no thing may be." (Heidegger 146-47)

3. All citations from Heaney's poetry are from *Opened Ground: Selected Poems 1966-1996* (OG).

4. The boy's expulsion also becomes an adult release from obsession, not so much with the memory of tadpoles in the flax-dam, as with the poem itself: an *other* that comes from within, that *is* oneself, but that in its strange difference provokes a fascinated prying and fingering. In the last stanza of "Personal Helicon" (his poem about staring into wells), Heaney acknowledges this narcissistic pull more directly, at the same time that he registers the relation between shame and language:

   Now, to pry into roots, to finger slime,
   To stare, big-eyed Narcissus, into some spring

Is beneath all adult dignity. I rhyme
To see myself, to set the darkness echoing. (*Ground* 14)

Suddenly caught at his rumination, he tries to recover himself (the comic pedantry of that "Now") from the embarrassment of exposing his naïve wonder and his self-regard. The poem is a well, as the verbal texture of "Death of a Naturalist" is a flax-dam. "Adult dignity"—however ironic the phrase sounds—requires the achievement of a windowsill clarity and a distancing frame; it requires a means of completing experience and being free of self-fascination.

5. In the earlier poem, he addresses Colum directly:

...in brimming grass
[I] gather up cold handfuls of the dew
To wash you, cousin. I dab you clean with moss
Fine as the drizzle out of a low cloud.
I lift you under the arms and lay you flat.
With rushes that shoot green again, I plait
Green scapulars to wear over your shroud. (*Ground* 146)

6. Heaney does not mention the great Romantics in "Station Island," but Wordsworth's complaint in the "Immortality Ode" or Coleridge's in "Dejection" are both poetic versions of this first dark night. Hopkins in his "Terrible Sonnets" voices yet another version.

7. The 1990 *New Selected Poems* contains significant revisions of Section XII and these are retained in *Opened Ground*. The 1984 text omitted from the 1990 editions is struck through.

~~so get back in harness.~~ The main thing is to write
for the joy of it. Cultivate a work-lust
that imagines its haven like your hands at night

dreaming the sun in the sunspot of a breast.
You are fasted now, light-headed, dangerous.
Take off from here. And don't be so earnest,

~~[let others wear~~] so ready for the sackcloth and the ashes.
Let go, let fly, forget.
You've listened long enough. Now strike your note.'

These first omissions take advantage of the opportunity to heighten the poem's clarity and avoid jarring claims. The metaphor of being "in harness" is laboriously at odds with writing "for the joy of it"; letting others wear sackcloth and ashes is a note of arrogance about the poet's privilege (his willingness to let others sacrifice instead of him) that Heaney rejects, even from the mother's-last-wish-refusing Joyce. But his next revisions are more important ones:

Raindrops blew in my face

as I came to –'~~Old father, mother's son,~~
~~there is a moment in Stephen's diary~~
~~for April the thirteenth, a revelation~~

~~set among my stars––that one entry~~
~~has been a sort of password in my ears,~~
~~the collect of a new epiphany,~~

~~the Feast of the Holy Tundish.' 'Who cares,'~~
~~he jeered any more?~~ and heard the harangue and jeers
going on and on. 'The English language
belongs to us. You are raking at dead fires,

[~~a waste of time for somebody~~] rehearsing the old whinges at your age.

In the seven lines omitted, Heaney alludes to the famous scene in *A Portrait of the Artist as a Young Man* in which Stephen Dedalus discovers that the Dublin word for a funnel, "tundish," is an older English word that the English themselves have forgotten. This specifically *Irish* English liberates Heaney as well, it would seem. But on second thought, he finds this explicitness unnecessary, not to say jejune, since the tundish scene is implied in "raking at dead fires"—not a cliché but literally what the old priest is doing in *Portrait*. The line "a waste of time for somebody your age" is simply wooden, and the revision introduces the interesting tundish of a word, "whinges." I take the text in *Opened Ground* as authoritative.

8. Heaney writes:

Now that the other children were older and there was so much going on in the kitchen, I had to get close to the actual radio set in order to concentrate my hearing, and in that intent proximity to the dial I grew familiar with the names of foreign stations, with Leipzig and Oslo and Stuttgart and Warsaw and, of course, with Stockholm.

I also got used to hearing short bursts of foreign languages as the dial hand swept round from BBC to Radio Eireann, from the intonations of London to those of Dublin, and even though I did not understand what was being said in those first encounters with the gutturals and sibilants of European speech, I had already begun a journey into the wideness of the world beyond. (*Ground* 416)

9. Even Dante's own "I" as pilgrim, the reader's threshold into each moment of the poem, multiplies personal consciousness in such a way that it becomes polysemous itself. The reader's "I" finds itself translated onto an allegorical plane where it is "Dante" in a journey through the afterlife, at the same instant that Dante's "I" is realized and becomes itself only within the particular consciousness of each reader. In a sense, the literal or historical level of the poem takes place in the time and place that the reader inhabits.

10. Turner writes about ritual, but his point applies equally well to poetic composition, when he speaks of "the subjunctive depths of liminality.... Actuality takes the sacrificial plunge into possibility and emerges as a different kind of actuality" (Turner 83-84).

11. Dante sees a river of pure light with almost the same sandy, waterweed high up in the Paradiso. He "drink[s] of the waters" with his eyes, after Beatrice explains the difference between what he sees and cannot see:

> She added this: "The river and the gems
> of topaz entering and leaving, and
> the grasses' laughter—these are shadowy
> prefaces of their truth; not that these things
> are lacking in themselves; the defect lies
> in you, whose sight is not yet that sublime." (*Paradiso* XXX, 76-81)

12. Given Heaney's allusion to Joyce in "Station Island," the word *claritas* invokes both the Thomistic definition of beauty and Stephen Dedalus' explanation of it in *A Portrait of the Artist as a Young Man*. Dedalus associates it both with radiance and with "the enchantment of the heart."

13. Some of the poems in "Squarings," however, strike me as flat, such as, I.xii, where he defines "lightening" as "A phenomenal instant when the spirit flares / With pure exhilaration before death—" (66).

4. OTHELLO AND THE MARRIAGES OF POLITICS

1. Regrettably, Brian Vickers makes no mention of the Shakespeare criticism influenced by Leo Strauss in his magisterial work, *Appropriating Shakespeare: Contemporary Critical Quarrels*.

2. If what Seamus Heaney writes about lyric poetry also applies to the speeches of Shakespeare's plays, then "any interference by the knowing intellect in the purely disinterested cognitions of the form-seeking imagination constitutes poetic sabotage, an affront to the legislative and executive powers of expression itself" (*Government* 93). Heaney is writing of what he takes the opinion of Robert Frost to be; perhaps he overstates his point. It is not that "the form-seeking imagination" has no truck with knowledge, as one might infer, but that in this instance the "knowing intellect" does not know as much as the imagination, which has to feel its way along, especially "to allow the first alertness or come-hither, sensed in a blurred or incomplete way, to dilate and approach as a thought or a theme or a phrase" (*Preoccupations* 49). Imagination, heeding the "come-hither" that attracts it, constantly ventures into areas off the conceptual map in order to bring them into the domain of the knowing intellect. In this regard Heaney agrees with Keats' famous comment about "negative capability" in a letter to Benjamin Bailey: that Shakespeare is preeminent in being able to remain in "uncertainties, mysteries, doubts, without any irritable grasping after fact and reason." What Shakespeare sees, he sometimes sees like old Gloucester, feelingly, yet he feels what he feels, on the other hand, knowingly. No internal border guard prevents his imagination from seeking what it will or from wording the souls of both Iago and Desdemona, and at the same time, nothing prevents him from immediately and actively understanding the implications of what he imagines. The knowing intellect acts through the form-seeking imagination, because the imagination is both closer to sense-knowledge, like Levin's dog Laska, who can smell out the hidden snipe, and more godlike, more like the "divinity that shapes our ends" in having at every point a sense of the whole action as a distinct form being shaped.

3. Some of the most recent criticism has fastened on precisely this dimension. Ferial Ghazoul, for example, writes that *Othello* involves "a double circulation of the Other and a complex intertwining that combines the effect of an African/Arab (i.e., Othello and his background) on European imagination and, in a reversed way, its impact on Arabs/Africans" (Ghazoul 1).

4. When Conrad's Marlow speaks of Lord Jim as "one of us," he means it in the same sense that the Venetians will consider Cassio one of them; they could never accept Othello in the same way.

5. Bloom says that Cassio is "the perfect disciple of Othello" who "expresses what his faith in Othello means when he says that reputation is the immortal part of himself (II.ii.291-92; cp. 117-35; Romans 9:18; 8:24)" (70n25). These parenthetical citations point to Cassio's remark in his cups that "there be souls must be saved, and there be souls must not be saved," to the passage in Romans to the effect that God shows

mercy or hardens the hearts of whom he will (9:18), and to the earlier passage arguing that "we must be content to hope that we shall be saved" since salvation is not yet in sight (8:24). Bloom's treatment of Cassio, in other words, understands the concern with salvation to be virtually identical to the concern with reputation: everything depends upon the favor or disfavor of one's god. The "immortal part" of oneself in both cases remains strangely removed from one's own control.

5. THE INTELLIGENCE OF FEELING
AND THE HABIT OF ART

1. Maritain goes on to explain that "intentional" is used in the Thomistic sense reintroduced into philosophy by Brentano and Husserl. It refers to "the purely tendential existence through which a thing—for instance, the object known—is present, in an immaterial or suprasubjective manner, in an 'instrument'—an idea for instance, which, in so far as it determines the act of knowing, is a mere immaterial tendency or intention toward the object" (120). I wish he would explain his explanation, as Byron said in another context.

6. THE SACRIFICE OF ACHILLES

1. When Achilles first asks Thetis to go up to Olympus, he reminds her that, inside the house of Peleus, she has often boasted that she alone "beat aside shameful destruction from Kronos' son the dark-misted, / that time when all the other Olympians sought to bind him, / Hera and Poseidon and Pallas Athene" (1.398-400). Calling attention to the "metaphysical nature" of binding a god who cannot die, Slatkin argues that the attempt that Achilles mentions "thus constitutes a mutinous effort at supplanting [Zeus] and imposing a new divine regime—on the pattern of his own overthrow of Kronos and the Titans" (69). As Slatkin mentions, the reference to a son greater than the father strongly invokes the greater Thetis myth.

    Perhaps there is another explanation, though, especially since the time of this attempt is unspecified. Why *else* might these gods, including the loyal Athene (who loves it when her father calls her his "dear girl of the grey eyes," 8.373), seek to bind Zeus? Might it not be to save their own regime because he was about to do something disastrous: sleep with Thetis? The aid of Thetis in this particular circumstance would signify her consent to marry Peleus—that is, to submit to her own substitute "binding" as the consolidation of the regime of Zeus—and as an allusion it would therefore bear a particularly trenchant irony.

NOT CONCLUSION

1. The Higginson-Todd version concludes after the twelfth line (word changes italicized):

> It beckons and it baffles;
> Philosophies don't know,
> And through a riddle, at the last,
> Sagacity must go.
> To guess it puzzles scholars;
> To gain it, men have *shown*
> Contempt of generations,
> And crucifixion *known*.

Dickinson's original, on the other hand, goes for twenty lines, the last two quatrains of which did not pass her well-meaning censors:

> It beckons, and it baffles —
> Philosophy — don't know —
> And through a Riddle at the last —
> Sagacity, must go —
> To guess it, puzzles scholars —
> To gain it, Men have borne
> Contempt of Generations
> And Crucifixion, shown —
> Faith slips — and laughs, and rallies —
> Blushes, if any see —
> Plucks at a twig of Evidence —
> And asks a Vane, the way —
> Much Gesture, from the Pulpit —
> Strong Hallelujahs roll —
> Narcotics cannot still the Tooth
> That nibbles at the soul —

Index